Suzanne Chick was born i
in the Sydney suburb of M
Charmian Clift and Geo
return from Greece in 1964. From an early age a love of line and colour was shared equally with a strong love of words. Her schooling at North Sydney Girls' High School was followed by the National Art School and Sydney Teachers' College.

After a long career in art teaching, and bringing up three daughters, Suzanne now spends most of her week in her paint-splattered studio or at the word processor. To keep her hand in she still teaches: adults, the developmentally disabled and, occasionally, schoolchildren.

She lives on the shores of a beautiful bay on the south coast of New South Wales with her husband Doug and their daughters' dog, Christmas. Native birds share her garden, and at night the resident possum allows her to stroke its current baby.

This is her first book.

Dear Lovey,

I hope you get as much out of this book as I did.

I 'dips me lid' at your fortitude and for following through with the courage of your convictions.

To one gutsy lady.

Love Nadia
XXXXX

PO Box 707
Leichhardt NSW 2040
Australia

Searching for Charmian

THE DAUGHTER CHARMIAN CLIFT GAVE AWAY DISCOVERS THE MOTHER SHE NEVER KNEW

with line drawings by the author

Suzanne Chick

Pan Macmillan Australia

First published 1994 in Macmillan by Pan Macmillan Australia Pty Limited
St Martins Tower, 31 Market Street, Sydney

This Picador edition first published 1995

Reprinted 1995 (twice)

National Library of Australia
cataloguing-in-publication data:

Chick, Suzanne, 1942– .
Searching for Charmian.

ISBN 0 330 35654 2.

1. Chick, Suzanne, 1942– — Family. 2. Clift, Charmian, 1923–1969 — Family.
3. Birthparents — New South Wales — Sydney — Identification.
4. Adoptees — New South Wales — Sydney — Biography.
5. Journalists — New South Wales — Sydney — Biography.
6. Authors, Australian — New South Wales — Sydney — Biography.
I. Title.

362.8298092

Typeset in 12/15pt Plantin by Post Typesetters
Printed in Australia by McPherson's Printing Group

For Gina, Danielle, Kristin and Rebecca:
the grand-daughters of Charmian Clift.

ACKNOWLEDGEMENTS

Many voices speak from the pages of this book. When I first began to discover my mother I didn't know enough to ask questions, so I just let people talk. Even when I knew more I found that this was still the best way to allow her friends to paint her for me. So to those people I owe a great debt. To Mary Andrews, James and Sylvia Calomeris, Betty Nunn and Fred Ring, my thanks.

Because I gave myself a time-span of one year for the story to unfold there were people I met after this time who had much to contribute to the coloured portrait I was forming of my mother, but unfortunately I could not include them in the body of the text, much as I would have loved to do so. My thanks to Tess van Sommers, Ken and Jean Wilder and Rodney and Bet Hall.

When I met Barbara Veldhoven (then Blackman), I found a woman of great strength of purpose who had firmly drawn memories of my mother. She would not let me flag and through her friends Denis Pile and Shirley Fenton-Huie I met journalist Charles Sriber who had been an intimate of the Johnstons on Hydra. He not only told me some delightful anecdotes but supplied me with photographic negatives of my mother that he had taken so long ago. I owe him my heartfelt thanks.

I can't adequately express my thanks to Nadia Wheatley who in the first months of my search gave me so much, not just information but friendship. I am looking forward very much to reading her biography of my mother.

Much of the background to my understanding came from books, bookshops, libraries and theses. My thanks to Lisa Highton and Tom Thompson, then of Collins/Angus & Robertson, for their interest and the copies of Clift's and Johnston's books. I owe a debt to Garry Kinnane, whose biography of George Johnston gave me a sense of time and place into which I could fit my discoveries and against which I could juxtapose my life. The poetry of my half-brother, Martin Johnston, showed me new aspects of his/our family. My thanks to Marie Fitzpatrick and her sister Bernice Berriman of my local A & R bookshop who went to great lengths on my behalf. School librarian Dot Beaupeurt went out of her way to find historical details and to contact libraries for me. Graham Tucker shared with me the photographs in his possession and his enthusiasm for my mother's writing. Libby Harkness of *Looking For Lisa* fame pointed me to information I needed and Judy McHutchison lent me her honours thesis, *Relinquishing a Child: The Circumstances and Effects of Loss*, and another paper, *Adoption in N.S.W.—An Historical Perspective*. Thanks are due also to Mark Cranfield and Valerie Helson of the National Library and to the technicians of the State Library.

One of my most shattering discoveries was made amongst the files at the Post Adoption Resource Centre. Manager Margaret McDonald and social worker Petrina Slaytor were a great help to me there.

Some of the people who were my mother's friends have become my friends in turn. I cannot thank Cedric Flower and his wife Wendy enough for their unfailing interest and 'encouraging noises' (as Cedric puts it). The letters and negatives which Cedric lent me made Charmian Clift tangible to me for the first time. June Crooke and I have maintained a correspondence and for her sympathetic help she has my heartfelt thanks.

Because of my voyage of discovery I have gained new family. My new cousin Diana Bradshaw, daughter of Charmian's brother Barré, and I first met at the grave of our grandfather, Syd Clift. I thank her for her friendship and the insights and the photographs she gave me. My daughters have found a new cousin, and I my only blood-niece, in Rebecca, Shane's daughter, and I thank her too for the photographs she has provided for this book. Friend and sister-in-law both, Roseanne Bonney, widow of Martin Johnston, has provided unfailing encouragement, affection and practical help. How do I say thank you for all of that? I must not forget my existing family, adoptive brother David and sister-in-law Carole Shaw, who have supported me from the beginning.

To the friends who read my manuscript and gave me helpful feedback my grateful thanks: Pam Cotterill, Anne Stanley and once again Roseanne Bonney. To the Johnston Estate my gratitude for allowing me to use photographs from the family collection and to quote from my mother's books. Jane Palfreyman and James Fraser of Pan Macmillan had the task of guiding me through the foreign country of book publishing. It can't have been easy at times. My thanks to them and to Linda Funnell whose editorial suggestions have never been less than astute. Human whirlwind, Debbie McInnes, has dragged me in her slipstream through the perils of publicity, and for my safe emergence on the solid shore I have her to thank.

Now to my two Tonis. Toni (Antoinette) Mackenzie has been chief midwife to this book. Through three distinct drafts as well as continuous rewriting her lead pencil has been busy. Despite all my doubts she has been determined that this book should happen. That it has been written is due in no small part to her. My deepest thanks go to a good friend.

Toni (Antonia) Burgess was my mother's best friend, one of the few people who knew of my existence. My turning up was a great shock to her and, even though it caused her great pain, she delved back into her life to unveil for me the real Charmian Clift, as she had known and loved her. Toni has become an honorary member of my family, and has made me feel a member of hers. To her go my love and my undying thanks. I know what that delving cost her.

Finally I would like to thank my husband Doug, who critically read every chapter, hot off the printer, in his role as the 'common man'. He dealt with the emotional peaks and troughs of my search, with the absence of wifely comforts, with the absence quite often of a wife, entombed as I was in the workroom. He encouraged me to find myself, to change, to fly. Without him, the events described in this book would not have happened.

QUOTATIONS

The author and the publishers would like to thank Roseanne Bonney, Jason Johnston and Rebecca O'Connor for permission to quote from Charmian Clift's work in this book and for the use of passages from George Johnston's *Clean Straw for Nothing* and *Cartload of Clay*.

Thanks also to the following for permission to use quoted material: to Roseanne Bonney for extracts from Martin Johnston's poems 'Letter to Sylvia Plath *i.m. c.c.*' and 'Biography'; to Corona Publishing Co. for extracts from Kathleen Silber and Phylis Speedlin's *Dear Birthmother, Thank You For Our Baby*; to David Higham Associates for the extract from Dylan Thomas' poem 'Do Not Go Gentle into That Good Night'; to Doubleday, a division of Bantom, Doubleday, Dell Publishing Group, Inc. for extracts from Arthur D. Sorosky, Annette Baran and Reuben Pannor's *The Adoption Triangle: The Effects of the Sealed Record on Adoptees, Birth Parents and Adoptive Parents*; to the National Library of Australia for extracts from Hazel de Berg's interview with Charmian Clift; to the New South Wales Department of Community Services for extracts from its booklet *Adoptees and Birthparents Guide to Searching, Adoption.*

ILLUSTRATIONS

The author and the publishers would like to thank the following for permission to use photographs and line drawings:

Mary Andrews: 67 (photograph by Gordon Andrews); Roseanne Bonney, Jason Johnston and Rebecca O'Connor for permission to use photographs from the Johnston family collection: 12, 13, 14, 17, 33b, 39, 45, 50, 51, 53, 76, 78a, b, c; Jill Crossley: 38; Cedric Flower: 19, 41, 42, 46, 60, 61, 62, 63, 64, 65, 66; the *Herald and Weekly Times*: 79; David Moore: 22, 23; Rebecca O'Connor: 108a, b; Charles Sriber: 35b, 36b, 47, 69, 70, 71b.

All other photographs and drawings are from the collections of Diana Bradshaw and Toni Burgess, for which permission is gratefully acknowledged, or the author's collection.

Thanks also to Dean Chick for the illustration for the chapter openings.

Every effort has been made to identify individual photographers and permission holders, but for a number of photographs this has not been possible. The publishers would be pleased to hear from any copyright holders who have not been acknowledged.

AUTHOR'S NOTE

The names of some minor figures in this story have been changed to protect their privacy.

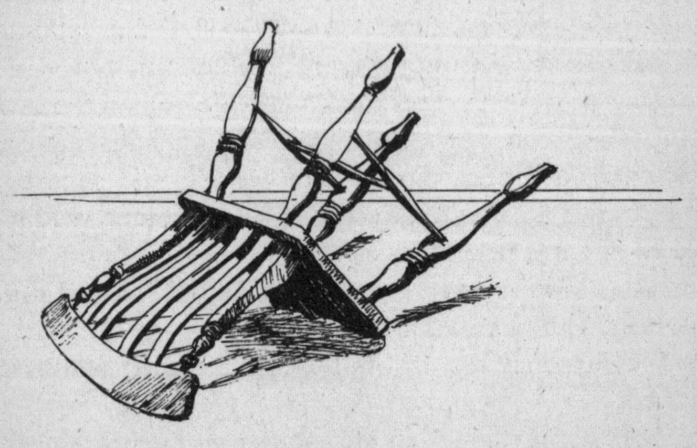

CHAPTER 1

The name is the symbol of her lost identity.[1]

The Indonesian chair is looking at me accusingly.

On Sunday, with its five fellows, crammed nose to tail in the back of my little station wagon, it had bumped and swerved around the hairpin bends of the mountain road lined with ranks of tall straight blue gums and short radiating tree ferns. In the driveway of the sprawling house overlooking the bay, it had been unloaded with its fellows. It had been carried up the steep wooden stairs, over the missing plank in the deck, and into place around the oval pine dining room table. All Monday long, one after another, the chairs had been rubbed with beeswax and polished, then buffed up with the electric drill attachment, sending flecks of lambswool spinning out into space like orbiting satellites. By Monday evening, five chairs glowed and gleamed with rich golden lights.

Tuesday came and my enthusiasm for chair polishing waned.

Until recently, my adult life had been spent as a teacher. Days had been doled out in forty-minute intervals separated from each other by bells. I was still awash with joy at my new freedom to lay down tasks, to walk out of rooms, whenever I wanted to. My dilettante thoughts and feet turned towards the world outside, which was bursting with its special winter life.

Rainbow lorikeets were screeching and quarrelling over white blossom in the tops of the surrounding blackbutts; two red wattlebirds, husband and wife, bills clacking, were chasing insects amongst the orange banksia cones; and a group of adolescent currawongs was practising aerial manoeuvres around the eaves. Floating up towards me from somewhere down near the water came the strident honks of cormorants hanging out their wings to dry in the dead gum tree.

The lawn needed mowing. Winter grass was shoving its way vigorously through the buffalo. I would deal with that. Chickweed was rampaging through the flowerbeds. I would deal with that too.

Bulbs were pushing green spears through the cool earth. Already the heavy perfume of jonquils and daphne was making my head spin. Purple splashes down amongst the green revealed themselves as violets by their clear, clean scent. Early primula were rearing tiny white and pink balls on furry green stems, ready to unfurl in another week or two. It was going to be a glorious spring.

My head was full of flowers, time flowing seamlessly around me, no bells at all. I was tying up sweet pea plants when my dreams were interrupted.

'Cup of tea, Suzie-love?' a deep familiar voice called from the back door.

Was it *that* time already? My husband was framed in the doorway, home from his day at school.

'I'll come in. Hang on just a tick while I tie this last plant.'

Sitting on the newly glowing chairs around the oval table,

the mail scattered amongst the tea mugs and biscuit crumbs, we talked of his day, my day. One chair waited upside down in the corner, matt and unfinished. A large manila envelope waited innocuously alongside the little rectangular windowed ones.

'Don't the chairs look nice, Doug? Would you please give me a hand to finish that last one?'

'Sure, after I look at the mail . . . here, this big one's for you.'

So at about 4.30 p.m. on that Tuesday in June 1991 I opened the large manila envelope. The first thing to be pulled out was a flat blue booklet printed in large white type:

Adoption Information Act 1990
Adoptees and Birthparents
Guide to Searching
ADOPTION

And the next thing, oh God, was a bromide of my original birth certificate.

It seemed so long ago that I had walked into the country town registrar's office tucked behind the old brick courthouse. The leaves were still on the giant plane trees, casting their dappled patterns on the curves of the brick paving. My sandalled feet kicked the spiky seeds over the path as I walked. My stomach was churning rebelliously. In fact I almost didn't walk in at all. Here was I, secure in my identity of forty-eight years, an art teacher, a painter, a wife, a mother . . . a daughter. Did I really want to know the truth?

'Can I help you, madam?' A polite dark girl in a skirt and blouse came up to the counter.

'Yes, please.' I screwed up my courage. 'You see I'm

adopted and I've decided to apply for my original birth certificate under the new *Adoption Information Act*. What do I have to do?'

The girl looked at me with eyes that had seen all human conditions, reached into a file and said, 'Fill this form in. It will cost you one hundred and seventeen dollars. One hundred for the search, and the package you will receive. Seventeen for the certificate, if they find it.'

One form to be filled in, a cheque to be handed over the counter, in exchange for that truth. If the truth could be found.

Only the name, I thought, *I need only find out the name and do no more.*

With a fluttering, sick-feeling stomach, I read:

> *Mother's name and maiden surname, age and birthplace:*
> *Charmian Clift*
> *19 years*
> *Kiama*
> *N.S.W.*

My eyes seemed to go out of focus; my heart seemed to be bumping around outside my body. My trembling hands belonged to somebody else.

As a young art teacher, I had read George Johnston's *My Brother Jack* and knew that his wife was the author Charmian Clift. But it surely couldn't be *that* one. There must have been another girl with the same name. There must.

Too late now to get to the town library, forty kilometres away. Dozens of books in my study about Australian artists, but none about authors. And where was my old copy of *My Brother Jack*?

Almost incoherent with emotion, I sobbed against Doug's shirt, a child again, clutching at an adult, needing adult comfort. How could I have thought, even for a moment, that the talisman of the name would be enough? Now nothing would content me but to know everything.

So it began, my journey, the search for my beginnings. A pilgrimage that has been as obsessive as any quest for a holy grail. On the way, unimagined doors have opened to me, revealing glimpses of different pasts, and possibilities of different futures. And one chair is unpolished still.

CHAPTER 2

In the place of real answers to the many questions, myths are created. The most pervasive of these is the myth of the 'chosen child'.[1]

It happened in Sydney in January 1943, when the dreary business of living in a country at war was at its most dreary. For ordinary Australians life was a matter of making do. Rationing for most commodities was in force, austerity regulations governed people's lives, pleasures were few. The very cityscape had changed; Sydney city buildings were sandbagged and the G.P.O. clocktower, symbol of the business centre, had been dismantled and stored, block by block, in case of air attack.

Harold and Marjorie were down from their temporary home in Orange, he attending to business at his head office in Hunter Street, she visiting her mother and catching up with the few friends who had not moved out of the city. The two of them had checked on the little worker's cottage in Cremorne that Marjorie had persuaded Harold to buy before the war with tears and entreaties. Tears and entreaties were strategies totally foreign to her nature but had seemed necessary in the circumstances. One of three identical small bungalows overlooking Reid Park, Mosman Bay, it had taken all their faith and savings. Now it seemed too dangerous to live there.

Their ninth wedding anniversary was only two months away but they were childless. Harold, a tall and heavy man, was already forty-five years old. Accustomed to pre-war double-breasted suits, he felt improperly dressed in his single-breasted 'Victory' variety, the only style allowed within the austerity regulations. He was glad of the formality of the newly permitted waistcoat. His round, good-natured face was topped by a soft felt hat and enlivened by a rabbity smile and twinkling bright blue eyes. Marjorie, at thirty-nine, had a long gypsy face surrounded by an explosion of unmanageably curly, wiry black hair, greying slightly. Tall and slim-hipped, she had the kind of figure that looked good in its austerity skirt and blouse, so she didn't mind them so much. What she did miss was the pre-war feel of good stockings. Leg-paint did not seem quite the same. It felt a bit 'fast', somehow. However she wore her little felt hat with a jaunty air.

Harold was the youngest of six children of a Church of England rector. The eldest child, Edna, had become quite a public figure. She was Matron Shaw of Crown Street Women's Hospital, and was already earning her hospital a reputation as the best in Sydney for mothers and babies. One of Marjorie's city entertainments was to visit her sister-in-law at the hospital and look at all the newborn babies.

It's astounding, she always thought, *how many babies keep coming into the world. Such an uncertain world. As though nature is working overtime to replace the lives that are being lost in their thousands.*

On this particular summer's day, as hot and humid as Sydney can make it in January, she dutifully cheek-kissed Harold's sister, tall and impressive in her matron's uniform, and together they made their way to the hospital's adoption nursery.

Marjorie peered closely at all the small bundles, swathed and wrapped, some sleeping, some squalling, all identical in appearance to wanted and loved babies, but in reality relinquished scraps of humanity. She searched their tiny secretive screwed-up faces for meaning.

All these little lives, each one with its own destiny.

At Edna's order, one little cocoon was unwrapped, and into Marjorie's arms was placed a baby girl, the gingerish fuzz on her head covered by a pink bonnet, feather-and-fan-pattern knitted pink jacket and matching bootees floating overlarge on her skinny arms and long thin feet. *Just like a kangaroo's*, Marjorie said to herself.

The baby squeezed shut slatey blue eyes, opened a large mouth and bellowed.

'Now this one, Marjorie, is special. She is three weeks old. She was born on Christmas Day.' Edna paused for effect. 'Have you never thought of adoption?'

The idea had never occurred to Marjorie. She had been startled into her late marriage and had taken the kidney complaint that had made childbirth inadvisable with philosophical acceptance. She had always tended to let life happen to her rather than forcing it to follow her wishes. But the baby girl had surprisingly long and slender fingers, and they gripped her forefinger as though they would never let go.

'But... but... but how could I? What about Harold?

What about her own mother? What about feeding her? What about napkins? How could I get enough coupons?'

'I'll tell you what we'll do. Harold's at the office, you say? Let's ring him and get him to come up here and see what he says.'

Harold found his wife and sister clucking over the baby, who was by now bubbling slightly and looking vaguely cross-eyed.

'Here, you hold her, Harry. This way. Make sure you support the head.' He was used to obeying his eldest sister.

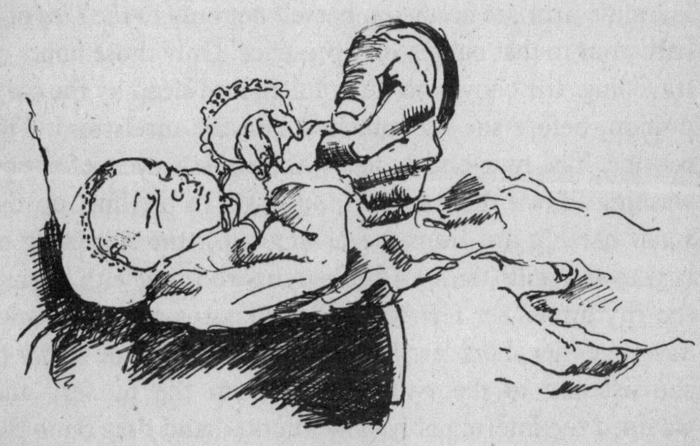

'Here, by Jove, Marj. She's smiling at me!' A fatuous expression appeared on his round face. 'We'll call her Suzanne,' he said. 'And Edna will be her godmother.' It had the force of a proclamation.

*

By the time Harold's official business in Sydney was completed, the baby's official business was completed too. And so, with a few scrawled signatures, the baby was taken home. Home to Orange, an inland country town, safe from overflying enemy planes, air-raid sirens and Japanese midget submarines. Home to a little upstairs flat in an ugly red-brick block in Sale Street.

Not for Marjorie the customary nine months of thinking, dreaming and preparing. Not the body changes and the birth experience. Not the milky weeks in the maternity ward bonding with the flesh of her flesh. Instead a brief time of frantic preparation and then four and a half hot hours in the Ford V8 with its hooded headlamps and white-lined running boards (its precious rationed petrol provided by Harold's firm), to accustom herself not only to the *idea* of a baby, but to that baby's very presence. Only those hours of travelling, the baby mercifully lulled into sleep by the car's motion, before she was plunged into the maelstrom. The routine. The four-hourly feeds, the endless cycle of nappy washing (down the stairs dripping wet to the line, up the stairs harshly dry from the baking sun), the sterilising of bottles and milk (the little kitchen superheating with steam), the rhythm of her feet walking, walking, a crying, colicky baby over her shoulder. The lack of sleep. And the worry as she listened to the rising howls from the nursery and watched the interminably slow minute-hand drag on to the hour when she could properly pick the baby up and feed her.

Is she all right? Can I go in? Does the clinic sister really know what she's talking about? Does Edna know what she's talking about? She's never had babies of her own. Should I really let her cry?

On the second Sunday in May that year, Marjorie clattered down the steep concrete outdoor stairs to check on the baby, now almost five months old. Suzanne had been left asleep in her pram, well wrapped, for half an hour's airing in the garden. She was still asleep, but in her gently curled hand was a white chrysanthemum and on the blanket a note in Harold's writing, wishing Marjorie a happy Mother's Day. Unaccustomed tears—tears of joy—sprang to her eyes.

It's true, she thought. *It* is *true. I am a mother.*

'Tell me again, Mummy, how you chose me.' It was Suzanne's favourite bedtime story. She knew it by heart. 'And why couldn't my real mother keep me? And where is my real daddy?'

'It was very sad, darling. Your mother died having you. Your father was a brave soldier in the army. He was killed in the war.'

And so the little girl believed.

In September 1944, Harold needed to go back to Sydney on business. He was nervous leaving Marjorie and Suzanne after the breakout of Japanese prisoners of war at Cowra the month before. But his wife insisted: 'You go, dear. It's only for a week, and if any Nip breaks in here and threatens Suzie, he'll be sorry. That's all I can say.'

So he went.

A week later the cream Ford pulled up outside the flats, softened a little by an early spring flowering of peach blossom in the otherwise bare yard. Harold ran up the backstairs fast for a heavy man of forty-seven.

'Coo-ee . . . Marj, I'm home!'

'Dadda. Home.' Sue was swung up onto his shoulders, her fat little arms twined around his neck. 'Lol-lol, Dadda?' She already knew the protocol of returning fathers.

'Here Suzanne, one for you and one for Mummy.' He reached into his pocket. 'Hop down now like a good girl while I talk to Mummy. I say, Marj, I've brought you a present. A special one.'

'Oh, Harry. What have you done? You know we can't afford—'

'Guess what I've got for you.' He could barely conceal his excitement.

'Heavens, I don't know. Is it a dress? Some stockings? Harry, you haven't been buying things on the black market?' A time of strict rationing still, presents were rare and always exciting.

'No, Marj, it's alive in a box in the back of the car, and I'll have to get it out soon. It needs a feed.'

'Oh, it's alive! Is it a puppy for Suzanne? Or a kitten?'

'No . . . It's a brother for Suzanne. A baby, a baby boy!'

And so David, barely two weeks old, a small thin baby with a head of black hair, arrived in his well-provisioned cardboard box to challenge Suzanne's infant supremacy. What Gordian knots of red tape had Matron Shaw cut this time?

Now his story was added to the family myth.

'Your mother died having you, darling. Your father was a brave pilot in the air force. He was killed in the war.'

And so both children believed.

CHAPTER 3

The most common unknown mother is between the age of fifteen and twenty-five. She was most likely around nineteen years of age when she relinquished her newly born child . . .[1]

'Do you remember, love, I told you there was a new *Adoption Information Act* so adoptees can now apply for their original birth certificates? Well I did, and it's here!'

My knuckles were white on the telephone receiver. I was on fire with the need to talk. A painful bubble of knowledge had lodged somewhere under my diaphragm. I was frantic to disperse it. To talk it out of me. It was a miracle that the telephone wires hadn't melted with the heat of my desperation.

I have three daughters. Danielle, the middle one, sleeps in a flat in Mosman, Sydney. Her life is lived elsewhere. She is twenty years old, refuses to answer to her full name, has dropped out of her economics/law degree, sends a small part of her brain to work in an office while the rest of it contemplates the complexities of life's journey. She has the eyes of a particularly loving angel and is the most empathetic of my children.

She was the only one of them I had been able to reach.

'So, tell me, tell me! Who is she? Who is your mother? How old was she? Why did she give you away? Who *are* you?' the questions streamed down the red-hot wires.

'Slow down, Dan. All I've got is the birth certificate. Her name is Charmian Clift. She was born in Kiama in 1923, she was younger than you are when she had me, only nineteen . . . and this is the scary part: there's a very well-known Australian author of that name.'

'Oh, Ma! That's incredible! An author! No wonder you have all those dictionaries and thesauruses and the house is overflowing with books—it must be in the blood! When are you going to meet her?'

'Hang on a bit, love. I've only just found out the name. And there may be another Charmian Clift entirely. And she'd be about sixty-eight. And she could be anywhere at all. And, whoever she is, she gave me away once and she may not want to meet me now. And she may not even be alive.' My voice was wobbling a little on a wave of emotion.

My daughter's voice sounded blurry and unfocused as well. 'What else does it say? Who your father was?'

'No, there's a big diagonal line through that part. Don't forget that having an illegitimate baby was a terrible sin in 1942. She would have kept my father's name out of it. But she did give *me* a name—Jennifer.'

There was a silence as she got used to the idea.

'Jennifer? Jenny?' She tried it out. 'No, sorry, Ma, it doesn't sound like you at all. So when are you going to find out? I'll bet it is that author. It must be.'

'I'll have to wait till the morning. It's too late now to go into town. The library will be closed.'

'Oh Ma, how can you bear to wait? This is just amazing!'

We said our goodbyes rather tearfully, and the need-to-talk bubble dispersed a little. As if to fill the pain vacuum, another kind of ache rushed in and took its place. A need to know. Right now!

Now, who could help me? An English literature kind of person . . . I knew the very one. The head teacher of English at Doug's school. Bill, a friend. He lived close to the school, and surely the English department would have some sort of dictionary of Australian authors.

I rang him, and told the story of my adoption and today's incredible discovery again. Excitement fairly crackled down the line from this man of immense energy. And yes, of course, he would duck into school and look up Charmian Clift for me. He would ring back.

No sooner had the receiver hit the cradle than the phone rang again.

I snatched it up. 'Hello.'

'Hi, Ma. This is Dan again.' She was tripping over her words in her agitation. 'It *is*! *The* Charmian Clift. It *must* be! I've just raced up to the Mosman bookshop. And—and—and—the lady in the shop was a fan of Charmian Clift and she's got all these books—and we looked at the dust jackets—and she was born in Kiama in the 1920s. It's *got* to be her! And the lady was so excited she could hardly turn the pages, and she asked me what you were like. I said you were artistic, intelligent and a very strong person, and she laughed and said, "That sounds like Charmian Clift's daughter." Oh, and there's a biography coming out soon by a writer called Nadia Wheatley. Maybe you'll be in it.'

'Oh, love . . .'

'And she lived *here*, in Mosman. But Ma,' there was a silence, 'she's dead. She died in 1969.'

Tears started out of my eyes and streamed down my face.

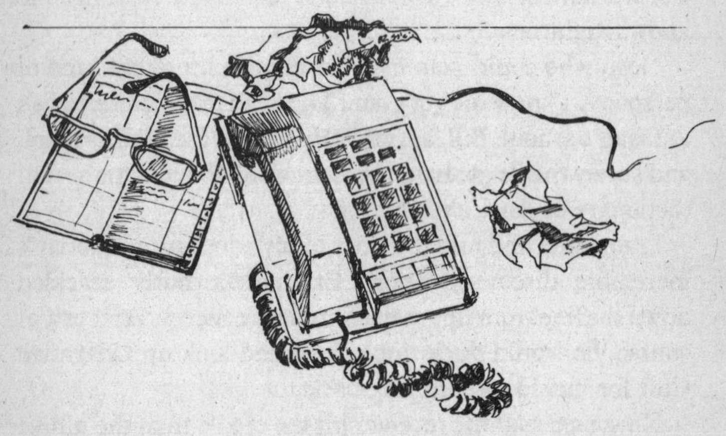

So I'll never meet her. Why am I crying? Why? WHY? Because she's dead? This is ridiculous. I always thought my mother was dead anyway. How can you cry for a mother you've never met?

The phone was ringing again. It was Bill. He had looked up his references and discovered Clift's birthdate: 1923. The same as the date of my mother's birth on my birth certificate. It was looking more and more probable.

He wanted to know if George Johnston could have been my father. It seemed most unlikely. If that were true, she would not have had to give me up. And the dates were wrong. The two had married in 1947, five years after my birth.

Half an hour and two cups of coffee later, the phone rang.

'Danni, you *again*!'

'Hi—Jennifer. Just listen. You had a great-grandfather called Will, and a great-grandmother Emma . . . and she had a *huge* contralto. I'll bet that's where you got your singing voice from.'

'Where on earth did you find that out?'

'I bought one of her books, something to do with being alone with yourself. I told you, didn't I? It's a collection of essays she wrote in 1968 and 1969. I started reading it for facts—and now I seem to be just reading it.'

Once again, the act of putting down the receiver seemed to trigger the phone's ringing. Bill again. He had unearthed more details. She had worked as a model, as a nurse and as an usherette at the Minerva Theatre in Kings Cross. She and George and their three children had lived on the Greek island of Hydra for years. Had I read George's trilogy, *My Brother Jack*, *Clean Straw for Nothing* and *A Cartload of Clay*? I had read the first one, many years ago, when it was first published in Australia. I had not enjoyed it much. It seemed irrelevant to the young woman I then was.

So it continued for the rest of the evening. Phone calls from my daughter and friends with tiny scraps of information that I wrote down on tiny scraps of paper. Scraps of paper that, in my nervous agitation, I shredded into confetti. The flutters in my stomach were now mimicked by this confetti, which seemed to have entered my brain, and was acting like one of those snowstorms inside a small glass dome. The smallest movement stirred it up, and it clouded all rational thought.

In bed that night, even the familiar comfort of Doug's large warm bulk failed me. There was no sleep. The rhythmic repetition of *Charmian Clift*, *Charmian Clift*, like some sort of maternal mantra, took over from my alpha rhythms. There were tears on my cheeks again. And the next moment I was grinning in the dark.

For one as pragmatic as I am, there was an intensely mystical element to this finding of a mother. It was revelational. Transcendental. I sensed myself tapping into some universal mother-to-daughter continuum. It stretched back into time: me, my mother Charmian, her mother. And it stretched into the future: my three daughters, Gina, Danielle and Kristin, and their unborn daughters, and theirs after them. Womb to womb to womb.

I didn't understand what was happening to me, but I couldn't stop it happening.

Who am I, then? Only seven hours ago amongst the sweet peas I was totally certain of my identity. Now . . . Sue Chick, adopted as Suzanne Shaw, born Jennifer Clift. Born as one person, adopted as another, married as another. Can I be all these people? And still be me?

CHAPTER 4

Take your search slowly, step by step.
Take your time to assimilate each piece of information as it is discovered.
Don't rush . . .[1]

From my present vantage point, when many of the mysteries (not all—never all) are mysteries no more, the first few days of my search for Charmian Clift seem the most frenetic. They remind me of a book that Doug and I used to read to our babies, entitled *Are You My Mother?*[2]

In the first pages, a mother bird flies off her nest, leaving the just-hatching egg. The newly hatched yellow baby bird can't find its mother. It goes looking. The first creature it meets is a kitten.

'Are you my mother?' it asks.

It tries a hen and a dog and a cow, a derelict car, a boat and a front-end loader, if my memory serves me right. None of them is its mother. Finally, as in all good children's stories, there is a happy ending. The baby finds a large, maternal-looking yellow bird. And yes, she is its mother.

In my just-hatched state my question was, *Can you tell me about my mother?*

At eight-thirty on the morning after my rebirth, eyes hot and aching, I set out. Everything in town opened at nine o'clock.

Angus and Robertson's bookshop was my first stop. Much as I love bookshops, to go there at all always needs a special effort of will on my part. It is situated in a shopping mall of such hideous aspect that it constitutes my own private expectation of Hell. In this particular Hell, I am forced to shop continuously, my ears assailed for eternity by the local commercial radio station at full volume, the noise overlaid with bawling barkers crying the beauties of some cut-price trinket or other. My eyes (I am forbidden by Lucifer to wear a hat or sunglasses) are blasted by the fast-cycle flickering of a thousand, thousand, thousand blue-white fluorescent lights reflecting from shiny glass, shiny mirrors and shiny tiles. I gag at the smells of an infinity of greasy takeaway foods and every horrible tattooed child I have ever taught is whirling around me on roller-blades. Forever. (The nice ones, of course, are all in Heaven.)

Once inside the bookshop, it is peaceful. A teaching colleague runs it. She has frequently supplied me with art books in my recent and outgrown incarnation as head art teacher of one of the local high schools. She is a very simpatico young woman.

Her eyes starred with tears as she heard the story. Mine, with the tears banked up, overflowed even faster.

Marie had a lot of help to offer. Collins/A & R had recently reprinted Johnston's and Clift's works. There was a new collection of essays, edited by Nadia Wheatley. Now *she* would be the one to talk to. She was the authorised biographer. Did she know that Charmian had given birth to an illegitimate baby? It might change the thrust of her biography. I could contact her through the publisher. The representative would be in this afternoon. She would get the publishing director's number from him.

Also, there was a local ex-teacher who was writing a post-graduate thesis on Charmian Clift. No doubt he would be only too happy to meet me. He had a print of a wonderful portrait of her. In fact, he had borrowed the actual painting for a while. In this painting my mother is stunningly beautiful. Marie had his number somewhere.

So the baby bird staggered out of the shop, feathers awry, weighed down by names, phone numbers and promises, and by the combined reprinted works of George Johnston and Charmian Clift (thankfully in paperback).

My second stop was the town library. I knew the head librarian slightly. As a mother of daughters she had faced my teacher-self across a desk a number of times at parent-teacher nights. Now I faced her across her desk in the bowels of the library, a daughter seeking her mother.

She had always been a Charmian Clift fan.

'Such a warm and wise writer. Her columns for the *Sydney Morning Herald* in the sixties were just wonderful. I couldn't wait for Thursday's paper to read what Charmian Clift had to say about her world each week.'

'Isn't it ironic?' I replied, 'I've never read one.'

'I'll tell you what I'll do, Sue. I'll ring the National Library for you. They'll be sure to have Nadia Wheatley's phone number. She is a well-known children's author after all. Will you be home tomorrow?' She looked at my face intently, then said, 'There is quite a look of her about you, once you know.'

I borrowed some more works by Johnston and Clift from the library. What could I do next? I had already drained all the founts of knowledge I knew about. So with the weight of my mother's warmth and wisdom dragging at my shoulder I walked out to the car park.

I don't remember the actual drive home. For half an hour the auto-pilot took over while the idea that I might actually *look* something like my mother chased all the other confetti scraps around and around in my head. Then I was home. Home. Lug the supermarket shopping up the stairs, over the missing plank in the deck, unpack it and put it away, walk back down to the mailbox—only envelopes with transparent windows today—put on the kettle, and at last rip open the parcel of books.

Start at the essays, I said to myself. *They will probably be autobiographical.*

It was in *The World of Charmian Clift*, in a piece entitled 'Taking the Wrong Road', that I thought I had found my first clue. It was the second essay in the collection.

> *When I was seventeen I took a wrong road (asphalt) that led me to a couple of crazy painters and an introduction to poetry . . .*
>
> *When I was eighteen I took a wrong road through great Norfolk pines, that led me to disaster.*[3]

The words leapt off the page at me. Was she writing about me? Was my birth her disaster? Where were the Norfolk pines? Manly? Or were they the ones at Kiama I knew well and she must have known even better? It was all questions and no answers.

I started reading those essays for information, making little pencil marks in the margins, underlining phrases and whole paragraphs. Page followed page and essay followed essay. She had grabbed me and pulled me with her into the world of Charmian Clift.

Wednesday night was always practice with the Lydian Singers for me. I felt at once so exalted and so despairing that I thought I ought to go, just to play out an enjoyable ritual, to keep myself in the normal continuity of my life. Though I wondered, as I drove back into town, whether my life would ever be normal or continuous again. Great-grandmother Emma's 'huge contralto' sang through my mouth that night as I tried to concentrate on the alto line of Mozart's *Coronation Mass*. In the little hall where the forty of us who were practising for 'An Afternoon with Mozart' love to sing, the acoustics concentrated and amplified our sound, great-grandmother Emma's and mine, and the weight of all our voices. But somehow Mozart's elegant repetitive melodic phrases and strictly adhered-to rhythms were at odds with the *Charmian Clift*, *Charmian Clift*, *Charmian Clift*, going around in my head like the turning wheels of a train gathering speed.

She was with me that night in bed. I know. She was looking through my eyes as the night-picture in the tall vertical frame of the open bedroom window kept changing. She was with me as the fragile crescent moon drifted into the frame, limning with its faint blue light the bare branches of the liquidambar. She was still with me as it sailed out of the top of the frame, growing smaller and smaller. She stayed with me until dawn, when my hot eyelids finally slid together.

The insistent shrilling of the telephone jarred me awake. It was my bookshop friend with the phone number for Collins/A & R's publishing director. I rang her immediately. Coincidentally, she too was an adopted daughter. A sympathetic listener to my by now well-rehearsed story, she promised to ring back with Nadia Wheatley's number. No sooner was the phone down than it rang again—the library this time—with that very information.

Stomach churning, confetti-cloud awhirl and eyes gritty and hot, I dialled.

'Hello, is this Nadia Wheatley? My name is...' I launched into the story again.

There was silence at the other end. Had she gone?

'Sorry, Sue—' a reassuringly broad Australian voice '—I'm weeping... I've been waiting for years for you to turn up.'

I was weeping too. 'So you knew about my existence, then?'

'Well, yes. There was evidence that Charmian Clift had had

an illegitimate child. A few people knew about it, but Margaret, her sister, totally denied it when I interviewed her. When did you say you were born?'

I told her again.

'I had thought that she was younger than that when she had the baby—had you. This helps clear up a lot of details for me. There are a few years—1939 to 1943—that I think of as the lost years. She more or less disappears. We can't find out what she was doing. Clearly she was covering up your birth.'

'Could George Johnston have been my father?'

'Definitely not. She didn't meet him until 1945. Briefly.'

I didn't think finding a father was going to be that simple. 'I know she's dead. But do I have anyone? Are my brothers and sister alive? Do they have children?'

A long silence. 'Prepare yourself for this. Do you know that she committed suicide?'

'No! *No*!'

'She took an overdose of barbiturates. It's a tragic story. Her eldest son, Martin, died a year ago this week. That's part of the reason why I was so emotional. You have turned up so close to the anniversary of his death.'

'Oh.'

'Martin's sister, Shane, died many years ago. She had a daughter, who must be about the same age as your girls.'

Poor mother, poor brother, poor sister, poor me.

'Jason is the only one left. He was a fair bit younger than the other two.'

So, I have a brother and a niece.

'Do I have aunts or uncles or grandparents? No?'

Dead. All dead.

We exchanged lots of excited information. We must meet. Next week? Your place? Or mine? Nadia issued me with warnings. Periodically the press liked to rake up the whole Johnston/Clift story. If they were to get hold of me they would have a field day. Or publishers with an eye to their sales might want to use me as publicity for the recent reissue of Charmian's books. I was to watch what I said.

She was concerned that the story might get out before Jason had been told. So she would get onto him herself as soon as possible. She would ring me back.

Next, Collins/A & R contacted me. They had spoken to Nadia and would keep quiet about it at their end, but it wouldn't remain a secret for very long.

There are politics to finding a mother. It had never occurred to me.

As for me, at this stage keeping quiet was the last thing I wanted to do. It was such an immense discovery. It felt like being in love! I would have stood on rooftops and shouted if I could. I would have bought space on Aussat and beamed my new knowledge into millions of satellite dishes. To have found my mother! And *such* a mother!

The flat blue book, the one that had come with my birth certificate, was at last consulted. Like most people, I read the instruction manual only when all else fails.

> *Adopted people may have a number of conflicting feelings about their birth family and birthmother in particular. They may feel anger, resentment, compassion, longing, hope and love—some or all of these at different times of their life.*[4]

Compassion, longing, hope and love. I could relate to these. I could never meet my mother, but her past existence, the reality of her life, was imprinting itself indelibly on my mind. What a burden of shame the word 'illegitimate' must have carried in 1942! I ached for the nineteen-year-old girl feeling the first butterfly touches of life within, her breasts swelling, her belly growing larger and tighter, labour starting, hours of relentless pain to give birth to a baby girl. But no euphoric climax. No bonding of young mother to newborn baby. Did she ever see me or touch me? Both of us were to be punished for our sin by never, ever meeting again. Yes, *compassion and love*. And for the connections that must be there, connections that I could dimly sense, *longing and hope*.

Anger and resentment? Not at all. But it was early days. My emotions were roller-coasting so violently that anything might be around the next loop.

> *Having finally met the person they have been seeking, the searcher may experience euphoria or be on a 'high', which may last for some time.*[5]

The white-hot telephone rang one last time that evening. It was Nadia again. She had caught a train to Sydney. She had seen Jason, and he was shocked but seemed to be coping. Could we meet tomorrow in Kiama, Charmian's town? She would show me where my mother had lived. I was to drive up and meet her from the train.

The flat blue book said:

> *—Take your search slowly, step by step.*
> *—Take your time to assimilate each piece of information as it is discovered.*
> *—Don't rush . . .*[6]

The search had taken on its own momentum. It obviously had not read the flat blue book.

Thursday night, with eyes so red and hot that they felt like twin dams for forty-eight and a half years' build-up of tears, I collapsed. And slept and slept and slept.

CHAPTER 5

The overprotectiveness of the adoptive parents is a big factor in the problems many adoptees experience during their childhood.[1]

Charmian Clift first met George Johnston, war correspondent, briefly in May 1945 in Melbourne.

In May 1945 the Shaw family was living in a rented house in Lord's Place, Orange. The house was bigger than the flat but built of the same ugly red brick. Its great advantage was the fact that it had a front yard with a path flanked by thick plantings of pinks, a fenced-in backyard with a sandpit, and a vacant block next door.

Suzanne was in her third year. A sturdy little girl with slightly wavy brown hair tied in two oversized bows, her short nose and round cheeks flushed red with the late autumn cold. Sue looked at her small world with wary, watchful eyes. David, her baby brother, reacted to life with

howls or sunny laughter, but she regarded the goings-on around her with serious, unsmiling attention, as if trying to work out the rules before committing herself. To the consternation of her mother, this small vigilant observer preferred to watch other children rather than join in their play. She could not bear to be parted from her mother. She had lost one mother. She couldn't risk losing another.

'Mummy come too,' was her frantic wail if separation seemed imminent.

Marjorie, like all wartime mothers, was trying to make do. Trying to pad out the food rations with the spinach and rhubarb and tomatoes that Harold grew along the corrugated iron wall of the garage (when the locusts and black frosts permitted) and with occasional eggs and fruit from friends on surrounding properties. Trying to make the clothing coupons last by devices such as unpicking one of her old jumpers and reknitting it into new cardigans for her children; by making all their clothes with plenty of room to grow. Trying to make exciting toys from scraps of old wool, fabric and a few buttons. Trying not to mind wearing the same straight grey skirt and grey cable-knit cardigan with the same lace-up medium-heel black shoes (which Harold kept in good repair and polished daily) and a much-darned pair of thick lisle stockings. Trying to cut down on her Capstan cigarettes. The corner grocer kept some under the counter for her but there were never enough. There was no alcohol in the house because Harold was a deeply religious man who believed that drink was the work of the Devil. Marjorie had other ideas, especially about a Penfolds sherry before dinner, but had promised to honour and obey.

Despite the Allied victory in Europe in May, the war in the Pacific dragged wearily on. The winter, a cold and bitter one, dragged on too. Orange, like the rest of Australia, was waiting.

Early in August, with the first tiny green and white snowdrops, the headlines in the Sydney papers screamed:

SINGLE BOMB WIPES OUT JAP CITY;
ATOM HARNESSED TO WAR.

Hiroshima had been destroyed. Two days later Nagasaki was wiped out.

The war had to end soon. News came of the Japanese surrender and the last acts of defiance of the kamikaze pilots. Surely now this terrible no-man's-land of waiting would be over. It could not go on any longer.

On the morning of Wednesday 15 August, Sue and David were happily playing on the kitchen floor. The breakfast things were drying on the sink, the high chair had been wiped down and Marjorie was sitting at the kitchen table glancing idly at the local paper, the *Orange Leader*, while 2GZ broadcast 'Food Facts' on the wireless. Her eyes skimmed the advertisements:

> *FAT LOST*
> *Safely—Quickly—Simply*
> *NO DIET—NO EXERCISES*
> *Glandular Extracts cause loss in weight of from 1–6 lb per week without any ill effect on health. Wartime discoveries have rendered this loss in weight permanent. Write now...*
>
> *THE THEATRE ORANGE. Showplace of the Stars.*
> *Last Two Days. Nightly at 7.45. Thursday screening at 2, 5.30 and 7.45.*
> *Wallace Beery and Marjorie Main in "RATIONING" (A)*

She and Harold never managed to get out these days, with two little children. And she was so sick of rationing. And she was too thin, if anything. She certainly didn't need glandular treatments. Did they take the glands from monkeys? She hoped not. She had always liked monkeys.

Then, in its own box, she read the discreet announcement:

> *The public should note that victory holidays do not occur until the Prime Minister officially announces 'cease fire'.*
>
> *If announced before noon, that day becomes the first holiday. If after 12 noon, the next day is the first holiday.*

Just as Marjorie was reading this, the dance tune on the radio suddenly stopped. Over the static came the voice of the Prime Minister, Ben Chifley.

'Fellow citizens, the war is over...'

Marjorie was prepared for this moment, as was every citizen of Australia. Letting out a wild whoop, and not bothering to turn off the continuing voice, which was announcing a two-day public holiday, she grabbed David off the floor, stuffed him in his stroller, yanked Sue by the hand and ran out of the house. The procession was due to start at ten o'clock. It had been organised for days now, just awaiting the announcement.

Harold was at the entrance to his office, but Marjorie and the children had to force their way through the growing crowds to get to him. Office workers, shopkeepers and customers, off-duty nurses, housewives with children let out of school, toddlers and babes in arms, a local policeman and numerous servicemen and women in uniform, graziers in their wide-brimmed hats with their well-dressed wives, ministers and town councillors were being joined every moment by scores, then hundreds more, as the wonderful, longed-for news spread.

As they hurried along with the crowd, Harold swung Suzanne up on his shoulders while Marjorie pushed David in the stroller. All around them was jubilation, exultation, triumph. Reserved strangers changed in an instant into cheering, laughing, singing friends. A conga-line wound through the crowd, more and more people joining onto the end until it stretched around the next corner.

'Lookit that, Daddy. What's that man made of? Why's that man on a bike?' From her vantage point Sue had seen an amazing sight. Marjorie saw it too.

'Harry, look. It's the girls from the munitions factory and they've made a straw man. Oh, it's meant to be Hirohito, the Emperor of the Nips. What's the sign around his neck say?'

'*I've got A-TOMIC ache.*' Harold laughed. 'Come on, Marj, they're wheeling him off. Let's follow.'

They let themselves be pushed along with the surge of the crowd, Sue getting more and more excited by the minute.

'Traw man ride a bike, Daddy! Traw man ride a bike!'

Outside the post office the procession halted. The laughing munitions workers shouted to the crowd, 'We'll cure his a-tomic ache!' as they poured kerosene over the effigy. One of them struck a match, and they all jumped back, dragging the bicycle with them.

Whoosh! Up went the Emperor of Japan.

Sue hid her face in terror against her father's shoulder.

'Let me *down*, Daddy. Don't want to see bad man. Let me *down*!'

David in his stroller had missed it all.

Fortunately the first official march for the day was starting up and the brassy strains of 'Colonel Bogey' soon had both children enthralled.

Suzanne has a few fragmentary memories from this time. One has to do with visual delight.

Late one evening her mother was making over a thick pre-war dressing-gown for herself. She was sitting at the Singer treadle sewing machine, poorly lit by a low wattage bulb, inexpertly hand-embroidering flowers with lazy-daisy stitches onto the shawl collar with stranded cotton. Awoken by a recurring nightmare of abandonment, Sue padded sobbing down the long cold linoed hall to the source of light. Instantly the tears dried. Her nose barely reached over the baseboard of the old black iron monster, and her dazzled eyes blazed with the glory of the brilliantly coloured blossoms growing and blooming one by one, transforming, devouring the mud-toned woollen fabric.

'Make a purple one! Now a yellow one! Now a green one! Go faster, Mummy, go faster. I want to see the colours!'

Another has to do with flight.

The swing in the park was a natural magnet for a father with a small daughter to amuse. Harold would push her over the mud puddle (a wide dangerous lake that had to be circumnavigated in order to clamber up to the towering wooden seat), higher and higher, till she could see over the scaly grey stegosaur backs of the peeling paling fences, then a little bit higher till she could see the repeated patterns of silver iron and red tiled roofs.

'Higher, Daddy, higher! High as the clouds! I want to touch the sky!'

'No, darling, that's quite high enough. Hang on tight. My little girl must be careful. My little girl might fall.'

CHAPTER

Adult adoptees . . . express an almost childlike delight in at last knowing someone who looks like them.[1]

My eyes opened on a sharp blue sky framed by a border of knife-edged gum leaves. It was Friday morning. There was a knot in the pit of my stomach. Why was that? Memory seeped back. Today I was going to meet Charmian Clift's biographer. Now I was feeling apprehensive. *Very* apprehensive.

Skimming through the family photograph albums and ratting through a cardboard box full of memories, I abstracted pictures of Mum and Dad in youth and old age, my husband and daughters, myself from adolescence on. The flattering ones, of course. Charmian had been stunningly beautiful, hadn't she?

I dressed carefully in clothes that concealed the fat bits. Forewarned by recent experience, I raided Doug's drawers for a couple of his big handkerchiefs.

drive to Kiama seemed to go on forever. My usually eptive eyes were blind to its beauty. The bare, rolling reen hills slid down unremarked into the pewter, back-lit sea. My car wound automatically around them on the smooth looping curves of the Princes Highway. A secret fear was nibbling at me. The same sick fear one experiences going unprepared to a job interview, where the interviewer holds all the cards. Would I be good enough? Nadia Wheatley would know so much about my natural mother and would be in a position to judge me. Would I get the job?

In my mind was a mental picture of the author I was about to meet. She was in her early forties. I knew that from my daughter's investigations at the Mosman bookshop. She would be very sophisticated, I decided, with simple, elegant clothes. Tall and thin with short blonde-streaked hair and gold jewellery. And a chain-smoker.

I had never met an author.

I walked down the steps onto the platform of Kiama station. How would she know me? I had not described myself. I had brought with me one of Charmian's books, *Peel Me a Lotus*, as some sort of identification. (Shades of all the spy stories I had ever read!) Pretending to read the book, I waited on a railway seat that slowly froze me through my clothes.

The red rattler from Sydney drew in. I was glad to stand up. People passed. No, that woman's too old. No, she's with that man. She's too young. Those two are together. Then a small girl with long blonde hair, big glasses and no make-up, wearing a sloppy joe, jeans and well-used sneakers, was hurrying towards me, arms outstretched.

'My dear, I'd have known you anywhere,' she smiled as we hugged. 'You're so like your mother!'

The knots in my stomach strangled each other with the grip of anacondas. Then unknotted themselves in a rush.

Tumultuous emotions clashed and grappled within me. Confusion—utter confusion. *Charmian, oh Charmian! Or is it Nadia who is my mother?* Time was slipping, warping. Who is it I am searching for? And when? A forty-eight-year-old woman looking for her girl-mother, all of nineteen! Then who is this and what am I doing here? Our hugging arms unfolded. It was Friday morning once again and I was standing on Kiama railway station under a brittle blue sky with Nadia Wheatley, my mother's biographer.

As we walked side by side up the stairs to my car, Nadia carrying her backpack, me my tote bag, she told me that she too had felt sick with apprehension on the way down. Would I be there? Would everything be all right?

It was. More than all right.

Sitting on the grass near the railway bridge beside Bombo lagoon, her face to the late morning sun, Nadia began at the most logical place: the beginning.

Charmian Clift was the youngest of three: Margaret, Barré and then Charmian. She was born in that house *over there*. I followed the direction of her pointing finger to a two-storeyed renovated weatherboard house on the corner with an Angus and Robertson's van parked outside. Of course it didn't look like that then—more like *that* one two doors down. Her father, Syd, was English and the foreman at the quarry on the headland up there. It's disused now. Later the family moved across the street to this house up the hill behind us.

Her mother, Amy Lila, used to write poetry and crumple it up in the fire.

'Was it Amy's mother who was grandmother Emma?' I had grandmother Emma of the contralto voice on the brain.

'No. She and Pardie Will were Syd Clift's parents. Amy's mother was said to be a beautiful Irish Jewess, who danced with eggshells on the heels of her slippers, and had a hand so small she could put it into the glass chimney of a lamp to clean it. Her name was Sara Carson.'[2]

Nadia went back to her chronology.

The lagoon in front of us had been the Clift children's playground. It was a different shape in those days. All three of the children had been taught to swim and surf by their father. They even rescued adults from the rip out there . . .

So it went on, a chronological life-history of my mother. Unlike most people when telling a story, Nadia did not weave back and forth in time. Instead she progressed directly in an arrow-straight narrative. My mother's life was clearly her subject, and a subject she knew very well.

I wanted to hear and remember every word, and concentrated fiercely on her storyteller's mouth as the sun climbed higher over the straddling shape of the railway bridge. Nadia's face was getting quite flushed with sunburn, mine with emotion. We pulled off our warm tops, our T-shirted arms now catching the winter rays.

Nadia continued with the story. Charmian's unquenchable thirst for life, her suffocation in the small town that Kiama was in the late 1930s, the Miss Pix Beach Girl prize that had let her escape to the big glamorous world of

Sydney, where her sister Margaret had been to art school and was, by then, working in a photographer's studio.

'The National Art School? East Sydney Tech?' I asked. 'I was an art student there myself in the sixties.'

National Art School, 1960. Heads together (one black, one brown, one red), three girls dangled their bare legs over the warm sandstone parapet, their suntanned arms resting lightly on the hot iron railing, their full skirts kilted above the knee. The walkway behind them was littered with sandals and flat-heeled shoes and drawing boards, half-finished charcoal sketches clipped to them. Shoulder bags, stuffed with art materials, leaned at drunken angles in the doorway.

'Are you sorry you didn't become a journalist?' Sandy, the redhead, asked Sue.

'A little. But you know Dad. He freaked out, said it was too rough for a girl. Sometimes I wish I'd taken the Commonwealth Scholarship and done Arts at Sydney Uni. I've always had a love affair with words. What about you, Vanda?'

'I love it here. In any case, there wasn't any choice. The Teachers' College Scholarship is the only one that pays us an allowance.'

'That's true for all of us, really. We *have* to become art teachers. It's the only thing we can afford to be.'

My thoughts jerked themselves back to the present. *Stop it. Stop it*, I told myself. *Listen to Nadia!* She hadn't noticed anything. She was still answering my question.

'Yes. Mind you, if there had been any more money in the Clift family, your mother would have liked to have gone to the National Art School too.'

Did this explain my artistic talents or did they come from my unknown father?

I was doing it again. Annoyed with myself, I tried to focus on Nadia's words.

... Some modelling ... the Minerva Theatre, a live theatre, where she worked ... the dates are difficult to get straight. Then her enlistment in the army in 1943.

The year after she had me. Was that deliberate—the beginning of her new life?

Her posting to Melbourne, recruitment to the *Argus* and her love affair with the 'golden boy', war correspondent George Johnston. He was married with a child, but the marriage was already dying. The scandal their affair stirred up, causing George to resign flamboyantly after Charmian was given the sack. Their move to Sydney and George's divorce from his wife, Elsie, when Charmian became pregnant with Martin. Their marriage in 1947 and Martin's birth. The flat in Bondi. The collaborative novel, *High Valley*, that won the two thousand pound *Sydney Morning Herald* prize in 1948 and made a celebrity of Charmian. The birth of Shane in 1949. The leaving of Australia when George was made chief of the London office of Associated Newspaper Services.

As the sun moved across the sky, we crunched barefoot along the coarse gold-ochre sand of *her* beach, and sat, still talking, on the sharp eroded rocks, slippery with Neptune's necklace, while *her* sea, placid today, played lazily with our feet. The giant bites of the quarriers, *her* father amongst them, had formed the silhouette of the headland at the northern end of the beach.

Nadia told the story with a wealth of detail. She had ideas about what had motivated the characters. She used internal evidence from both Clift's and Johnston's writing and external evidence from research she had carried out over the last ten or twelve years. If anyone knew the story of my mother, she did. In fact, in half a day I had heard more about the history of my natural mother than I ever knew about my adoptive mother in a whole lifetime of knowing her. I wanted to know and understand Charmian Clift, of course I did, but there was just too much to take in. She was trapped in the thickets of her own life, and I could only catch glimpses of her. I tried again to pay close attention.

Post-war London in the early fifties, the home of expatriate writers, actors, playwrights, artists, designers. Charmian's initial excitement with its sophistication. Then trapped in a smart London flat in a fashionable district, with two small children to amuse, doing little of her own writing but still collaborating with George. Their holidays by the cold bleak sea in Cornwall (nothing like golden Kiama) while George slogged away at the office. Respites of Continental trips, the children packed off to a dreadful English 'holiday camp'. Ideas of Greek Islands. The beginning of the romantic myth when they decided to move to Kalymnos. The sponge divers. Her two Greek books, *Mermaid Singing* and, after the move to Hydra and birth of Jason, *Peel Me A Lotus*. The island's community of expatriates. The growing number of summer visitors who changed the character of the island and eventually turned it into an Aegean resort. George's TB. His impotence. Her reputed affairs. His jealousy. The drinking and fights. The disastrous trial return to England, and the later backtracking to Greece. George's *My Brother Jack*, whose characters David Meredith and Cressida Morley were fictionalised versions of George and Charmian. George's Miles Franklin Award.

'What colour eyes did she have?' I interrupted. Nadia turned to stare at my querying, slightly tilted green eyes. There was a pause.

'Green,' she said.

Why, why did it matter? Why experience such elation at every newly discovered similarity? Was it that I had never looked like anyone before, had no visual links with my past, the links unadopted people take totally for granted? No-one, as far as I could see, had left their mark on me. Was this the reason I was so passionately interested in the faces of my husband Doug's family? Was this why I had made copies of all the family photographs I could find, going back in time to sepia-toned collodion plates of stiffly posed wedding groups and little boys in dresses? None of whom looked like me.

Was this why I had gazed with such satisfaction on the face of my first newly born daughter? Here at last was someone who was related to me by blood. Someone who looked like me. Here at last was my genetic legacy.

Meanwhile, in Nadia's narrative, George had returned to Australia, a literary hero, in 1964. Charmian and the children followed about six months later, as assisted migrants. They lived in Mosman, Sydney.

Mosman, Sydney!

Sue grew up in Cremorne, on the western ridge overlooking the filled-in part of Mosman Bay. Mosman starts on the eastern side of this land-fill park, rising steeply up the opposite ridge. The park is shaped like a long green finger, dividing the two suburbs.

Five days a week, she and her younger brother, carrying little brown cardboard cases whose insides smelt of ancient crusts and dried orange peel, slithered down the steep path through the bush, pelted past the cave where the bunyip lurked, and skipped across the narrow suspension footbridge to catch the bus to Mosman Infants and Primary

School. At least *she* skipped. Avoiding the cracks. He was just as likely to be balancing precariously on the conduit outside the guardrail, a dizzying, head-spinning height above Reid Park, where microscopic life was laid out for their inspection. A tiny dark circle with two moving extensions was a walking man, a blurring rectangle a running dog. With a child's sense of ritual, David always climbed back over the fence before they got to the middle. From the exact centre of the bridge (the only place unscreened by trees) the two children would wave up at their mother, a tiny tea-towel-wielding figure under her doll's clothes line in her minute backyard on the ridge.

Coreopsis like a collection of concentrated, tethered suns always seemed to be blazing by the bus stop, where an old drooping jacaranda bough made a wonderfully springy horse to ride while they waited. In November they were showered by its mauve bells as one of them pushed the horse up and down for the other.

As the bus drew in, Sue envied David his pockets, for she would be scrabbling for her fare up the leg of her navy bloomers, the tight elastic cutting corrugated grooves into her legs.

After living in a rented house in Kirkoswald Avenue with a view over Balmoral Beach and out through the heads, the Johnstons moved to a flat in a new block of units at Neutral Bay, then eventually purchased an old two-storeyed house in Raglan Street, Mosman.

Raglan Street, Mosman.

It was in Raglan Street that Sue had spent so many hours of her teenage years. Hours and days with the youth fellowship in the ponderously ugly church hall. It had been her red-brick clubhouse. How many times had she and her best friend, Sandy, paraded giggling under the viciously pruned camphor laurels whose roots were already levering up the footpath? They were playing their teenage girl duo song-and-dance act, full circle skirts over even fuller petticoats, starched and edged with rope to make them stand out, demure shirts with one too many buttons undone, Ming blue or Presley purple cummerbunds pulled tighter than possible, ponytails—Sandy's long, straight, thick and a glorious red; Sue's short, wavy, fine and an ordinary dark brown—sheer stockings hooked to unseen suspender belts, flat black pointy shoes. They knew they looked seductive. They hoped the boys thought so too.

Sandy and Sue had sat together since the day Sandy arrived in second class, with black-rimmed glasses, thick copper-red hair dragged back tightly into two bunches, a few large orange freckles and a dense Birmingham accent that sounded as foreign as Cantonese to the rest of the insular seven year olds. They were instant enemies. How could anyone like a new girl who said *pooppy* instead of *puppy*, and rhymed *grass* with *gas*.

Sandy had moved in one-street-down-and-around-the-corner from Sue. Her parents had bought a decaying two-storeyed house overlooking the watery part of Mosman Bay, divided it into cubbyholes and were running a guesthouse.

The enemies walked to school and back together, picking bunches of sweet-smelling freesias from vacant blocks, stopping off at one another's places. The saved fares would be spent after agonising indecision on musk sticks or licorice straps or milk ice-blocks or tiny marshmallow ice-creams covered in hundreds and thousands, or sherbet in little packets that they sucked through straws till it exploded in tingles on their tongues.

Both of them liked to draw and paint. They would sit either side of the table on Sue's back verandah and quarrel and draw all Saturday afternoon.

'What'll we draw, Mum?'

'What about Tony-the-Greengrocer's on a Saturday morning?'

And they'd be off, competing like crazy. The little round trays of scrabbly watercolour soon proved inhibiting, and they moved on to glorious poster colours in squat glass jars. Such strong blues, reds and yellows, but heaven help the child who wanted to make purple. Brown was all she could get! Ink served for black, horribly runny and spilly, and Kiwi tennis shoe cleaner made white. It had the advantage of making the brushstrokes stand right out of the paper. But it could get them into terrible trouble if Wednesday morning (Marjorie's tennis day) came and they had had a particularly creative weekend.

Both children sent in black ink drawings to the *Sunday Sun* children's pages. Sue's were smudged and blotted as the mapping-pen nib crossed, or the ink flowed too fast to control, or she impatiently rubbed out the pencil lines before the ink was dry. Sandy's were immaculate and were often published. With monetary rewards. Her friend's jealousy was uncontainable! Until one day a letter arrived from some kind children's page editor, suggesting that if she were to clean up her drawings they would like to publish them. It wasn't easy, but with such a glittering prize as bait, she tidied up her work. The editor kept her promise. From then on it was a contest. Who was in this week?

Marjorie cajoled Sue into writing stories, writing about what she knew—none of this fantasy rubbish. She liked to write but she preferred to draw.

Some days the girls would clamber barefoot around the rocks and wharves of Mosman Bay with drawing pads and

3B pencils, often trailed by David with his fishing lines. Cleaning the tiny yellowtail and baby bream he caught gave Marjorie severe dermatitis (David wouldn't clean them himself), and like many fishermen he couldn't bear to eat fish, either. Sue hated it too. Marjorie suffered her red-raw hands in silence.

I was deep in the recollection of sun-warmed bare grey planks on a pontoon wharf gently curving up and down on a deep green swell, when Nadia's voice penetrated my consciousness.

'Sorry Nadia, I lost concentration then. You were telling me about Charmian and George living in Mosman.'

George's growing illness and hospitalisation in the Royal North Shore Hospital. The 'shark-bite' operation which took away a section of his lung. Charmian having to be the breadwinner. Her column in the *Sydney Morning Herald*, which brought in the necessary money and an increasingly devoted following. Her celebrity status, reactions to the inevitable fading of her beauty, the escalating drinking problem and the continuing fights. Conversely, their loyalty to each other. His writing *Clean Straw for Nothing*, which developed the characters of David Meredith and Cressida Morley. Her refusal to read it.

I heard it all, the whole Greek tragedy, culminating in her suicide in 1969. An overdose of sleeping pills and a poignant quotation from Keats: 'I shall cease upon the midnight with no pain.'

All of them dead. George, Charmian, Martin, Shane—even George's daughter by his first marriage—all self-induced deaths, if not actual suicide, and all far too young. Only Jason alive. And now my turning up had made the odds better. Apparently the curse hadn't reached me.

The winter sun was floating above the hills to our west when we moved from my mother's beach to the Terraces for a late lunch. It was growing cool, and our shoes and tops were put on again.

In the restaurant, one of a line of converted nineteenth century workers' dwellings, the photographs I had brought fanned out across the table.

'Yes, you look particularly like her in *this* one and *this* (a nineteen-year-old Sue in Moulin Rouge cancan dancer's costume at an art students' ball at the Trocadero, head flung back, black-ribboned throat, wide triumphant smile, one black-stockinged leg propped up on a model of the Eiffel Tower) and in this colour print you even have exactly the same pattern of freckles (Sue at twenty-seven, with jasmine in her long hair and a baby on her hip). And now you look as she might have looked if she had lived to your age.'

Nadia looked through the prints of my daughters. 'What lovely girls! I can see her in this one especially. In spirit more than features. Your husband looks very nice. How is he coping with all this?'

'Better than I am. Doug is one of the world's best men. Always ready with the listening ear, the strong shoulder and the none-too-clean handkerchief. He's a believer in growth and change. He really wants me to know who I am. To be myself.'

I handed her a copy of my birth certificate across the littered table. Do biographers want such things? I had imagined they did. It was neatly tucked away into her backpack, as her capable-looking hands pulled out copies of photographs of Charmian Clift. I could hardly contain my excitement. I had never seen a picture of my mother. This was the moment I had been waiting for.

The photographs were a proof sheet. They were of a woman of about my own age, in pants and a checked shirt, cigarette in hand, curled up on a divan covered by a Greek rug. A series of prints. Probably part of an interview, because she was obviously talking animatedly. Nadia was right. I *was* like her. This woman had *my* bone structure—high obvious cheekbones and a strong jawbone, slackening now—*my* eyes, tilted under *my* eyebrows, and *my* mouth, large and full-lipped. The sort of lips starlets today obtain with silicone injections, but which in my adolescence were embarrassingly out of fashion. She was putting on weight—well, so was I—and the hand that waved her cigarette around was the same strong, long-fingered hand as this one holding up her image. Even her simple wedding ring looked the same as mine. Her wide smile was similar, but her teeth looked better.

'Capped,' said Nadia. 'Hers were in a dreadful condition when she arrived in Sydney in 1964. There were no dentists on Hydra. Both Martin and Jason had trouble with their teeth.'

That explained my dental history, too. Never had teeth been better looked after than mine. Regular brushing, six-monthly check-ups, large square strong-looking teeth that sheered off like icebergs in spring, the despair of my dentist and me.

I looked back at the proof sheet. Her nose was different from mine. Longer and straighter than my turned-up one, it made her face appear longer, and therefore thinner. Perhaps on second look her forehead was slightly higher, and her chin slightly longer, too. Yes, that was it. That was the main difference. Her face was longer than mine.

There was no slipping of concentration now. I couldn't take my eyes off these images. They formed a bridge between Charmian and me that was undeniable. *I am her daughter. See! I even look like her.*

'Did she get migraine headaches? They've been a monthly torture for me since my sixteenth birthday.'

'No not her, but there is a mention of someone—was it her mother Amy? A passage about excruciating headaches somewhere. I'll look it up for you.'

'This might sound silly, but do you know about her collarbones? Unlike everyone I know, I have dead straight collarbones instead of the usual V-shape.'

Nadia sounded amused. 'Sorry, Sue, I've no idea. It might show up in a photograph somewhere.'

The unimportant details of eye colour, dentistry, facial planes, hand shape, collarbones, even headaches, were far easier for me to relate to than what I had been hearing about all day, the big significant issues of her life, her writing and her death. What kind of superficial idiot was I?

Later, feeding coins and photographs into the Kiama library photocopier, I asked Nadia how she had come to write the biography. What was Charmian like when she met her?

To my utter amazement, she said, 'I never did meet Charmian Clift. She was already dead when I started going out with Martin Johnston. He was a romantic figure, tall and very thin, a poet already, with great charm for women. At one time he was trying to write the memoirs of both his parents. But it was a subject too close to him and he asked me to collaborate. Somehow I inherited her. George Johnston's biography has since been written by a Victorian academic, Garry Kinnane.'

'Could I get hold of that?' I asked.

'It's still in print, but you might be upset by the portrayal of your mother,' she answered.

'I want to read it. I want to know everything,' I said.

Our combined supply of twenty-cent pieces was exhausted, and I was exhausted too. Dropping Nadia off at her lodging for the night, with heartfelt thanks from me and promises from her, *anything you want to know, ring me, anytime*, I drove on home, the precious photocopies of my mother's face looking at the pictures of me, her daughter, that I had packed that morning.

Waiting for me was a very curious husband who wanted to hear it all. And as a bonus for the most extraordinary day in my life, a large cardboard box was also waiting for me, sent by courier from the publishing director of Collins/ A & R. It contained a selection of the current Charmian Clift publications, photocopies of newspaper articles, bookmarks adorned with the images of George and Charmian, a calendar of Australian authors similarly illustrated, and a little note:

> *Dear Sue,*
>
> *Here's as much material on Charmian as I can get my hands on today and still make the courier.*
>
> *Anything else you think I can help you with, please let me know.*
>
> *With all best wishes,*
>
> *Lisa*

Help was being offered from all directions. Today through Nadia I had found a mother. Now I had to get to know and understand her. If such a thing were possible.

CHAPTER 7

Adopted people are often brought up in a different environment and have totally different values, attitudes, standards and outlook from their birthmother and her family.[1]

It was two o'clock in the morning. I had tried to sleep. Now I was sitting at the oval table in the magic circle of golden light from the low-hanging Filipino shade. The embers in the handmade copper-hooded fireplace still glowed; the only other spots of light were the tiny red rectangles of the pilot lights on the kitchen appliances. Doug's full-bodied snores from upstairs nearly drowned the geriatric whuffles of our ancient Siamese cat, stretched out on the fire-warmed bricks of the hearth. The appliances chattered away quietly to each other, as they do in the night. On the outside edge of consciousness, from the mysteries of the dark world outside, came the beat of the southerly-whipped surf.

If I'd been a drinking person I would have got drunk. Instead, and far less romantically, I made myself a cup of tea and a toasted cheese sandwich and sat down to think.

The snowstorm in my head wasn't clearing. I needed to pin down my thoughts to stop them circling, but they were elusive and wouldn't let themselves be caught. Just as I snuck up on one, mental lasso at the ready, it would turn transparent and float out of reach. A strategy was called for.

I needed to start a journal. If only I could remember what my childhood had been like, as well as writing down everything I learned about Charmian, I might be able to connect myself to both my mothers. I might be able to find a position between heredity and environment.

Sydney, autumn 1947. Charmian Clift, now twenty-three and pregnant for the second time, was working with George Johnston on their first collaborative novel, *High Valley*.

Sue had turned four the previous Christmas. Her family had just moved back to Sydney, where Harold had been posted by his firm. The cottage in Cremorne that Marjorie had pleaded with him to buy in 1937 now proved its value. Although it was small, dark and old-fashioned, and so close to its neighbours that to get down the side passage to the back you had to walk crabwise between the high paling fence and the house, it had two advantages. It was only minutes from Mosman wharf, so Harold could catch a ferry to work, and from the back it looked out over an expanse of differing greens. The foreground was filled by twisted old angophoras, and way down below was the grass of Reid Park. Jacarandas and camphor laurels partially screened the red-roofed Federation houses of Mosman that climbed the slope in the background, rank on rank. And on the skyline a few remnant cabbage tree palms flew their fronds like miniature pennants.

Marjorie soon set to work to modernise the place. Lack of money, continuing post-war rationing and a shortage of building materials slowed her down, but over the next few years her steamroller determination flattened most obstacles. First to go were the picture rails. Then the dark cedar doors were painted shiny white. She would have taken down the ceiling roses if she had known how to do it without collapsing the ceiling as well. The main tiled fireplace was blocked up and a new black Kosi heater installed. The coal merchant had to bend double to deliver his load to the hewed-out area under the house. One day when Harold was at work, Marjorie single-handedly knocked out the corner fireplaces in the other rooms. It had to be done quickly before he could stop it, because if there was anything Harold hated, it was change.

These guerilla tactics, hit and run, became the pattern for household alterations throughout their life together.

Harold painted the outside of the house cream with a dark green trim, and the paths with dark red paving paint. They were to stay these colours, painted and repainted, for the next forty years. Long enough to come into fashion again.

Harold owned one original painting, an age-spotted watercolour of the pulpit in Westminster Cathedral, all gloomy browns and greens. This sombre relic had belonged to his father, the Church of England minister, and had pride of place above the mantelpiece. Sue much preferred the brightly coloured print of Chinese junks in the sunset that Marjorie had hung in the entrance hall above the nest of tables. There were no other pictures.

It was a life of unalterable routine. Meals were served on the dot. Fish and chips on Friday night, roast dinner at one o'clock on Sunday, after Sunday school and church. 'For what we are about to receive' before every meal. The final ritual of the day for the children was a kind of baby Last Post:

Now I lay me down to sleep,
I pray the Lord my soul to keep.
If I should die before I wake,
I pray the Lord my soul to take.

Sue invariably struggled to keep her eyes open in case The Lord swooped down and removed her soul, whatever that was. It sounded bad. Like having a splinter taken out of your finger. Invariably her heavy eyes would close.

Every morning before seven o'clock, Harold and his little daughter would open the front door with its dimpled glass panels. There on the verandah, white against the red-painted concrete, would be the rolled-up newspaper that the paper man had left, and the enamel billy that the milkman had filled earlier that morning. Harold carried the pail, Sue the precious *Sydney Morning Herald*. If the milkman's horse had left a steaming present on the road outside, Marjorie would rush out in her dressing-gown with dust-pan and broom and thoughts of lush rose gardens. But she had to be quick, before other broom-bearing women appeared over their scrubbed marble doorsteps.

The iceman came early every day, his pick-work on the huge block of ice leaving puddles in the road, irresistible to small feet. Bread too was delivered daily, a still-warm high-topped white loaf. Brown was for poor people who couldn't afford better. The ham-and-egg man used to bring his mobile delicatessen to the door twice a week. Although a fruit and vegetable truck did the rounds, Marjorie preferred the lately emigrated Italian greengrocer up on the corner of the main road near the bus stop. David and Sue were warned not to play with the greengrocer's little daughters. They were dagos, Roman Catholic *and* had their ears pierced.

Midmorning was the high point of Sue's day—*Kindergarten of the Air*. The optimum listening position was on the floor, right beside the dominating feature of the room, the wireless cabinet. Sue would lie on her stomach, chin propped on her hands, feet in the air, and remain like this until the kindergarten lady released her.

'Gallop, children! Around the room like spirited horses! Listen to the gallopy music on the piano.'

In future years the wireless set would become rather bald. Years of little fingers picking and plucking in a life of their own while their owners listened to the unseen heroes in the big brown cabinet—the Muddle-Headed Wombat, Hop Harrigan, Biggles—would gradually reduce the fabric covering the speakers to something resembling furry chicken wire.

On sunny Saturday afternoons in summer, to give Marj a break Harold would load children, towels, buckets and spades into the Ford V8 for a swim at Balmoral Beach.

There was a tremendous feeling of exhilaration in hurtling down that steep sweeping road with its wide expanse of sequined blue at the bottom. The barefoot children would have to be carried through the minefields of bindiis in the yellowing sunburnt park beside the park. Then they would run very fast over the burning sand.

'Don't jump off the wall, Suzie, you might hurt yourself. Stay in the shallows, you might drown. Don't go out of sight, David. Sue, hold on to your brother's hand. Now don't wander away, a bogey man might get you.'

'Getting a good colour' was an important part of summer. Salty, red-raw children with zinc-creamed noses were stripped of wet costumes in the laundry under the house, hosed down on the lawn to squeals of protest, towelled vigorously, then finally allowed to come inside. The car would also be ritually washed, dried with a chamois and hidden under its homemade calico cover until it was needed again for church the next day.

Then it was the sacred office of lawn worship. The three tiny areas of buffalo grass (back, front and on the street) were weeded, mowed with a push mower, and swept with the hard millet broom. The edges were then cut with a sharp spade and geometric precision. Perhaps the purple lantana hedge had dared to grow beyond the line of the front fence and had to be pruned back, or the twin golden cypresses by the front verandah had spoiled their straight-topped accuracy by growing above eye level and needed the points cut out of them. Finally, with a glass of cold lemonade from the icebox, Saturday's paper and sport on the wireless, the man of the house could relax.

It was Sue's first day at Danvers, a private nursery school just around the corner. Her sturdy lengthening legs trotted after her mother's long thin ones. Pedalling his sister's birthday dinky furiously, two-and-a-half-year-old David brought up the rear. Possession of the dinky was a blatant bribe for not being able to go to school, too.

Today Sue's mother had dressed her in a blue and white gingham dress with white braid trimming, specially made for this occasion on the Singer treadle machine. She had the usual two oversized bows in her hair. Her mother said they made her face look just like a pussy cat's. A very serious pussy cat.

She bawled when Marjorie had to leave her. She wanted to go. David bawled too. He wanted to stay. The teacher enticed her with brightly coloured beads to be threaded, while Marjorie dragged a protesting little boy out of the room. Gradually the howls died down to sobs. By the time she found the easels and the paint table, it was obvious that kindergarten was going to be a great success. She was still happily engrossed when it was time to go home.

'Most unusual,' the teacher told Marjorie when she arrived to pick up her self-important daughter. 'Children usually have very short attention spans, but Suzanne spent the whole morning painting. Paid no attention to the other children. See all the details she has painted on this picture. She says it's her Daddy. Hat and coat with lapels and buttons, laces in the shoes, briefcase in this hand, the other one waving. And I think this is meant to be a ferryboat here. She really is a most observant little girl.'

Words were her other delight. The glorious nonsense sounds of them made her smile. The power of them made her feel strong.

Marjorie had left school at fourteen, but was an omnivorous reader. Shakespeare, Shaw, Sartre, Stendhal, Scott, second-hand books were piling up on the shelves. Beside them were the old favourites she had carted around with her from state to state since she had first left her mother's home. They would later be joined by Salinger, Steinbeck and Simenon (every one of his Maigret detective novels), Gide and Galsworthy, Huxley and Hemingway, Conrad and Colette, Dostoevski and Durrell (both Lawrence and Gerald), by all the letters of the alphabet, even Zola. But very few books by Australians. Her precious collection would be read and re-read over the years, until their bindings came apart in the hands of the eighty-year-old woman.

Harold, who had left school equally early, read nothing but his oracles, the *Sydney Morning Herald*, the *Sunday Sun*, the church news-sheet and the Bible.

Marjorie had a highly developed sense of humour and would make silly songs out of Shakespeare to lighten the housework. Sue would happily join in.

Oh, to be or not to be
Eei, eei, oh.
That is the question now you see,
Eei, eei, oh.

The magical quality of names was important. Sue refused to answer to Suzanne. She refused to call her Mummy 'mother', or her Daddy 'father'. Pompous formal words were all very well written down on paper, but they were not to be spoken.

This was a year for magic, the year that the black-and-white squiggles of the bedtime story gradually coalesced into words. Simple words. But words that spoke directly to her. No intermediary needed. Words that made pictures in her head. There was no stopping her now.

As Charmian's pregnancy progressed, she took her typewriter home to Kiama for long stretches of time. Her father,

Syd, had died earlier in the year, and perhaps she thought to be of some comfort to her mother. Barré and his new wife, Bobbie, were living in a rented house not far away and the couple had privately decided to offer to adopt the coming baby if George didn't do the right thing and marry Charmian.[2] But there was no question of that. It was only a matter of time before George's divorce became final.

In post-war Sydney accommodation was hard to find and for a while George was living in a depressing room in Kings Cross. The weatherboard house on sunny Bombo beach was much more pleasant. Charmian and George were both working hard on *High Valley*, in their separate ways. In Kiama Charmian was working painstakingly slowly, as was her habit, while back in Sydney George was working at lightning speed, as was his. When he travelled down to be with her, both their typewriters clattered a duet amidst clouds of tobacco smoke and cooperative good will.

They married in August that year at the registry office in Manly, and found a flat in an ugly block at Bondi. In November, about six weeks before Sue's fifth birthday, Charmian's second child, Martin, was born.

He was born at Crown Street Women's Hospital, where Edna Shaw was still Matron.

CHAPTER 8

A tragic end to a search could be the discovery that the birth parent . . . had died. This will not be easy to accept . . . When a search ends this way people naturally feel a deep sense of personal loss and grief. It means that many, perhaps most questions will never be answered and dreams will never become reality.[1]

It was my first weekend as the daughter of Charmian Clift.

In between desultory housework and bouts of uncontrollable weeping, I was ringing all my family and friends. Or writing long letters to those too far away to ring—in particular to Sandy, who had been living in America for the last fifteen years, but who had visited me just before Christmas. Or writing in my sanity-preserver, the journal. Or reading Charmian Clift's essays. I was filled with a compulsion to think and talk about her.

If an hour went by when I wasn't telling someone my news or talking about my reactions or writing them down or reading her work, I felt totally empty. It was as though the me parented by Harold and Marjorie Shaw, the me that had inhabited my body for forty-eight and a half years, had gone away somewhere, and I was waiting to see what Charmian Clift's eldest child was like. Making her up from moment to moment. Trying her on for size as different pieces of the pattern turned up at random.

On Tara, at Trunkey Creek near Bathurst, New South Wales, the youngest daughter Margo had just come in from the paddocks where she had been helping her father hand-feed the cattle. She found her mother Jeannette sitting on the telephone chair with tears streaming down her face. A very unusual occurrence—in my husband's family, his sister Jeannette is noted for her strength, pragmatism and commonsense. She is the family's rock.

'What on earth's the matter, Mum? Who've you been speaking to?'

'Sue's just been on the phone.'

'What's the matter? Nobody's ill, are they? Uncle Doug hasn't had an accident on the motorbike? The girls are OK?'

'No, no. No-one's sick or hurt. It's Sue. She's just found out who her mother is.'

In an untidy student house in Weetangera, Canberra, eighteen-year-old Kristin answered the phone. Kristin is the youngest of my three daughters. An uncomplicated, forthright girl, she has an overdeveloped sense of humour and a natural ability to manage other people. This is her first year at university, away from home. She is immersed in the wonderful external world that only the young can inhabit.

'Hello, Mum... You've *what?* ... *And it's who?* ... But that's great, Mum! I haven't heard of her myself. But I'm really pleased for you. How do you feel? ... Mum, can I ring you tomorrow? Do you mind? I've just organised some friends and we're off to the Hoodoo Gurus. I just ran back to get the phone... Bye.'

From a high-ceilinged, old-fashioned flat in Clanalpine Street, Mosman, just around the corner from the Johnston house in Raglan Street, twenty-one-year-old Gina rang home. Gina is the eldest of the three sisters. She is supposed to be finishing a Communications degree, but is spending most of her time having fun, loving and being loved, composing on her piano themes that may one day be a concerto, writing on scraps of paper short pieces that may one day grow into a book, dancing all night, and making money working in a Mosman gym. When the fairies gave out the talents at her birth, they overdosed her with the self-expressive ones. Her greatest talent is for high-diving into the deep end of life.

'Hi, Marmee. It's me, Gi.' Her effervescence threatened to bubble out of the receiver. 'This is fantastic news! I've just been up to the bookshop and bought a biography. Of George Johnston. By some guy called Kinnane. But listen to this: it's got pictures of *her* in it. And she looks just like *us*! Like you and me. The big mouth and the eyes and everything. And the cheekbones. And just listen to this!'

The carbonated voice flattened out slightly as she read: '"At some point in her teenage years it seems likely that she had an illegitimate child, which she regretfully had adopted out, though whether this was with the knowledge of all her family is uncertain."[2] That's you, Marmee. They must have known about you.'

There was a short silence. A deep breath.

'You know... you might find this hard to believe... but sometimes I think I'm *too* flamboyant, *too* over the top.'

She was right. I did find it hard to believe. She has always revelled in gilding every lily in sight, and since she was a small child she has insisted on her right to do so.

'Finding out that my grandmother is Charmian Clift has somehow made it all right. From what I've read about her, she's just like *me*. It's given me an excuse or at least a reason, if you know what I mean.'

I finally managed to launch a word against the current. 'I know what you mean love, only too well.'

In her airy split-level house in Clareville on Sydney's northern beaches, with its spectacular view up Pittwater to Lion Island, my dearest friend Vanda was taking my call. As close as a sister since we first met at art school thirty-two years ago, this French/Italian/Egyptian/Australian art teacher was trying to convince me that it was fate.

Charmian's spirit was guiding me. How else could I explain how I had found all this at just this time, when I had stopped teaching? She had led me to this discovery at the first time in my adult life that I had leisure to pursue it. Her spirit now knew that giving me away had not harmed me. Now she was content and at rest.

It would have been comforting to have believed Vanda. But I didn't. I knew there was nothing left of Charmian but her words, any effects those words may have, her reflection in other people's memories, her ghostly image on film, and her genes. Her genes in her two surviving children and in her four grandchildren: Shane's daughter Rebecca and my three girls, Gina, Danielle and Kristin.

In his big raw unfinished house in Melbourne my brother David was astounded to hear my news. But he didn't seem at all anxious to look for his own birthmother.

Interesting speculations arose. Why didn't he want to know? Because he was a *he*? Was this a woman-to-woman thing? After all I wasn't desperate to find out who my father was.

I had asked a friend who worked for Family and Community Services to enquire about the ratio of women to men looking for their birthparents. My instinct told me that it would be heavily weighted towards women.[3] It certainly was deeply rooted in the primal female role of life-giver.

Perhaps for my brother it had something to do with the magic of the name. I had already changed my name once, when I married. It didn't particularly disturb me to find that I had a third surname. But David's name was part of his being. His identity was tied up in it. To find out that he had a different name might disturb not only his sense of ego, but his whole world.

There was also the element of risk. Of opening a door into a hitherto locked room. Who knew what might come flying out? That feeling I could understand.

The days dragged on.

Shreds and scraps of ideas kept insinuating themselves into my consciousness—tags and tatters. Perhaps they could eventually be cobbled into a whole piece one day. I wrote them down.

The 'if onlys':

If only she had kept me. All my childhood creativity could have found its place in a richly creative environment. I might have achieved something in my art world, like Charmian did in her world, instead of being sucked almost dry by generations of students.

If only I had tried to find her when I was in my early twenties. We had probably passed each other in the streets of Mosman, or Sandy and I might have glanced into her open front door as we walked along Raglan Street. Maybe she wouldn't have killed herself. Maybe now we would be wonderful friends.

If only I had started looking a couple of years ago. At least

I could have met Martin, my half-brother, the poet. We would have liked each other. I was sure of it.

If only she could have known my daughters, her grandchildren. Each of them has inherited something from this unknown grandmother: intelligence, feeling for the written word, creativity, beauty, love of life. This last quality is especially strong in the eldest. How those two would have enjoyed each other!

If only I could have told her that it was all right. That I understood why she had to give me up. That I felt no resentment, only compassion for her pain. That I had had a good life, and been happy and loved.

If only she were alive!

Then followed the 'yes, buts':

Yes, but if she had kept me, she wouldn't have met George Johnston and the whole myth wouldn't have happened. Or would it? Would she still have been a celebrated author? Would I have survived? Two of the children she had kept with her, living as a family with their own father, had died tragically by their own will. How would I have survived with her as a single mother? Would I have been the bastard child?

Yes, but if I'd achieved the fantasy of my ambitions in the art world, would I have had the long, loving marriage I've enjoyed? Would I have been able to give my children that most precious of gifts, their mother's time and focused attention? Would they have grown up able to cope with life? Are the pursuit of greatness and the nurturing role mutually exclusive for a woman?

Yes, but if I really hadn't wanted to teach, would I have continued to do just that for twenty-seven years? I would have missed the shaping of those lives, the fostering of the emergent talent of others. I would have missed knowing those hundreds of young people who have found release from the frustrations of school, and sometimes life, in my art room. The most interesting teenagers were often the ones who didn't fit in. The outsiders.

Yes, but if I had met her in Mosman when I was a green and unformed girl in my twenties, could I have thrown her a lifeline? She was a complete, very complex woman in her forties, riding the crest of her powers as a writer while slowly sinking in her personal life. Could I have helped her, or would her despair have swamped me too?

Yes, but if she were alive now, might she not reject me a second time? She might not want to meet me. Or she might not like me when we did meet. We might make impossible demands of each other.

A science fiction writer could make something of all this. Other possible pasts, leading to other possible futures. If Charmian Clift had made one different choice.

It was Tuesday again. One week since I had opened the brown manila envelope. I would have liked two heads. At least two. I was trying to read as fast as possible, and at this stage had finished *The World of Charmian Clift* and *Trouble in Lotus Land*. I was well into *Mermaid Singing*, shedding more tears over my mother's fresh and beautiful writing. Particularly poignant was her description of the Greek islanders calling out to Martin and Shane on Kalymnos. They found the children's names hard to pronounce.

> *. . . often the last thing we would hear, drifting very faint and sad across the water, were the names of Martin and Shane.*
>
> *'O Martis! Say!' they would call from the rigging. Very faint, very sad, it would drift to us. The talismanic words. The golden children of the new world.*[4]

Golden children with the Fates poised above them.

Another shred of thought. Do the children have to be sacrifices for the parents if the parents aren't sacrifices for the children?

One passage in particular kept tweaking at my memory. The family had just arrived on Kalymnos, leaving suffocating London behind. They couldn't speak Greek, had very little money, but were supremely and romantically optimistic. A friend had said that they would live to regret their folly, but that 'although the mermaids are mute it is necessary for everybody, once in his life, to go down to the sea and wait and listen.'

> *'Hey Mum!* Mum!*' Martin whispered urgently in my ear, his blue eyes amaze with hope and on his mouth the little deprecating smile of the disenchanted. 'Does he really mean* mermaids? *Or is it just grown-up talk? Are there mermaids in Greece too, besides the donkeys and the longest sausages in the world?'*
>
> *'Silly,' Shane said sleepily, 'there are mermaids everywhere.'*
>
> *'Oh,* I *know they're not true,' said Martin quickly, with the lordliness of disappointment. 'Excepting perhaps for a* rare *one. Mum, might there still be a rare one?'*[5]

Sue and David, aged about eight and six, were on the ferry to Circular Quay with their mother. On the top, up the front, outside. As always. The children were kneeling up on the seats, faces turned into the sea wind. Much to their delight, the wind was plastering their clothes to their bodies and threatening to uproot their dark hair. It was doing its best to unpin Marjorie's hat and blow it overboard into the deep green harbour swell. The tide was out. The Admiralty

House flag was snapping in the gusts. The Governor-General was in residence. The wide flat rock platform at the bottom of his green swathes of lawn was exposed, revealing its hairlike covering of bright emerald weed.

Sue had lately been reading and crying over Charles Kingsley's *The Water Babies.*

'Look Suzie,' said Marjorie, pointing. 'That must be where the water babies play. Wouldn't they have fun in that water grass?'

'Don't be silly, Mum! They're only pretend. Everyone knows there's no such thing as water babies,' said Sue, crushingly. 'That's a rock for *mermaids*!'

Was it still only Tuesday?

On Tuesday night I rang Martin Johnston's widow, Roseanne Bonney. Nadia had given me her number. Remembering that it was only a year ago that Martin had died, I felt sadness and extra tension on top of my nervousness in approaching anyone who might have known Charmian. Nadia had already told Roseanne about me, to prepare her for the shock. This was the last week of the school term, and Doug and I were due to go to Sydney on Friday night for a few days—I to sing in Mozart's *Coronation Mass*, Doug to cheer me on. We were planning to see our Mosman daughters, Gina and Danni, and stay with friends for a few days. So we made a date to meet Roseanne the following Monday night. Her voice sounded welcoming.

Somehow the leitmotif of babies and births kept on cropping up in magazines, newspapers and on television. The A.B.C. drama series *GP*, which I watched to try to wrench my mind off its obsessive track, featured a woman, twenty-seven weeks pregnant, who went into premature labour with an incompetent cervix.

Babies and births! More tears. It brought flooding back the memories and feelings of giving birth to my very first baby, twelve weeks early. She had been living, kicking and turning, when the spotting started at the beach. A few days later in hospital, my cervix dilated, the waters broke and the cord eventually prolapsed. I could both see and feel that baby's self, its very being, pulsing along the thick twisted lifeline as it lay looped along my inner thigh. Until one morning the rhythmic beat stopped.

It was all of twenty-three years ago, but I've never forgotten. After a few hours of induced labour while the humidicrib was being warmed up (but they couldn't fool me), my dead baby was born. And the sister held my head down so I couldn't see the tiny body. To be kind. To be kind. The nurses pushed me back down as I struggled to see my dead baby. Never to see her, never to hold her. How could I ever grieve properly?

Well-meaning acquaintances said, 'There's plenty more where that one came from.'

'Most heifers lose their first calf.'

Even Doug couldn't get close to me, couldn't understand my continual mourning.

I'll never forget the pain. The physical pain as the milk came into my breasts, hot and caked and aching, the hooks of the maternity bra laced up with wool to let it stretch far enough, and milk, sticky and warm, leaking through my clothes. The mental pain concentrated in this empty, empty space inside me, where my baby had been.

The premature baby on *GP* on Tuesday night hung on to life, tiny and pincushioned with tubes in its humidicrib. Mine died. Yet what Charmian had to face was worse.

Eventually you come to some kind of terms with death. But to lose a live baby, and never know—that would be eternal grief. Did she see me? Or did some triple-certificated sister force her young head down, too?

It was Wednesday and my thoughts would not let me alone. They nudged and poked and pushed their way past any guard I could put up. They brought with them storms of tears or hours of depression or even manic and slightly hysterical laughter.

Ideas of the potency and magic of Charmian's beauty whirled in my brain. I had recently read Naomi Wolf's *The Beauty Myth*, a frightening analysis of the pressures that work on women to keep them docile consumers.

To me, beauty is a two-edged sword. Its possession can cut to the quick, severing cleanly all other aspects of a woman until there is nothing left *but* beauty. It can also be the loneliest thing. Is a beautiful woman loved for herself, or for the way she looks? The social pressures in Charmian's youth had been different, of course. Was it easier to be beautiful in her time? She had managed to grow despite her beauty—or because of it? Had its loss been unbearable for her? Had that been a large part of her tragedy?

I do look very like the photographs I have seen of my mother. Old photographs from my album prove it. But beautiful I have never been. Yet I am totally addicted to beauty. Other people's. Despite everything my mind believes about the superficiality of mere outward appearance, the importance of character and strength of mind, I can't stop my eyes from devouring beauty. A really beautiful man or woman can make me stare and stare.

I need to consume wholesale the enormous cosmic beauties, and snap up the tiny detailed ones that nature casts in my path. I am a consumer of beauty. That is what I am. My whole being can be stopped abruptly by my eyes. The flash of jewelled colour on a mistletoe bird, the subtle curve of a long and lovely throat, moonglint on corrugated iron roofs. One glimpse is enough to do for me.

Years ago, in another country town, in my early thirties, after the birth of my youngest, somehow all my features settled into each other and I was the closest to beautiful I would ever be. It happened at a party. I was sitting on the floor, leaning back to back with a male friend, talking over my shoulder. I don't remember if Doug was in the room. A stranger, slightly drunk, came up to me and said, 'God, you're beautiful.'

'Hands off,' said the friend, 'she's married with three children.'

Later that night the same man, drunker, came back and said, 'You're getting more and more beautiful as the night wears on.'

'Sure,' I laughed it off, 'you're getting more and more drunk as the night wears on.'

And yet I've never forgotten it. I am not without achievements. I have heard words of praise. And forgotten the words and the speakers. But I remember in crisp detail the only time I was ever called beautiful.

Wednesday was limping slowly to its close.

In desperation for some peace, I planted daffodil bulbs in a big terracotta pot I had bought a fortnight ago in another life. My need to touch the earth was very strong. I was suffering from mental indigestion. I had consumed too much, too quickly.

The post brought a parcel from Nadia. Audio tapes and a videotape. The video was a documentary about the artist,

Russell Drysdale, with his mate George Johnston doing a boozy interview over a period of weeks. The point of interest for me was not that Drysdale had painted a portrait of George over the course of the interview, but that, for about thirty seconds at the end of the film, there was my mother in her Raglan Street house, taking delivery of the portrait. I had to freeze-frame it to see her, and I'm still not sure what that blurred ghost really meant.

The audio tapes were a Radio Helicon programme that Nadia as Clift's biographer and Garry Kinnane as Johnston's had made a few years ago. It was fascinating. It painted a picture of the two long dead authors using their own voices culled from past interviews, as well as actors' voices. The narration of the two biographers tied it together. Doug and I lay curled up together on the lounge, listening with hypersensitised ears to the voice of a woman dead for over twenty years. My mother.

Her voice was a shock. It was very deep, very slow, very deliberate and cultivated. My children later called it 'posh'. Her sister Margaret's voice was also on the tape, and it sounded unmistakably Australian. My mother's could have been English.

All of a sudden I knew why Matron Shaw had persuaded her brother to adopt me. Not because of Charmian Clift's loveliness, vivacity, health or vigour. Not because of her talent, because surely that hadn't been apparent at that stage and would not have impressed my aunt for a minute, even if it had been. It was because of her voice. My adoptive father's family was fervently Anglophile. They spoke of England as Home, though all of them, even their parents, had been born in Australia and most of them had never set eyes on Home. If Charmian had spoken like that when she was nineteen, Aunt Edna would not have been able to resist her.

On the tape, an actor read from George Johnston's novel *Clean Straw For Nothing*. He read a passage which for me conjured up the living beings of George and Charmian, despite their fictional guises of David Meredith and Cressida Morley. It was 1946. They had abandoned Melbourne unlamenting, leaving behind a journalistic world aquiver with the scandal of their affair. They were on their way to Sydney. Cressida wanted to stop and see her parents in Lebanon Bay, a thinly disguised Kiama.

> *One of what Cressida's mother calls the Blue and Gold Days, or the Illawarra Days . . .*
>
> *We swam in the toss and turbulence of a deep gut between the rocks . . . and we came naked from the tingling water to the shallow rock pools . . .*
>
> *Cressida floated on her back in the rock pool while I uncorked the bottle, floated in a dreamy abandon, arms flung and legs wide apart and eyes closed against the sharp blue radiance, and I was a long time over my trivial task because I could not take my eyes from the stupefying loveliness she presented.*

I found the passage for myself and continued to read:

> *I could live a thousand years and never again know such loveliness—the honeyed domes of her small sharp breasts, rose-whorled and dark-pinnacled, floating above the gentle water lap, and there was a golden glint of down, wet and metallic, brushing her thighs across curves of umber flesh, where water-drops dewed like tiny pearls, and fading on the pale cool silk-soft slopes within, and the pink hint of cloven mysteries below the flat gold plane of her belly where the neat mounded triangle of her hair,*

> *tangled and sun-spangled, crimped and flowed and curled into tiny ringlets, moving with the water.*[6]

This, to me, was one of the most erotic descriptions in Australian literature. But this was my *mother*. So young, so beautiful and so rapturously alive.

My journal grew. My emotions rode roller-coasters. I walked down to the shops for yet more tissues.

Wednesday night brought a farewell to a colleague. My news had spread throughout our teaching community by now and I arrived at the function carrying a little bundle of photographs and photocopies. I behaved like a new grandmother with a brag book. Shamelessly. *Here! Let me show you photographs of my mother! Look, and here's me at the same age. See how alike we are!*

My defence, apart from my own need, was the acute interest of my questioners. Tears would spring instantly to female eyes. I was beginning to feel that we women lived lightly on the surface of our world, skimming daily over a thin crust of existence. And that underneath that crust lay an enormous, deep, primal flooding reservoir of atavistic experience. The experience of archetypal Woman. Something mystic about the telling and the hearing of my story broke through and connected us to this flux.

Male listeners, while equally interested, never wept. They would offer opinions, make conjectures and give offers of help. Women would silently press my hand while their eyes overflowed.

Thursday morning saw me break down yet again. I felt like a fish jerked suddenly out of my watery environment onto the shore. A jerking, twisting, turning creature who did not belong on the land, and could never go back to the water again.

By Thursday night I was halfway through re-reading that terrifying book by Nancy Friday, *My Mother, My Self*, dipping in and out, interspersing it with *Peel Me a Lotus*, Charmian's story of life on their second island, Hydra. Nancy Friday's book strikes fear into the hearts of women, as it seems that our inner selves are formed by our mothers, and most of us are incapable of resisting that preordination. The ultimate horror is that we may eventually turn into those mothers. A year or two ago, when I first opened this book, I had felt smugly complacent and kept on reading, while others amongst my friends had flung it across the room. My genes, I had thought, so completely different from hers, must protect me from becoming my adoptive mother. And now? Surely the upbringing so different from my brothers' and sister's would protect me from turning into my natural mother?

As these tatters of ideas joined the rest of the ragbag in my head I realised that I *couldn't* turn into my birthmother. I was already older than all the Charmian Clifts who had ever been.

Would this terrible week never end?

On Friday afternoon Sandy rang from America. She had just picked up my letter as she got home from work, taken it into the toilet with her and howled for fifteen minutes.

'Don't you remember, Suze?' her familiar voice echoed from the far side of the Pacific Ocean. 'We always thought your mother had to have been someone really special—a Russian princess at least. Because of the cheekbones. Well she was, wasn't she? Really special, I mean. I'm so *glad* for you. But I'm not really surprised. I always thought you could have been a writer. It'll be your turn next. You'll be writing a book. About us as kids, and your Mum and her crazy doings and about all this.'

'Not me,' I said. 'Never!'

CHAPTER 9

Since I am just as prone to snobbishness as anybody else it has given me pleasure and satisfaction to keep my Rembrandt in the kitchen.[1]

She lives in a terrace in Darlinghurst. From the street it is one of an unprepossessing row of houses. The facades would be right on the narrow footpath, except that the slope of the hill means that a flight of concrete stairs is needed to get to each front door. It is not one of the tarted-up streets with iron lace, steam-cleaned sandstock brick and brass doorknobs. Few of the houses are painted. Some have their first-floor balconies boarded up. One is totally encased in a security cage of vertical iron bars. The bars act as support for a riot of vines and hanging flower pots, making an easy ladder to the top storey for any intending thief. Lovely little feathery-leafed golden robinia trees soften the harshness of the lane.

We had parked in the nearest available space. Doug locked Christmas, the dog, in the car, while I balanced tote

bag, bundle of photographs and a bunch of early daffodils. We counted the house numbers, 80, 82—oh, here it is. We were keeping our appointment with Roseanne Bonney, the widow of Martin Johnston and therefore my sister-in-law. Roseanne is a distinguished criminologist and I had never met a criminologist before.

The door opened on a small, elegantly slender woman of about my age in tailored pants and jacket, with a short sculptured haircut, bright brown eyes and a big welcoming smile.

'You do look just like her, don't you?' she said.

Behind her was an airy, cool, tiled space with white-painted walls and a distinctly Mediterranean feel. Paintings glowed on the white, some by artists I was sure I recognised, and it was hard to keep my attention from wandering.

Stiffly at first, but with increasing ease, we talked. For Roseanne it had been a second marriage. She and Martin had met after the deaths of Charmian and George, so she had never known my mother. She had loved my poet brother and missed him sadly. In the good times he had been a fond stepfather to her teenage children and the four of them had made a happy family unit. It was obviously distressing to Roseanne to have to focus her memory on him a scant year after his death. But she talked about him freely.

An intellectual, even a brilliant man, he had long been a heavy drinker, after the manner of both his parents. He drank heavily at night to slow down his mind so that he could sleep. He smoked very heavily too, also like George, who had never been able to give it up even when suffering most acutely with TB and emphysema. But in his last few years Martin's drinking had taken on a new quality. That of a life's work.

Roseanne told us that Martin was convinced that he was fated to die (in the sense of Greek tragedy) and that he might as well get on with it. His death in 1990 was nothing less than a passive suicide.

She found her photograph album and showed him to us. A four year old with a face I recognised, a feather stuck in his hair. A young man of the seventies in flowing shirts and flared jeans. Martin in Greece with Nadia. Martin in Greece, Martin in Rome, Martin in London with Roseanne. A very credible poet. You'd say he had been typecast. A tall, very thin man with shoulder-length fine dark hair, thick glasses and familiar facial planes.

Apparently neither Charmian nor George had ever noticed how myopic their elder son was. It wasn't until he was thirteen or so that they finally got him glasses. His teeth were terrible, too. Roseanne said they literally fell out of his mouth. This sounded familiar. And in a photograph of Martin in a swimming costume I found my straight collarbones.

As we talked, Roseanne's eyes would occasionally well

parents as children

1

2

3

1. The Clift children: Barré (19 months), Margaret (5) holding Charmian (6 months). Kiama 1924.

2. The Buttemer children: Dorothy (3) on left, mother Alice, Marjorie (4) right. 1907.

3. The Shaw children: Harold (6 months) in the centre, supported by 8-year-old Edna (later to become Matron Shaw). 1899.

CERTIFIED COPY FURNISHED UNDER PART V OF THE REGISTRATION OF BIRTHS, DEATHS AND MARRIAGES ACT 1973.

BIRTH REGISTERED IN NEW SOUTH WALES, AUSTRALIA

NOT FOR OFFICIAL USE

WOMEN'S HOSPITAL, CROWN STREET.

SYDNEY

I, VERNON MARK BENNETT, HEREBY CERTIFY THAT THE ABOVE IS A TRUE COPY OF PARTICULARS RECORDED IN A REGISTER KEPT BY ME. THIS BIRTH RECORD HAS BEEN SUPERSEDED BY A LATER RECORD AND IS ISSUED UNDER THE ADOPTION INFORMATION ACT 1990. NOT TO BE USED FOR OFFICIAL PURPOSES.

PRINCIPAL REGISTRAR

ISSUED AT SYDNEY

17 JUN 1991

Registrar General's Department,

Sydney.

28th October,1965.

CERTIFICATE OF PARTICULARS OF BIRTH

I hereby certify that, according to an entry in a Register kept in this Office,

Suzanne Shaw,

was born on 25th December,1942 at Sydney, N.S.W.

Registrar General.

ML 21080 V.C.N. Blight, Government Printer

4. Matron Edna Shaw of The Women's Hospital, Crown Street, Sydney.

5. Harold and Marjorie Shaw, the adoptive parents. Early 1940s.

6. Two birth records and a change of identity for an adopted baby.

7

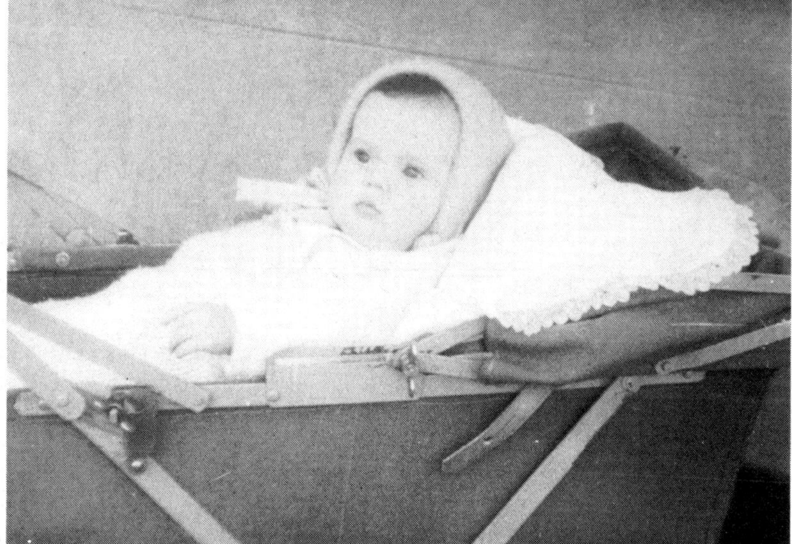

8

7. The mother who went home alone. Charmian at Kiama, 1943.

8. The baby. Suzanne at home in Orange, 1943.

9

9. Marjorie with Sue (2) and the new baby-in-a-box, David. Christmas 1944, Orange.

10. Proud father: Harold with his adopted children (3 years and 16 months) on Balmoral Beach. January 1946.

11. Sue (4) off to nursery school, on the north side of the harbour. Cremorne, February 1947.

12. Charmian and husband George Johnston, winners of the *Sydney Morning Herald* prize. Their collaborative novel, *High Valley*, had won them £2000. 1948.

13, 14. Charmian with Martin (born 1947) and with Shane (born 1949) on Bondi Beach.

on the north side of the harbour

10

11

on the south side of the harbour

12

14

the England experience

15

15. They're changing guard at Buckingham Palace. Shane, London, 1951.

16, 17. Martin and Shane, English children. 1953, 1954.

16

17

and back in Australia

18. Sue (11) and classmates from Fort Street Opportunity School with radio personality Keith Smith. Sue with arm around Smith's neck. The occasion is the first episode of *A Word From Children*, 1954.

19

19. Greek primary school children, Martin (6) and Shane (5). Kalymnos, 1955.

20. Australian primary school child Sue (11), on the right with friend Sally and art critic Wallace Thornton. David Jones Gallery, 1954.

20

Charmian Clift's children

21. Sue (4) Sydney, 1948.
22. Martin (4) London, 1952.
23. Shane (3) London, 1952
24. Jason (3) Hydra, 1959.

25

26

28

29

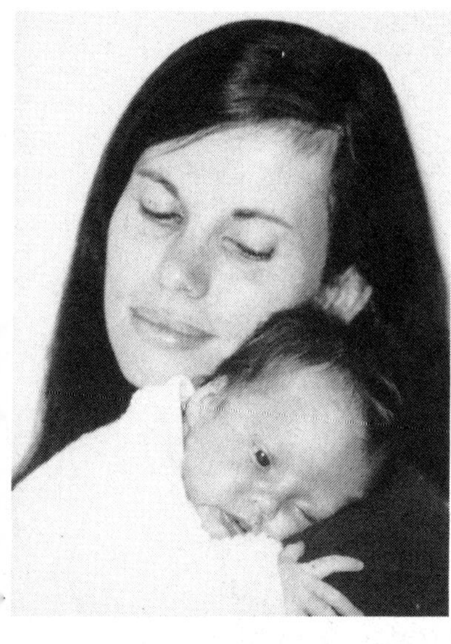

four generations of Clift women

25. Amy Lila Clift.

26. Charmian.

27. Sue with baby Kristin.

28, 29, 30. Sue's daughters: Gina, Danielle and Kristin.

31. Sue (15), Charm (mid 30s).

32. Sue (21), Charm (mid 20s).

33. Sue (34) with daughters, Charm (40).

34. Charm (35) with Jason, Sue (31) with Kristin.

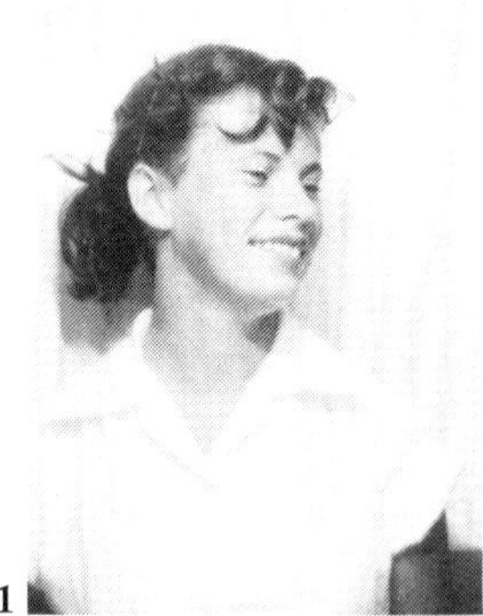

31

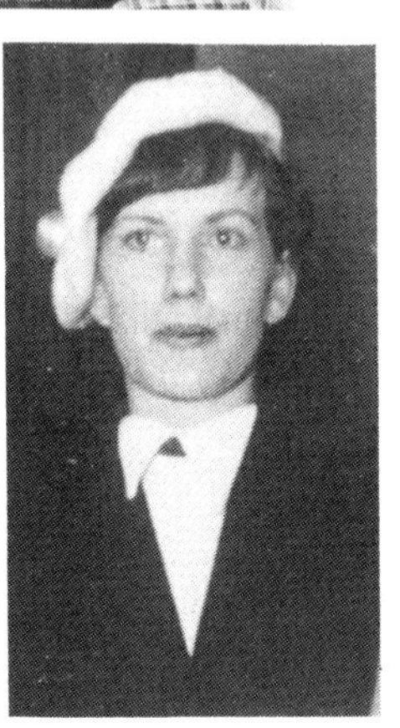

32

33

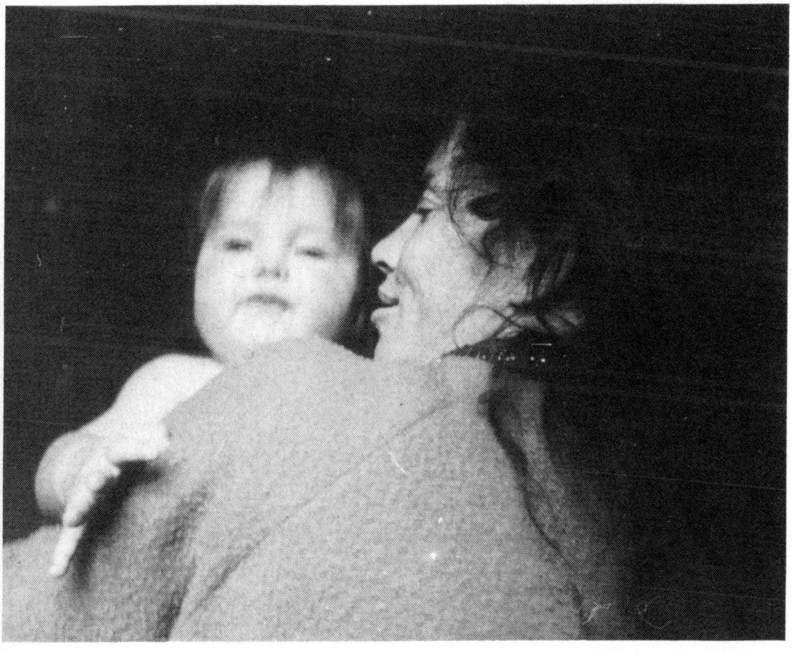

35

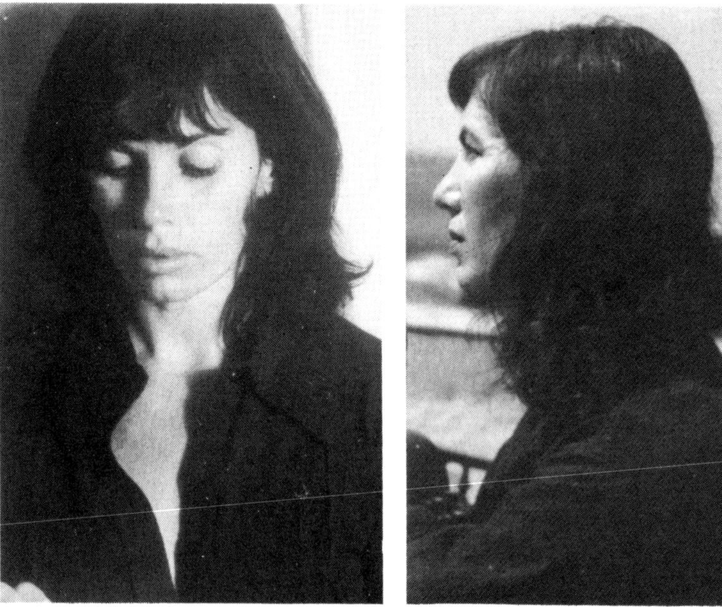

36

35. Sue (22), Charm (35).

36. Sue and Charm (mid 30s).

37. Sue (32).

38. Charm (44).

39

40

39. Charmian Clift with the sad eyes. Mosman, 1968.

40. Self-portrait by 13-yea old Sue. Cremorne, 1956.

with tears when she looked at me. She saw the lineaments of Martin's face in mine. The smile crinkles around my eyes, the mouth, the way my hair grew out of my forehead. An unnerving experience for someone who had only known of my existence for slightly over a week. I felt guilty because I couldn't feel as distressed as she was. I was sad for her, and sad that I would never meet my brother. But I was so glad to have found her, a member of my family.

The paintings behind us signalled for my attention. An icon, painted in gold and jewelled colours on a worm-eaten fragment of wood, spotlit. Eighteenth century, said Roseanne, not Byzantine, brought back from Greece by the Johnstons. A Nolan sketch for an Icarus and the Minotaur, from the Hydra days. And leaning non-chalantly against the wall a miniature Dobell, a birthday present expressly painted for Charmian. This was so dark and mysterious that I could only just discern a tiny fat water god frolicking in his element and a host of ghostly white horses behind him. Best of all this treasure was the Rembrandt of an oriental merchant, an etching that used to hang in Charmian's kitchen. I had only just read about it in her essay in *The World of Charmian Clift*, and there it was. About three inches by four inches and exquisite. He had been three hundred and ten years old in 1966 when she wrote the piece, so he must now be a venerable gentleman indeed.

And glowing with their own golden radiance were my daffodils in their vase.

My new sister-in-law gave me one of Charmian's favourite books, bought in London in the early fifties and carted around with her. She and George used to sell up or give away all but their most precious possessions whenever they moved. That this book had ended up back in Australia, to be inherited by Martin, proved its value. A book of Chinese poems translated by Arthur Waley, with George's inscription on the flyleaf:

> *For my favourite wife . . .*
> *George*

and hers underneath it:

> *Charmian Johnston*
> *Hydra*
> *Greece*

It was the first time I had seen my mother's handwriting: big, rounded and generous.

She also gave me a lovely old carved wooden picture frame that used to hold a picture of Amy (Charmian's mother), so I could have something tangible that my mother had obviously valued. And she lent me her copy of Garry Kinnane's biography of George Johnston—with warnings. It was a biography from a very male viewpoint, and the family had been upset by the way Charmian had been treated. So read it with circumspection.

We left with hugs and the feeling that we had been with family.

It had been a cathartic three days in Sydney. Mozart's Mass had soared and echoed in the high spaces of the church. We had seen our two elder daughters, and answered all their questions. We had spent Sunday and Monday sitting on Vanda's wide shade-dappled deck. Through the tall trunks of spotted gums the distant flotillas of white boats were sprinkled on the sparkling reaches of Pittwater. Vanda and Kathy, another friend from art school days, had listened for most of Sunday afternoon over endless cups of cooling tea and coffee while I recounted my story the way Nadia had told it, in strict chronological order, saving all the questions and speculations until last. Kathy had also been adopted, but she had spent time with her father and had always known who her dead mother was.

The usual chemical reaction took place and the tears flowed. Doug passed around the tissues.

I was a richer person. I had gained a sister-in-law. I had been given glimpses of my brother. I had seen and touched objects that my mother had owned and written about. And in my possession were things that her hands had touched and were now mine to touch in my turn. I was a little closer to Charmian Clift.

CHAPTER 10

Kalymnos declared itself only gradually.[1]

It was the third week of my knowing. Strictly according to the law of learning a new word—as soon as you learn a new word, it will turn up in everything you read for the next month—on television there was a *GP* episode and a *Couchman Over Australia* programme on adoption.

A girl on *GP* needed to find her birthmother for medical reasons, but the mother had a veto on any meeting. The girl was the result of rape. That was a very disturbing thought. Could it have been that way with me too? I hadn't been too concerned about a possible father up till now. One more question on my 'Ask Nadia' list.

While the *Couchman* programme flickered through its allotted hour, the phone kept ringing—friends telling me I should be watching it. They needn't have rung. I couldn't keep my eyes off the young women and the few young men who had found their birthmothers and were sitting with them in the studio. Or the birthmothers who desperately wanted to find their children. Or those who had found their children, erasing the terrible grief and guilt they had felt through the years. Or the desperate birthmother in her sixties, who had never told her husband and their three sons that she had had an illegitimate boy many years ago. He was attempting to contact her and she felt that her life would be destroyed. I was haunted by the hard, bitter face of one young woman, herself a mother. She could never forgive her birthmother for giving her up. Her face was a mask of anger and hate. A happy-faced group consisting of a child, her adoptive parents and her birthmother was in the audience as a unit—representatives of the new type of open adoption. The little girl understood that she had two mothers, one who had given her life and one who was bringing her up. And that they both loved her. What is more she had free contact with both her mothers.

The *what ifs* came back. What if...? What if...?

As soon as I had the chance, I turned eagerly to Kinnane's biography of George Johnston, and went straight to the photographs—clear and of good quality. Now I had something visual to fix on! Better than photocopies.

Some of the images I had already seen more than once, used to illustrate the newspaper articles that had arrived on my doorstep from many different sources. The young Charmian of Kiama and the later Lieutenant Clift of the Australian Women's Army Service was proudly beautiful, head erect, knowingly aligned to the lens. Charmian the successful young writer, the year she had given birth to Shane, glowed, full-lipped and full-faced, her hair in a simple chignon. The Charmian of London I didn't relate to at all—sophisticated, posed stiffly in an armchair, reading beside her bookshelves. The Charmian of Greece, now *she* looked like a mother to own. On Kalymnos, hair loose, a simple full skirt; and on Hydra, striped pants with a shirt, bare feet in sandals, or wearing a swimming costume; wide shoulders and wider smile, no longer young but sure of her powers. The Charmian of Mosman looked infinitely sad, her face pouched and coarsened, one picture in particular with her face turned to the light, so terrible that I wondered what point Kinnane was trying to make by choosing it. These Charmians looked more different to each other than the mere passing of the years could explain. They looked like separate women entirely. Which one was the real Charmian Clift?

I began to read, skimming over George Johnston's life until I reached the chapters where Charmian Clift appeared. It was essentially the story as told to me by Nadia Wheatley but with a paler Charmian. Diminished in some way. A satellite to her husband's sun.

It occurred to me that, apart from the direct source of her own writing, my entire understanding of my birth-mother had come to me from people who knew a great deal about their subject, but who had never met the living woman. I needed to talk to people who had been her friends, to see her through their eyes. I would ask Nadia for some addresses.

Meanwhile my own old friends network was in action. I was astounded to discover that the headmaster at one of my previous schools had gone to Wollongong High with Charmian Clift. Here was someone living in my town who had known her as a schoolgirl! I rang him. Fred remembered her well.

'Very like you and your girls,' he told me. 'Full of life. Looked like you when you were younger now I think about it.'

'Do you have a school photograph with her in it?' I asked.

'Oh no, you misunderstand me. She wasn't in my year. She was in third year when I was doing the Leaving. Then she left. She was a good sort, a terrific flirt though. She had a reputation at the school.'

'With the boys, you mean?'

He laughed. 'Well, yes. But there wasn't anything in it as far as I could see. Nothing to take exception to. It was just that she was lively. She liked everyone and was liked by everyone. I can still remember where she lived and that was about fifty years ago, so she must have made an impression.'

A small vivid fragment of my mother at fourteen. I had recently read her essay 'On Turning Slightly Sepia' in *The World of Charmian Clift*, about a school photograph that had been taken of the fifth form when she was in third form. She must have been describing Fred's year. How extraordinary! I had taught in his school for ten years, and all along in his memory had been living the mother I didn't even know I had.

A young teacher at Doug's school told me about a friend of her mother's who had been in the army with Charmian. Charmian and her sister Margaret had joined the A.W.A.S. together, after my birth, so perhaps this barracks-mate had been her confidante. She must have told someone about the baby she gave up, and this would have been the most likely time, soon after the birth, when her emotions were still at a peak. I would write to her.

A welcome letter came from Nadia in answer to all my questions. She had been interested to hear Fred's memories. No, she didn't think I was the child of rape. Possibly my father had been an American serviceman. Would I mind if she interviewed some of my contacts, if they agreed of course? She sent me the addresses of people who had known Charmian: Cedric Flower, artist and author, who, amazingly, lives quite close to me and who, with his first wife Pat, had been friendly with my mother since the days of the Bondi flat; June Crooke, wife of the painter Ray Crooke, who knew her in the last years in Mosman; James Calomeris, past editor of the *Hellenic Herald* in Sydney; and Mary Andrews, who had known her as a young mother in London, on Hydra and then again on her return to Australia. Enough to be getting on with.

There were quite a few Charmians here: the writer, mother and wife on Kalymnos; the celebrity who ended her own life; the political activist working towards the restoration of democracy in Greece; the mother of tiny children in London; the young lieutenant. I had already caught a glimpse of Charmian the schoolgirl. I would be moving backwards and forwards through the years, a form of time travel. I was reminded irresistibly of a television programme my children used to adore—*Dr Who*. This time lord had no control over his time machine. He travelled in time, certainly, but never knew where or more importantly *when* he would end up. I was beginning to feel a kinship with him.

I wrote a bundle of very carefully composed letters. And one extra to my half-brother, Jason. I posted them all except the latter, on Nadia's advice. *Give him time to get used to the idea.*

The replies came by phone or in the mail. Warm and accepting. No-one denied me. A series of invitations to morning tea, lunch and dinner with generous people only too pleased to help me.

Nadia had told me how she conducted interviews—well-prepared with the questions she wanted answered, and mostly with a tape recorder. I had to decide exactly what I was about to do. I wasn't an oral historian. I wasn't writing a book. I didn't know enough to ask many questions at all, let alone the right questions. I thought that I'd just let people talk and try to absorb the atmosphere. I wouldn't even take notes. When I got home I would write down in my journal everything I could remember.

I had known now for four weeks.

The moment our car pulled up, within sound and smell of the ocean, I could see that I'd brought coals to Newcastle. Cedric Flower's lawn was polka-dotted with old-fashioned white freesias in the late winter sunshine. Their fragrance rose like a visible mist in the warm air. In the garden was reproduced, shape by shape and colour by colour, the bunch of blooms I'd picked from my own garden beds. Nevertheless, I would take it in. Doug was carrying the chilled wine, and I had my collection of photographs of past Sues. The flattering ones. The twisting in my stomach was not unexpected. Cedric, as well as being an old friend of Charmian Clift, was a successful artist, presumably with little time to spare, yet he and his second wife, Wendy, had asked us to Saturday lunch.

As we walked up the drive beside the old, gnarled vermilion-starred coral trees, a slim figure emerged from the back of the white weatherboard cottage.

'Hello, you must be Sue and Doug. I'm Wendy. Ceddie is over in the studio. He won't be a minute. Oh, thank you. They're lovely,' as I handed her the flowers.

Wendy had a warm English voice, a profile drawn purely, the bluest of eyes and a gracious charm.

What we had taken for the house next-door was the studio. The Flowers live in a complex of buildings—two white houses, a guesthouse out the back, converted from the original garage. The banished car was kept in the carport.

Cedric and Buster, the black and white cat, two comfortably rounded figures, arrived simultaneously from the studio to greet us in their separate ways. Cedric shook hands and Buster wound around our legs, tail erect.

'Would you like a drink?' the artist's deep voice asked.

We sat in the sun at a timber table against the whitewashed chimney with its decorative wire sculpture. Buster balanced his way along the garden edging to disappear behind the guesthouse. Six tiny red-browed firetails were drinking and bathing in the birdbath, outlined in a cascade of backlit droplets. The distant purple escarpment quietly glowed.

'Doug probably would, but not for me thanks. I hardly ever drink. The pleasure isn't worth the after-effects.'

A surprised smile lit his face. 'Hardly your mother's daughter in that respect, are you?' He was studying me. 'But in other respects... there is a resemblance. Quite a resemblance. You have her eyes and her mouth...' *I look like my mother*. The accustomed feeling of joy washed over me.

Wendy came through the kitchen door, bearing cold beers and a mineral water.

'Do tell us,' she said, 'why you decided to find out who your mother was.'

I launched into the familiar tale. Out came the photographs. Wendy and Cedric listened intently, Wendy with all of womankind's instinctive reactions.

'It's the most extraordinary story. Who are you going to give this to? Or are you going to write about it?' asked Wendy. 'It's wonderful. I can see a magazine like the *Women's Weekly* jumping at it.'

'No,' answered Cedric. 'It would be awful if the media got hold of it. Can't you see the headlines? "Love Child of Fated Writer!" Leave it to Nadia in her biography. She'll treat it with sensitivity.'

Cedric took Doug and me to his studio with its heady, evocative art school smell of linseed oil. Here, waiting for us, he had laid out letters from Charmian to him and his first wife Pat, and a series of contact prints and their original negatives that he had taken on Kalymnos in 1955. Dedicated to the preservation of history, Cedric had kept these precious relics of my mother's life. Tactfully he left us alone while he went back to the house to help Wendy with preparations for lunch.

With Doug's arm around my shoulders, hardly able to see through the mist in front of my eyes, I studied the black and white thirty-five millimetre contact prints. They were incandescent with the light of Greece and showed an equally incandescent Charm and a happy, open-faced George with their young, spectacularly blonde children, Martin and Shane. A loving family in the sun. The first original photographs of my mother, brother and sister that I had seen.

The letters were particularly poignant—typed and written *by her hand* nearly forty years ago, kept by a friend all those years, and being read today by the daughter she gave up. I almost believed that her spirit was watching.

St Nicholas,
Calymnos,
Dodecanese,
Greece.
5th January[2]

Dear Cedric and Pat,

This is the life! Can't think why we didn't do it years ago. We live here in a little yellow house overlooking the harbour—all the sponge boats in—the big two-masters, and the little caïques, yellow and red and lime-green—fabulous colours. Our front windows and balcony are a grandstand for all the doings of the main street that runs along the waterfront. Casuarina trees and cafe tables and wedding processions and funerals (ever so grisly with open coffins) and flocks of turkeys and donkeys and sheep and pigs being dragged squealing to the slaughterhouse. Kids learning the facts of life fast...

Drink every night at one of the tavernas—tavernas very numerous indeed. All very clean and nice with sawdust on the floor for gents spitting and black and white check tablecloth produced clean for me. Big blue retsina barrels. Lots of singing, and a little brown-faced man with tiny white teeth and a black seaman's cap who plays wild music on a primitive sort of bagpipes made from a whole sheepskin (the skin not the fleece) with a horn of carved olive-wood shoved in one of the animal's legs, and a mouthpiece in the other.

We will be here until springtime I think. We want to stay until after Easter, partly because the Easter festivities are quite a thing and partly because we want to see the sponge boats go out.

. . . This is a tough, rambunctious, wonderful, colourful, piratical port. Must find something else as good, but with a few more amenities.

Love from us both,
Charm

I couldn't quite believe it. Here was *Mermaid Singing* from her own typewriter, complete with signature in her own hand.

And in the second letter, dated 1st March:

. . . we have made formal contact with the Church. Received by the Despot, a marvellous character in blue silk and black taffeta, hung with great silver chains and crosses—great black beard, and conical black hat, draped with silk—carries a tall silver-topped staff when he walks abroad. We walk abroad with him occasionally—sort of a royal procession, with little children and aged crones and strapping great divers too all bending the knee and kissing the hand of the Despot. Little children apt to kiss our hands too when in the Despot's company, which George enjoys very much. Great deal of church-going—in church Despot wears a fabulous brummy crown, all tinsel and paste emeralds which is very effective—ceremonies quite marvellous—all chanting and singing—and at the end the Despot dispensing little bits of bread from a basket, just like our Lord, and we all take one and kiss his hand. First few times at church George and I entranced—but ceremonies last about five hours and you have to

> *stand up so I've given Byzantium away for a bit and gone back to the fleshly pleasures of the tavernas.*
>
> *. . . Weather is now really lovely—all the blossom over and pinching green almonds over the walls when we go for a walk. Children swimming. Masses of flowers, irises and freesias and poppies and wattle. Mountains smell of sage and thyme . . . Kids at proper Greek school—can't understand what they're talking about any more. Shane abominable, Martin no longer a siss. Have hopes for them.*

Ending with:

> *We're dying for you to be here. Book going magnificently. Building ivory castles like mad. Very very happy. Even if it all fails will never be sorry we got away from it all for a bit, anyway.*
>
> *Love, Charm.*

What fantastic treasure! And Cedric was going to lend me the letters to be copied and the thirty-seven-year-old negatives so that I could print them. Did he realise how much that meant to me?

Over lunch at the long refectory table, Cedric spoke of Charm on Kalymnos in the happy days. He and Pat had stayed with the Johnstons in their rented yellow house but, unlike their friends, had hated the island: its poverty, bleakness, the sponge divers crippled by the bends. Even the Greeks didn't go there if they could help it.

Charm had been the greatest of romantics, extreme in her emotional reactions. For her, the poverty of the island served to underline the courage of the divers. On the home front she couldn't bear to listen to George tell stories about being beaten by his father as a child. She would burst into tears and retreat to the kitchen.

'And it was all lies. He wasn't beaten at all. Of course she was a great one for crying. I'll always remember a last poignant moment. They had moved to Hydra, and we had helped them. The time came for us to go back to Australia. The launch was waiting to take us out to the boat and we were saying the last tender farewells. George was at his charming best: *lovely to have had you, sorry if I've been a bastard*. Charm and Pat were hugging their goodbyes, when Charm suddenly burst into tears. "I'm pregnant!" she wailed.'

I could imagine only too clearly why she was crying. Her own writing, independent of George, under way at last. Her children growing up and less tied to her. And now another pregnancy! Snakes and ladders! She had slid back to the beginning again.

'We keep hearing how beautiful she was,' said Doug. 'What really was her attraction?'

Cedric thought a moment. 'She was magnetic, warm and fun to be with. She giggled ... to me she was always the chuckling girl from Kiama.'

'What about her voice?' I wanted to know. 'I got a real shock when I heard a tape of her voice. It sounded so fruity and English. Did she always speak like that?'

'Of course she was always an actress. In London the young sophisticate. In Greece she was more Greek than the Greeks.'

'So was that just her London accent?'

'Heavens, no! That was her *poetry-reading* voice.' Cedric's own deep, round voice became deeper and rounder, his mouth making a small tight *O*.

'Once we were on the waterfront, looking up at the little white chapels ringing the hills, and Charm put on her poetry-reading voice. "Look," she declaimed,' he made a dramatic gesture with his arm, '"just like little white droppings from Jove!" "Come off it, Charm!" I said, and she started giggling. You could always bring her back to earth.'

I was so glad that he had called her the chuckling girl from Kiama. It made her real somehow. And I felt a rush of affection for this man who had so obviously liked—loved—my mother.

Charmian was a happier person away from George. She had accompanied Cedric and Pat on a boat trip. They had sailed to Ermioni and she had been the best of company, George left far behind. The three of them had booked into an awful hotel and sat up all night playing word games because the beds were jumping with bedbugs. The next day they had taken a bus which eventually delivered them to Mycenae. When they had gazed their fill on the Lion Gate, they turned back to the coast, arriving at some Crusader port, where they looked for a way to get home. There was no boat to take them back to the island. Charmian ran around the waterfront for half an hour talking in her crazy Greek until she persuaded a fisherman to take them in his caïque. There was a lovely little print of them under the shadow of the sail.

She was happier away from George, yet she was intensely loyal to him. He was jealous of her work and destructive in his criticisms of her. When the Flowers arrived on Kalymnos in July 1955 Charmian was deep into *Mermaid Singing*. George was 'correcting' her manuscript, adding his own adjectives and purple passages. She had had enough of dual-control flying and was ready to go solo. She turned to her friends for advice.

'Communicate to George that it is *your* book and that you don't want him to touch it,' was Pat Flower's response.

Charmian did just this, and a furious George did not speak to any of them for a week.

'Awful,' said Cedric, 'when we were living in the house with him.'

In London, Cedric had already seen ample evidence of George's fury. George had shown the Flowers the manuscript of *The Piping Cry*, their second collaborative novel (which in the end was never published), and asked them what they thought of it.

'Wonderful,' said Cedric, who had not thought so at all. Paul Brickhill, the author of *The Great Escape*, was asked in his turn, and was foolish enough to make suggestions. Neither George nor Charmian ever spoke to him again.

'I valued the Johnstons' friendship more than honesty,' Cedric told me.

I liked him more and more.

The Flowers had stayed on Kalymnos with the Johnstons in the yellow house for eight weeks or so. When they first arrived, Sevasti, the middle-aged Greek woman who looked after the Johnstons, disliked them on sight.

'Jealous,' said Cedric. 'She didn't like sharing her family. There had been an outbreak of bedbugs and she accused Pat and me of bringing them in our valises.'

After a while Cedric and Pat convinced their friends that Kalymnos was no place to bring up children and that they would have to look for another island. So they offered to baby-sit while Charmian and George went looking at islands—the then unspoilt Hydra among others. Seven-year-old Martin, said Cedric, was superior and po-faced, correcting their Greek; Shane, wild and uncontrollable, kicking Cedric's shins then lying on the ground and having a tantrum. Swimming for the children had to be curtailed when Martin nearly drowned and was dragged out of the sea just in time by a fisherman. Cedric was very pleased to see the return of their parents.

They had all been caught in a terrible earthquake, which did not improve the Flowers' impressions of the island. They were still waiting for their ship when the Johnstons made their move to Hydra, and one of the little contact prints showed the furniture being moved out, surrounded by a crowd of curious Greeks.

The whole story of the Johnstons was like a Greek tragedy, Cedric thought. As if the gods had said to them: Take it all! Talent and beauty, popularity and fame. Then pay for it!

'Do you know who your father is?' he asked suddenly.

My heart beat a little faster. 'No. Nadia thought it might have been an American serviceman. Do you have any ideas?'

'Well, I could hazard a guess, but it would only be speculation,' and he named a notable stage designer who had worked in Sydney in the forties. 'I know from George that he and Charm had an affair when she was very young and working at the Minerva Theatre. She had not long arrived in Kings Cross and he could see that she would run into trouble, so he took her under his wing. They lived together. You'd have to check with Nadia but if the chronology is right he could be the one.'

'That would explain my artistic leanings then. When I think of the stage sets I designed and painted in my youth, it would be very fitting to have a father like that.'

'What I can't understand is why you are here at all. There was a place up at Redfern that performed abortions.'

'Perhaps she was scared. Not long ago I was reading something of hers where she writes about a girl who died from a knitting needle. I wonder if she told her stage designer? If they were having an affair, he must have cared about her.'

'Women don't always tell. Anyway he was quite a bit older than her and I've got a feeling he was married.'

Unexpectedly and unasked for, a possible father had been dropped into my lap.

What a lunch! Wendy made us feel completely welcome, and made me feel the most interesting person in the world. Cedric showed me my mother through his eyes. Showed me with the clarity of Greek light a wonderful, emotionally rich, independent young woman with the juice rising strongly in her veins, whose surface concealed the chuckling girl from Kiama. He gave me the hope of a father. He lent me negatives which had been taken in that faraway, lucent time. Lent me letters typed by my mother's own fingers so long ago. (*Had those fingers ever held mine?*)

I was full, of more than food and wine.

CHAPTER 11

The glories of the bathroom have spread streets away: aunts and cousins and grandmothers are brought to see it. Shane and Martin accept toffees and marbles and plastic ikons from an impatient army of children all labouring under the delusion that they are going to be allowed to pull the chain.[1]

It was ink-dark in the small room. It was meant to be. I turned on the safelight and a dull red glow illuminated my tools of trade: enlarger and timer, three developing dishes with developer, stop bath and fixer, tongs hung neatly above, boxes of photographic paper and, in an envelope, the negatives from Kalymnos, still in their original rolls. The same safelight drained all hue from my skin and turned my red jumper an eerie no-colour. The radiator pushed up the temperature to a comfortable twenty degrees centigrade: comfortable for the chemicals that operated best at that temperature, not too comfortable for me. A rolled up towel against the crack at the base of the door kept the light out and the heat in. The small bathroom attached to my studio had been purpose-built to double as a darkroom.

The negative carrier was set to hold a curled up roll of film, and I laughed aloud as I focused the first of Cedric's photographs on the white baseboard. Two extraterrestrial children on a nightmare animal, their faces dark grey with white shadows, their hair jet-black, the details of their faces sharp. White eyebrows, white pupils in grey irises in black orbs, black teeth exposed in grey mouths: images from a horror movie. Ten seconds at F-8. The timer clicked out the exposure. Paper into the first tray of solution and the developer began to work its alchemy. Faint ghosts slowly came to life at the bottom of the tray, growing, growing, growing until . . . there! The negative was positive. My very blond brother and even blonder sister, perched precariously on a little donkey; Martin's arm around Shane, both faces ecstatic with smiles—hers pearly with baby teeth, his gappy. Silvery olive trees lining a dusty road, a shiny dark-leafed citrus tree to one side, an out-of-focus peasant boy watching the foreign children from a patch of sunlight. Slanting early morning light and shadow patterns from that Greek sun, distant in time and space, making linear designs across the dust. Even the few scratches that the years had inflicted on the negative couldn't diminish the radiance.

What other riches were here to be unearthed? I felt very like an unimportant archaeologist who had by chance stumbled upon a fabulously important ancient treasure.

When a photographer prints up her own negatives, she knows what images are there. The only surprise is how well they will print. With this roll of film I did not know what was coming next. There! There was my mother beside a market caïque: baskets piled high on the waterfront, an old Greek produce-seller grinning toothlessly at the camera, Charmian in full skirt and white shirt choosing beans from a broadly striped woven basket. There was a line of young black-polled Greek fishermen, some mere boys, pulling up their net. There! Like an outdoor painting by Renoir. The whole family at a taverna table, dappled with sun and shade, empty clear glass bottles refracting the light. Both children bare chested. Martin and his mother (our mother) are fingering the texture of a paisley scarf with similar faraway expressions. *I know that look well.*

One by one the magical images progressed across the negative carrier, were transmitted to photographic paper, floated up in the developing tray, were 'stopped' in the acetic acid bath and then 'fixed' in the hypo. The running tap signified the washing clean of the earlier spells. Witchcraft.

And what was this? The inside of the rented yellow house? Charm and George at the dining room table, typewriter in front of her, typescript and fountain pen in his hands, burning cigarettes in the ashtray, cut watermelon in a large pottery bowl. The casement windows are open, an earthenware amphora on the window ledge, light flooding into the room, texturing the white walls. She is turned away from the light, reaching out her strongly contoured arm, its wrist encircled by an exotic heavy linked chain bracelet, to another large bowl full of—figs? olives?—that is held by the third person in the room. This woman is extremely thin and straight; her leathery, seamed face saint-like. A white coif, its folds delineated by light, is wrapped around her head.

Here is Donatello's wooden carving of Mary Magdalene come to life. It must be Sevasti, of whom Charmian wrote:

> *I think Donatello would have liked to carve Sevasti, cutting the lines deep in her thin face and tilting her head so that the leathery folds of her cheek emphasised the beautiful modelling of her thin fine nose and the flat plane of her brow. Her smile, for all the broken stumps of teeth and spaces of shiny pink gum, is enchanting, her hands truly marvellous. And in spite of the marks of obvious suffering—a pattern in flesh of the looting of her home by the Germans, its ultimate destruction by British bombs, the near-starvation and flight to Turkey, the nomad life of a refugee in Palestine and Egypt—in spite of an inherent gentleness that is calm and lovely, Sevasti carries within her an inextinguishable spark of raffishness.*[2]

And my mother, with her short fringed haircut and happy white smile, looks so young and carefree: the chuckling girl from Kiama. Cedric had asked me to print him one of the negatives, my choice. Here it was. The Kalymnos experience distilled in silver on a piece of resin-coated photographic paper, 20.3 by 25.4 centimetres. I made multiple copies. One for Cedric, one for Nadia, one for Roseanne, another one for me to frame.

Hours later, red-eyed and fume-drunk I emerged from the hot ruddy darkness, pupils contracting with a snap to flinch at the cold white light of the real world. With me were multiples of a dozen moments in Charmian Clift's life.

There had been some disappointments. Cedric had lent these negatives to the Mitchell Library to have them copied for their collection. They had given him back one roll of originals and one roll of copy negatives that were too bad to print. I presumed that they still had the originals. Mentally I added it to the list of questions to ask Cedric when I saw him next. Questions like: would he mind if I showed these pictures to Nadia and sent her a copy of Charmian's letters?

The cold white light of the real world had shone on some astounding events while I was locked in my magic room. The U.S.S.R. had been overthrown by a coup. Gorbachev had disappeared. There were tanks in the streets of Moscow.

Astounding news, but not as important to me as those priceless relics, which I kept on worshipping with visual fervour.

I made my benedictions: a letter of thanks to Cedric and Wendy, a phone call to Nadia. Had she seen the photographs and the letters? Was it possible that my father had been the stage designer suggested by Cedric? No, she hadn't seen the photographs or the letters and would love to. And as for my father, she would have to look at her files and would write to me. Nadia had become my Greek chorus, commenting on the action as the play unfolded. Indispensable to the narrative. Roseanne rang to say that Garry Kinnane had returned all the Johnston family photographs he had borrowed for his biography, and I could borrow them in turn when I was next in Sydney. There were plenty of my mother. She had obviously flung herself in front of a camera whenever she saw one. I might like to copy them.

What was I going to do with all this? I had been asked this question by almost everyone who had helped me, and an English teacher colleague had insisted that it was too interesting a story to keep to myself. I had a series of paintings in my head, *Charmian and Me* paintings, that I fully intended to explore when the frantic gallop of my present life had died down to a more normal plod. For now

I would keep up my journal, make notes on the letters and photographs, compare them to Charmian's written words, work out where they fitted in. And work out where the child who had been left behind fitted into all of this. Me.

I began to reassemble myself.

I went back to my parents' box of memories and to photograph albums. Once our children reached school age, and there were no more mother and baby images to capture, I became the photographer in our family, so I was rarely on the receiving end of the lens. There are hundreds of photographs of Doug, but not many of me. Now I wanted to find them, every one. I raided the albums, ripping out whatever I could find. I went through old albums of Mum and Dad's, doing the same. I leafed through bundles of loose box-brownie prints, turned out shoe boxes full of faded images. I bought a big new album. In bold white letters I labelled it SUE.

A blurred picture of a six-week-old baby in an antique christening robe, yelling blue murder; a little print of a small girl, elasticless wartime knickers drooping below the hem of her dress, holding the hand of an even smaller boy, he grinning, she scowling. One rare one with Mum's long face smiling self-consciously at the camera. She has the baby David on her lap and a serious round-faced Sue in a pretty print dress leaning against her. I didn't know I had this photograph. Pictures of Mum are very rare. She always considered herself ugly and avoided the camera. Dad's double image smiles at me from the wall: a blue-eyed, innocent nineteen and a blue-eyed innocent eighty-nine, but obviously the same man. But none of Mum. After she died, I had tried to avoid pain by not thinking about her. The last years were made a nightmare by a personality hatefully changed by Alzheimer's disease, a senile drinking problem, and a lifelong repressed anger expressed as a wish for death, which wouldn't oblige her. The horrible end somehow wiped out the decades before. No pictures of Marjorie.

I walked straight down to the shops to buy a tiny brass picture frame for Mum, my baby brother and my toddler self. The three of them could sit on my desk and look at me as I continued with my own reconstruction.

One after the other the images piled up: my life in chronological order. Some had my father's copperplate handwriting on the back, signposts to the past. Like this one. Stiffly posed in front of the severely pruned vines on the pergola, anxiety written on my tense face, wearing a new gingham dress and carrying a tiny school bag. 'Off to Danvers, '47', penned on the back.

A class group, Sandy's round face smiling next to mine. 'Mosman Infants School 2A' in chalk on a small blackboard, held up by the girl in the middle of the front row.

How many children? Forty-three faces representing forty-three lives, lived parallel to mine. Yet what were they to me, or I to them? Only a fleeting memory, activated by the action of light on this particular fraction of a second of time's continuum.

Here, folded into creases that had almost torn through, school reports. Mosman Primary, then Fort Street Opportunity School, 'excellent' for English, 'could do better' for Maths, 'outstanding' for Art.

A press photograph from 1954, my arm around radio personality Keith Smith's shoulders as he sat on the studio stairs with a group of children from my class before the first episode of *A Word From Children*. I had to say 'I love you' as the shutter clicked. Another press photograph with a classmate in primary school tunics, posed beside art critic Wallace Thornton at an exhibition of modern painters at the David Jones Gallery. I had hated the paintings, deeply offended by their distortions. I could paint better than that. At eleven, the Pre-Raphaelites were my favourites. A reply to a letter I must have sent Thornton after the exhibition.

My twelfth birthday party, early from necessity. Ten awkward simpering girls in full-skirted organdie frocks with flowing hair crowned by artificial flowers, feet encased in white socks and black patent-leather shoes. Posed in rows in front of the still severely pruned pergola that spanned our front gate. The grown-up present of a wristwatch on a black band. My twelfth birthday was on December the twenty-fifth, 1954.

Christmas Day was always extra special in the Shaw household because it was Sue's birthday, and Marjorie went to great lengths not to rob her of her day just because it happened to be Christ's birthday as well. The house was decorated in painstakingly made paper chains. Colour coordinated paper—Sue insisted on that. Christmas cards covered the venetian blinds. The best possible pine branch was picked from the dozens that stood in a bucket outside Tony-the-Greengrocer's corner shop. Sue had been saving silver milkbottle tops for months. Now she and David threaded them onto cotton twine and looped them around the tree. They were allowed to buy a few new tree ornaments every year from Woolworths. This year the prize had been an ice-blue hollowed out glass ball, embossed with beautiful crack-patterns. A crib was made in a shoe box painted realistically by Sue and topped with a silver star. Mary, Joseph and the Baby were tiny dolls dressed from the ragbag, the animals lead cows and horses from an old farm set. A week before The Day, Harold got out his stepladder and installed his precious set of multicoloured lights over the pergola. All the family assembled on the front grass for a trial view. The red, blue, yellow and green globes would be turned on every night thereafter until New Year's Eve. Mysterious parcels were smuggled into the house and hidden in the tops of wardrobes.

Tolerating no helpers, Marjorie slaved away in the superheated slot of a kitchen preparing the Christmas food. A birthday cake was made. Threepences had been saved up for the pudding. The once-a-year, long ago ordered chicken was stuffed, tied up and put on the ice. A salad and jelly and ice-cream were also prepared because Sue invariably gagged at the smell, let alone the taste, of a baked dinner.

On Christmas morning, the pillowcases left at the bottom of the children's beds were lumpy with surprises. Until their parents woke up they were allowed to feel, but not to open. David came into his sister's room before dawn.

'I gotta new cricket bat beside my bed. I felt it. What've you got, sis?'

'Don't know yet. Can't tell from the feel... hang on, Dave. Turn on the light while I look at my watch (precious, precious first watch). It must be nearly time.'

When Harold and Marjorie woke up they processed ritually into Sue's bedroom, bearing birthday presents high and singing 'Happy Birthday to You'. David's high treble rang out with the current rude version about the monkey.

Excited gift unwrapping followed. This Christmas, a fountain pen for the girl who was going to high school. The birthday watch she had already received. Homemade clothes, books, comics and sweets. *Don't you eat those until after breakfast.* Morning Service with a full choir and all the favourite carols, then home in the sweltering heat to Christmas dinner. Marjorie's mother and step-father, known to the children as Nan and Jackie, motored down from the upper North Shore suburb of Pymble, laden with more presents. Nan always smelled of violets and fault-finding, Jackie of cigars and good humour. After a stupefying meal, washed down with non-alcoholic cider, followed by birthday cake, lit candles and more *Happy Birthdays,* David and Sue left Marjorie and her mother washing up mounds of dishes, the men snoring open-mouthed in the lounge room, and raced out into the street to see what their friends had been given. At the far end of the road, the top of Sandy's red head was just visible. Slice by slice, the rest of her appeared as she trudged up the stone steps on her way to visit her best friend.

December the twenty-fifth, 1954, was the Johnstons' first Christmas in Greece. To the Greeks at that time, Christmas was a religious day only. There was no Santa Claus. There were no Christmas trees. There was nothing to buy. And there were two uprooted and upset children.

Their new Greek friends found them a tree. In her letter to the Flowers[3] Charmian says it was a couple of branches of pine, but ten years later she remembered—or embroidered—it as 'a salt tree branch still encrusted with hen droppings and with a couple of tentacles of dried octopus hanging from it'.[4] Charmian decorated it with balloons and sweets on brightly coloured ribbons. For some reason there was a plentiful supply of sweets and ribbons on Kalymnos. With Shane and Martin, she and George concocted a crib. They made:

> *haloes from chocolate wrappings, silver and gold,*
> *and a flock of sheep from scraps of sponges and*
> *matchsticks for legs, and a manger from bamboo*
> *and straw, and frost from a packet of coarse salt.*[5]

They painted a background of shepherds and angels with an old paint set of the children's, and 'a marvellous wobbly five-pointed star'.[6]

At three o'clock on Christmas morning the family stumbled down the stairs, shivering in the winter air, to answer the knocking on the front door. Their raised lamps showed a new neighbour and friend.

'My dear brother and sister,' he said. 'Christ is born!'[7]

As if the words were a signal, all the church bells began ringing. They dressed and followed their friend to the church of St Nicholas, lit candles with the Kalymnians to celebrate the turning back of the darkness, and stayed for the service full of wonderful chanting. It was daylight when they came out and processions of children were going from house to house singing Greek carols.[8]

Did Charmian think then of her secret, the daughter who had been born on Christmas Day twelve years ago? Did she wonder where the child was, if she were celebrating Christmas, if she were loved, as her other children were loved? Did she weep a little?

Here are two photographs of Sue the student at North Sydney Girls' High School in 1955 and 1956, first and second year. A lumpy, serious girl, ill-at-ease in her growing body. Box-pleated navy blue serge tunic (reaching well below the knee), navy blazer, both homemade, black stockings and shoes, navy felt hat with navy and bottle green band, and navy gloves. Woe betide the girl seen without hat and gloves in the street. Bike-riders had to tie their hats to the centre of the handlebars, visible to all. No talking to boys while in uniform, even to your brother.

By 1955 Charmian Clift and George Johnston, with seven-year-old Martin and Shane, nearly six, were beginning to settle in to their new life. It was a big risk. George had resigned, they had sold most of their possessions and moved to the bleak, bare, poverty-stricken Greek island of Kalymnos, more than two hundred miles by caïque from Piraeus. It had been the chance of writing about the plight and courage of the sponge divers that had inspired them. The divers had always faced retribution from the sea, which could suddenly cripple their bodies with the bends, and were now facing unemployment and poverty as synthetic sponges ousted the natural product. There had been a scheme to send the divers to Australia to dive for pearls (an ideal subject for an Australian writer to exploit) but it had fallen through. George and Charmian went to live on Kalymnos anyway, fired by optimism, the irresistible challenge, and a romantic dream of sun and sea and islands.

George was getting off the treadmill of Fleet Street. Charmian was moving away from her role of house-bound wife and mother in foggy London. She was moving back to the sea which had made her its own from childhood. They were going to try to live as full-time writers.

They spoke no Greek. The island had no dental facilities, only rudimentary medicine, no water supply, sporadic electricity, no sanitation, no transport apart from donkey-back and some decrepit cobbled-together cars that acted as buses on the road across the island. It was subject to earthquakes. But Charmian's romantic vision coloured its primitivism. She loved it. In the nine months they were on Kalymnos they worked with a will. This was what they had been looking for. George pounded away at *The Sponge Divers*, Charmian writing some of the descriptions. Although the book was published in both their names, she later described it as a 'phoney collaboration'.[9] But in a letter to the Flowers at the time she sounded triumphant. 'Roll over, Hemingway', she said.[10] On her own account she was working on *Mermaid Singing*, a lyrical and evocative account of the family's stay on their first Greek island.

By September they had moved to Hydra, helped by Cedric and Pat Flower. Charmian, who had just turned thirty-two, was pregnant again. Jason was born in April 1956, with no medical assistance except for the island midwife and a bottle of ouzo. Her fourth child and the only one not to be born at Crown Street Women's Hospital, Sydney. Two daughters, two sons. Did she, as newly delivered mothers do, remember her other confinements? Did she think about her first baby, the one so far away?

Some months later, in whatever snatches of time a small demanding baby allowed her, she began another gestation, a literary one this time—*Peel Me a Lotus*.

*

Sue had reached puberty. Even after forging herself a note to be allowed to miss the supremely embarrassing 'Mother and Daughter' film afternoon at school, it had still overtaken her. She had just turned thirteen, her initiation into the longed-for state of teenagerhood being the teenage accessory of the year, a black patent-leather belt. As yet she did not have a waist.

It happened on the way to The Entrance, a seaside town north of Sydney—the Shaws' annual pilgrimage. Same town, same rented house, same three weeks in January every year. The Ford V8, a well-preserved old lady of seventeen, had had her tyres and brakes and oil checked for the long journey. New swimming costumes (not, alas, the two-piece that Sue had coveted) had been purchased. The old surf-o-planes had been patched. Sandy had turned up late, as usual, to find all the Shaws, with the addition of David's best friend, waiting impatiently in the car. Her suitcase, overlarge as usual, had been squeezed, with much grumbling from Harold, into the boot. The kids' bicycles had already been put on the train.

They had stopped at the railway station in Mt Kuring-gai to go to the toilet when Sue discovered the brownish spots on her pants. Marjorie made a hasty detour to the chemist shop and after some self-conscious fumbling with elastic, safety pins, a bulky, uncomfortable pad, and an impassioned *Don't you tell Dad or David*, they resumed their journey. In the week that followed, while Marjorie swept and washed and cooked at the cottage, and Harold and the rest of the tribe swam laps in the sea pool, or body-surfed, or paddled in hired canoes over the thick layers of gelatinous jellyfish in the eighteen inches of water in Tuggerah Lakes, Sue sat on the shore and watched. With a face like thunder. No wonder girls called it 'The Curse'.

The Entrance in January 1956 was still a small coastal

town. The fibro house they rented stood alone in a sea of paspalum, half a mile from the next fibro house. Horses grazed in the paddocks between. A rusty corrugated iron tank provided water which had to last the three weeks if it didn't rain. Baths were a stand-up affair in an enamel basin. You washed all over with soap, then poured the contents of the basin over yourself. The dunny was out the back, a fibro and iron sentry-box, without even the usual choko vine: noisome and stewing in the relentless sun. Big hairy huntsman spiders, or worse, redbacks, were an ever-present possibility. Newspaper, torn into book-sized rectangles, hung on a nail beside the wooden seat. It created a weird kind of censorship as you sat and read fragmented sentences before you wiped. The dunny man came on Thursday nights. Friday morning was the best time in the week to go to the toilet. The sentry-box smelled harshly of raw disinfectant and the blowflies had not yet become interested.

Charmian in the past year on Kalymnos had learnt to cope with worse, as she explained in her letters to Cedric and Pat Flower:

> *No running water or hush-flush or anything like that. Have organised the dunny fairly decently and introduced Sevasti to Dettol. Don't know what we'll do when it's gone. One lone chemist here never heard of it.*[11]

and:

> *Thank you very much for the Dettol which arrived intact. Lovely scene explaining to customs what it was and its use. Never heard of such things here. Notice that it cost you a fortune to send. Will repay one day and bless you both.*[12]

Part of the coping mechanism was a bucket of seawater beside the lavatory and a bunch of basil hanging above it.

Shane and Martin had developed coping mechanisms of their own. Transplanted to a barren island from their comfortable, affluent London life, they had at first been foreign, frightened and friendless. But with the easy adaptability of small children they had gone to the local primary school, begun to absorb the Greek language through their pores, learnt to read in Greek as well as English, made friends with the peasant children and been petted by the adults. They had learnt to eat strange food like squid slippery with olive oil, run wild on waterfront and mountainside, watched animals being slaughtered for meat, ridden donkeys, made temporary pets of stray dogs, hauled water from the well, sailed with the fishermen, jumped from the rigging of sponge boats, swum in the warm Greek sea, sunbaked in the hot Greek sun. They had caught head lice, and developed jaundice. They had been part of the seasonal religious rituals. They had decorated the paschal lambs at Easter; eaten Koliva, the food of the dead, on the days set aside for All Souls; dressed up for Carnivale; held candles beside the baptismal font; joined in wedding processions and followed the unclosed coffins of the dead. They had waved goodbye to the divers as the sponge-fleet sailed away to the coast of Africa after Easter.

Shane turned six in February and Martin eight in November, 1955.

The Shaw family had become more affluent. Against Harold's wishes—*people will say I can't support my wife and family*—Marjorie, now fifty-two, had gone back to the job she had been doing when he first met her: typing. She was home every day by three-thirty, so her conscience was clear.

More important than the money—though that was her excuse—was her new freedom, her new sense of self, and a circle of work-friends who found her brand of cruel Irish humour hilariously funny. She was a chain-smoker, lighting one cigarette from the other, and one day, to their delight, had absent-mindedly tried to light up her morning-tea banana.

Harold thought that she had given up smoking, as she had promised. At home she would wait until dark, then wrap an old plastic shower curtain around her shoulders, put a shower-cap on her head, pick up her Craven As, matches and breath mints, and go down to The Deep. The Deep was a thirty-foot drop down a sandstone cliff, at the bottom of which most of the garden was laid out. A set of rickety sunbleached wooden stairs connected the upper and lower levels. Marjorie would crouch on the bottom step, puff her way frantically through three or four cigarettes, pocket the matches and the cigarette packet, then begin chewing the mints as she began the dark climb to the top. The shower cap and curtain would be stowed in the laundry under the house, and she would re-emerge indoors odour-free and in a much better mood.

Now the house improvements gained momentum.

Definitely not, Marjorie! It's out of the question. There's nothing wrong with the one we have. We can't afford it.

Marjorie obtained quotes, chose the fittings, organised the workmen, changed her work hours to let them in, made them cups of tea, let them out, cleaned up after them, paid the bills, and when the new bathroom was finished, Harold was quite convinced the whole thing had been his idea.

It was heavenly. The old freestanding cast-iron, claw-footed monster was retired to the back garden to become a fish pond. A lovely new pale green tiled-in version, with shower over, took its place. A matching ceramic toilet and hand basin nearly filled the rest of the space. A tasteful green terry towelling toilet seat cover, and a very with-it bath mat with two black footprints on it, added the finishing touches. Sue was ecstatic. She had been allowed to choose the mat.

A cunning walk-through cupboard called, with great accuracy, 'the squeezebox', now hid the bathroom door. It was an improvement. In the past the door, opening straight onto the toilet, had been barely five feet away from the dining room table. Afternoon-tea visitors had been, on occasion, greatly entertained by the performances of unembarrassed small children. Sue was mortified by the memory.

A big iron key turned the lock on the inside of this door and, once turned, was hard for children's hands to unlock again. The only way out of the bathroom was to climb up over the basin, squeeze through the narrow space at the bottom of the equally stuck sash window, and shin down the waste-pipe to the side-passage far below. By the time Sue was too big to squeeze out the window, her hands were strong enough to turn the key.

Marjorie's money had run out. The old gas heater had to stay.

Definitely not, Marjorie! We can't afford a hot-water system.

At night the bathroom was Sue's secret place. She locked the door, turned on the water, lit the gas, turned off the electric light, dropped a towel on the black and white tiled floor, and took off her clothes. Kneeling up on the toilet seat, she stared through the steam at her naked reflection in a wiped patch of the shaving mirror. Ugly, ugly! Big mouth and a gap between her two front teeth. Everything turning curved! Round, nipple-accented breasts. Rounding hips. Ugly dark hair starting under her arms. Why wouldn't her mother let her shave it off? She would anyway. That would show her! And the shadowing of pubic hair. It was the ugliest of all. Why did God let it happen? As for sex! She wished her mother had never given her that awful book about rams and ewes to read. Surely it couldn't be true. She was never going to let anyone do *that* to her. She was never going to get married, and if she did, she would adopt all her children!

Then she lay on her back on the towel, listening to the roar of gas and hot water (foaming closer and closer to the top of the bath), staring through the warm fug at the reflection of the flickering blue flames dancing on the shiny white ceiling. Hypnotised, she would dream thirteen-year-old dreams. Dreams of who she was, what she would be. Dreams of being beautiful. Dreams of her real mother coming to claim her. Not dead at all, but a young, fabulously gorgeous, unbelievably rich mother, who would understand her perfectly.

A sudden thumping on the door.

'What on earth are you doing in there! Get out of that bath. Now! There are others in this family besides you, you selfish girl, and they all want a bath too.'

And on their second Greek Island, Hydra, George and Charmian had bought a house, the first bit of property either of them had ever owned, their first bit of security. A large old house, built of stone in 1788 by a sea captain. The house by the well. To be christened by the Greeks 'the Australian House'.

> *'Here! Here is where you will put the pump.'*
>
> *'Pump. What pump?' George asked blankly.*
>
> *'You must have a* pump, *mustn't you? Do you*

intend to carry buckets of water by hand to the bathroom?'

'But there isn't a bathroom,' said George.

'You will construct one . . .'

'Look,' George whispered anxiously, 'for Christ's sake steer Creon away from bathrooms. He'll have a gang of workmen here tomorrow pulling the whole place down and rebuilding it. We can't afford a bathroom!'[13]

So in a moment of surrender so reckless that we dare not think of it we have allowed Creon to order from Athens a square porcelain shower tray and wash-hand-basin with a wonderful swivelling tap, and a gleaming white toilet bowl whose tank is labelled 'The Best Niagara'.[14]

CHAPTER 12

They brought the family photograph album too. So I sat there and saw all these people. And this is your brother and this is your sister and this is your aunt, and so on. All these people and I looked. 'Oh, I look like her, and I look like you, too.'[1]

'So, you're Charm's little girl!'

The greeting, with a faint trace of American underlying its Englishness, came from a small-boned woman with a Shirley MacLaine smile. Her arms opened wide and hugged me, almost crushing the bunch of early tulips I was carrying.

Finding her home unit had been no trouble. In my carefully chosen outfit (shamelessly plagiarising the casual elegance of my mother) of black pants and grey wool blazer over a red shirt that perfectly matched the lipstick on my Charmian Clift mouth, I was hoping to hear, from yet another pair of lips, those wonderful words: *You look so like your mother*.

'Nadia said you looked like Charm would look if she'd lived to your age. Nonsense!' she said. 'Now would I say you looked like her if I didn't know? Let me look at you. If I saw you walking down the street would I say: "That woman looks like Charmian Clift"?' She took the flowers. 'How lovely of you to bring me tulips. I adore tulips.'

So began an evening with a friend from Charmian's young-mother-in-London days, Mary Andrews. 'A warm and hospitable person . . . you two would get on well,' Nadia had written to me.

While Mary prepared pasta and salad in her kitchenette, she talked about her relationship with my mother.

'Now, just when did we meet? It was certainly in Sydney. I think they were living somewhere pretty seedy. We all used to meet in pubs. We were living in Wahroonga, so we wouldn't be staying overnight in the city. She was pregnant with Martin. In fact I lent her the dress she got married in. It was a sack dress, knee-length and straight and a sage-green. It went some of the way to hiding Martin, but didn't completely succeed.

'When they got to London in the early fifties (we were already there, you understand) Charm rang at our door. Gordon and I were working in our office. It was the year of the Festival of Britain. Gordon was working as a designer for the Design Research Institute for the Science Exhibition at South Kensington and we were very busy. There was a ring at the door, and there she was standing outside, wearing a black coat and a little hat and little white gloves. I remember those gloves clearly. She was acting very correct. Her impression of the London sophisticate. But I must admit that didn't last long.'

'Were you really good friends? Did you confide in each other?' I asked as I carried the bowl of salad to the table. Without causing a ripple on the surface of my face, an interior fanfare of trumpets sounded as I asked The Question: 'Did she tell you about me?'

The cutlery ceased to clatter, the thin stream of wine was frozen in mid-pour, the tips of the salad servers paused a hair's breadth from the lettuce leaves: the laws of the universe were suspended. I waited for her answer.

'We were very busy with our own affairs. It was a very busy life with young children. You've had children. You know what it's like. Routines. Taking them to nursery school. Picking them up again. We would take it in turns. To answer your question: no. We didn't talk about things like that. We were too busy *doing*. I didn't know she had had a baby before Martin.'

The world started up again. Her hand continued pouring the wine. My rib cage fell. The held breath left my lungs.

'Perhaps you can tell me this, then. How did she do it? How did she combine her writing with this domestic life?'

'She tried to write at night. In London she gave the impression that she had the first stirrings of the feeling that she could do it by herself. "What am I doing, being a mother? Where is my writing going?" And there was always the conflict. Especially on Hydra and back in Australia. She and George both had tremendous egos. About who was the better writer. In London it was only a debate, but back in Australia it was something more.'

'What I can't understand is how she managed to do it at all! Write that wonderful book, *Mermaid Singing*, on Kalymnos, at the same time as the events in it were actually happening. Coping with domestic crises, and two little children, later three. I can understand how George did it. He had Charmian to backstop for him, but she had all of her role as a mother and her role as a writer, too,' I said with some passion. (This issue has been central to my working life.) 'How does a woman juggle all these responsibilities, and still nourish her creative self? For the women I've known it has been either/or. They don't marry or they don't have children. Or if they do, they are lousy mothers. Or, more often, they marry and are good mothers, but the creative juice is sucked out of them. I haven't known any who could manage it all.'

Mary shrugged off the question. She seemed to think that it was nothing remarkable and that many European women combined their family and creative lives with great success: 'When you are young, nothing is impossible.'

She changed the subject. 'You know, George and Charm could be a lot of fun.' A reminiscent smile curled the corners of her mouth. 'A few weeks after they arrived in London, we took them on a weekend to Paris. It was April, Paris in the spring. We went to hear the chanteuse, Juliette Greco, sing. Somewhere very small and very smoky. The atmosphere was very intense. Riveting. Charm was fascinated. I remember us all getting drunk. We didn't have enough money and had to wash dishes. We ended up on the Quai d'Orsay—staggering along beside the Seine. And do I remember it right? Did George really fall in the Seine? Wait a moment. I've got some photographs somewhere.'

She produced a fat album full of memories; theatre programmes, tickets, photographs. There they were, leaning up against a Parisian wall, looking down their pretty noses (two young actresses straight out of *Irma La Douce*), Mary and Charm. My mother in slacks and a trenchcoat had one of her legs bent at right-angles, heel against the masonry. Gordon had taken the picture. To my eyes, my gay Parisienne mother with her tipped up chin looked the spit and image of my young self, but I said nothing.

'Here, you must have this!' Mary began impulsively tearing the pasted down photograph from its page.

'No, no, please, it's going to rip. I could always get a copy. Any photography place would make a copy,' I said.

She stopped. 'Yes, I suppose it does belong here, with all the rest.'

She kept talking. 'On Hydra, the Greeks were very uncomfortable with the Johnstons, though Charmian never realised that. She thought they loved her. The children ran wild. Oh, she fed and clothed them, and heard their homework... I don't mean that she didn't, but both she and George focused more on other things, less on their children.' (Maybe Mary was answering my question after all.)

'Do you mean that they were neglected?'

'Not exactly. You have to understand the Greeks. The Greeks adored the children. They were perfectly safe anywhere on the island. Any adult would care for them. And they were such beautiful children. Martin was a truly lovely boy, and Shane was a darling little blonde fluffy girl who just wanted a mummy. The Greeks didn't like the way Shane in particular was allowed to run around unsupervised at thirteen or so. Because she was a girl, you see. It was a bit different with Martin. Later, back in Sydney, Shane felt out of it in the family because she wasn't an intellectual. She tried so hard to be an ordinary girl.'

Mary drew me a vignette of the night-life of the expatriate colony on Hydra. 'All the tables at the waterfront taverna would be drawn together. The whole expatriate population would be celebrating something—someone's cheque for something or other. Everyone would be drinking and eating too much. The person who was celebrating would end up owing twice as much on the slate as the cheque was for. The generators would be turned off—was it eleven o'clock or midnight? We would all stumble home hurriedly in the dark. Someone, perhaps George, too drunk to make it home, would slide down a wall and fall asleep on the cobbles, then wake up and stagger home two hours later, but no-one worried.'

And, with the coffee, she described another party, back in Mosman in the sixties.

'It was a function. I can't remember what exactly. Everyone was dressed nicely. Dressed up I mean. Charm arrived late wearing just a sweater and slacks. A good sweater and slacks. She did a double-take when she saw how everyone else looked. She was obviously upset that she hadn't worn her glam and glitter. Charm liked to be the centre of attention. You could see her switch herself on. She turned up the voltage to compensate. I remember this architect—what was his name?—totally stunned by her, in love with her by the end of the evening. There was a group of people at her feet. And there was Charm, drinking too much, staying too late, perhaps trying too hard.'

Mary offered to drive me home—a kindness she had often performed for my mother who, after her return to Sydney with all those years of slow island life behind her, could never manage a car. But in my case it was an unnecessary offer. Driving back later that night to my eldest daughter Gina's Mosman flat, my car a cell surging along the bright pulsating blood-stream of one of Sydney's minor arteries, I kept screening pictures of Martin and Shane behind my eyes. The children of my mother. My half-brother and sister. Mary had thought well of them, had seen a need in Shane particularly.

It tied in well with what I had found out that morning.

*

'Come in the morning,' he had said on the phone. 'I am better in the mornings.'

As I drew up on a hilly street in a south-eastern suburb, a stiff north-easterly breeze whipped up whitecaps on the wedges of Prussian blue ocean visible between orange-red tiled roofs. A delicate superstructure of television antennas traced geometric scribbles over an airbrushed sky. I juggled my *Gregory's* road guide and my leitmotif—a bunch of cellophane-wrapped flowers—as I untangled my legs from under the steering wheel. I was in Sydney to see two of the contacts Nadia had organised for me, and one I had organised for myself. My first visit was to James Calomeris, who had been the editor of the anti-Junta paper the *Hellenic Herald* when Charmian and George were on the Committee for the Restoration of Democracy in Greece. Nadia had told me how glad Jim had been to hear that I existed and had three lovely daughters.

An attractive dark-haired woman answered the door. Sylvia Calomeris took me in to her husband's study, where he was waiting for me, sitting rather rigidly in his chair, a rug over his knees. A strong-featured man with fine brown eyes, he suffers from Parkinson's disease. We shook hands. He remarked on my likeness to Charmian Clift.

Waiting for me at the desk was a chair, and on the desk a pile of photocopies and papers. Sylvia came in with tea and honeyed Greek cakes.

Sylvia and Jim showed me the newspaper reports of the doings of the Committee. Unfortunately for me, most of the reports were from the *Hellenic Herald* and were in Greek. But there was Charmian's piece for the *Sydney Morning Herald*, 'Long Live Democracy', where she had written:

> *Last Saturday was the first anniversary of the colonels' putsch. The tanks rolled in and constitutional government rolled out and no democrat could raise a finger or a voice to stop it. To many Australian Greeks it was a day of mourning, falling as it did on their Easter Saturday, with Christ not yet risen and feasting not yet in order. It was a sad day. Fascism had been tolerated for a whole year . . .*[2]

Her words had touched thousands of hearts.

Jim remembered Shane's wedding well. The reception had been at Ray and June Crooke's place. Sylvia produced the original *Sydney Morning Herald* piece, 'Betrothing a Daughter', in which Charmian had written about Shane's engagement. They spoke more easily. This was whom they remembered best. Shane.

Shane, as a native Greek speaker ('with a strong peasant accent', said Sylvia), had worked on the *Hellenic Herald*. Up till now, I had heard very little about my sister and was curious.

She had worked as Jim's secretary.

'Always on the phone to her friends, a scatterbrain,' he said.

'You're too hard on her. She was just a normal young girl,' countered Sylvia. 'I feel guilty about Shane,' she added. 'She kept wanting me to come shopping with her in my lunch hour, to choose things for her wedding. And I was always too busy. I didn't have time. I can see now that she wanted a mother with her.'

Shane was in the office on Wednesday 9 July 1969, when the phone rang for her. Telling her of her mother's death. Jim remembered my poor young sister, then only twenty, turning ghost-pale and crying: 'She always said she would do it, and she has!'

My reverie shattered. The artery had branched off into a vein. My little car-cell had to choose. Right blinker flickl-flicklflicklflick. My little cell flowed its way in a stream of similar cells into the venous system of the suburbs. This way to Gina's flat and my bed.

Moonlight crept across my sleeping face. The distant howling and whooping grew louder, louder. Penetrated my dreams. My consciousness. I was awake. The room was drenched in blue-white light. And the noise! Of course: Taronga Zoo, just over the crest of the hill, hugging the harbour foreshore, under a full moon. Childhood memories surged back. Memories of wolf-howls, lion-roars, monkey-whoops reverberating across the valley dividing Mosman from Cremorne and pouring in with the moonstream to my little box of a room. How Sue had loved those jungle sounds. Sitting up in bed, she had seen with the eyes of imagination lions prowling the grasslands of Africa on huge soundless paws, a pack of wolves in a circle, heads thrown back in vocal worship, gibbons swinging from attenuated arms, dark against the moon-splashed forest, macaws exploding out of the blackness of the rainforest canopy, their colours bright enough to defeat moonlight. Even as a young woman, home on holidays from her teaching job in the country, the moon-sounds had held her in thrall.

And what about Charmian Clift? Her Mosman house was just around the corner from this flat. Had she too lain awake at night, in the studio at the back of the house, ears assaulted by the same soundwaves?

I slept.

The sun was streaming in the window, causing me to twist and tangle in my sleeping bag. Still half asleep I turned over searching for the warm presence usually in my bed. It wasn't there. *Where am I?* I woke in an instant. *Oh, here I am, at Gina's. Yesterday was wonderful. Two people who knew my mother. Today I'm going to Roseanne's to pick up that bundle of Clift/Johnston photographs.*

I couldn't wait to see them.

I wasn't disappointed.

There were all the family. My family. My great-grandparents, Pardie and Emma Clift, on what looked like their fiftieth wedding anniversary. Emma a diminutive virago, upright, thin-lipped and unsmiling. But look at the planes of that face and the high cheekbones! Mine! Mine and Gina's. There was Charmian's sister, Margaret, and brother, Barré. He shared the tipped-up eyes with Charmian. And with me. Their father, and my grandfather,

Sydney Clift. A long rectangular face, with very strong features and plenty of chin. Like Margaret's. I could see nothing of myself in him. Their mother, and my grandmother, Amy Lila, the one who had bequeathed me migraine headaches. Her shorter, squarer-jawed face, with a wide mouth, short chin and strongly accented cheekbones, was echoed in my face, but even more in the face of my eldest daughter. The same grandmother, sepia-toned, as a young girl. My second daughter to the life! I *belonged* amongst these faces. Here were bits of us, my girls and me, scattered back through the generations. To most people this phenomenon is self-evident. To me it was miraculous.

And here was my beautiful mother. Large glossy press photographs, studio portraits, model shots, and faded sepia snapshots from the family camera. I could see now what everyone meant. As a young girl, she had been stunning: classically featured, large eyes, chiselled bone-structure. I have photographs of my second daughter, Danni, looking very like this. After Charmian had produced Shane, she was plumper-faced with fuller cheeks and glowingly beautiful. I couldn't recognise myself in these images. On Hydra, in her late thirties, with her head tilted up (it was obvious she had once been a model) she could have been me! Even the way the hair sprang from her head was the same. And her mouth—my mouth! Here, too, were distressing images, taken in Mosman in the last, bad, sad time. One in particular: a shiny press photograph. She must have been about forty-five. Three years younger than I am now, though she looks older. She is looking straight at the camera, which has a cruelly sharp lens. The mouth (my mouth) is smiling, but the eyes staring out of the photograph are not. They are the wisest, saddest eyes in the world. They are staring straight into my eyes. And eerily they *are* my eyes. But full of despair greater than mine have ever known.

Yet again, mine filled up and overflowed.

Roseanne has said that I may keep these photographs until Nadia wants them for her book. I want to buy a copy-stand and make copy-negatives as professionally as I can. There are dozens of images of Charmian, my birthmother. I have only a tiny handful of Marjorie, my adoptive mother.

There was one more joy in store for me. Through a charming young woman who taught German to my youngest daughter, Kristin, at school, I had contacted Betty Nunn. Betty was the barracks-mate I hoped had been Charmian's confidante when she first joined the Australian Women's Army Service. She invited me to afternoon tea with her and her husband.

This time the leitmotif varied. I bought a red and white striped miniature rose, flowering in its pot. Betty and John live in a villa in a retirement complex. They had given me careful instructions, and I only had to drive once around the block before I found it.

I had hopes that Betty might be the one who had an answer to The Question: *Did she tell you about having me?* But they had not met in the barracks in Sydney in 1943, when my mother had first joined the army, full of sorrow and guilt at having to give up her baby. Betty had known Cliftie (as she was called in the army) in Melbourne in the winter of 1945. Charmian was nearly twenty-two. And there had not been the slightest whisper of the tragedy in her recent past.

The weather was awful. The two of them shared a room that leaked. 'The goldfish bowl' was how my young mother described it. Cliftie was the most alive person Betty had ever met. She could never sit still, doing nothing. She was always scribbling. She kept a notebook in her pocket, and would whip it out on the slightest provocation. She was sunny and gay (in the lovely lost meaning of the word), tremendous fun to be with, and beautiful to look at. People were irresistibly attracted to the warmth she radiated.

Betty recalled an officers' dance. All the men were in uniform. And all the women, too. All except one. From somewhere, Cliftie had conjured up a length of rainbow fabric and made herself a glorious frock.

'She was like a vivid butterfly amongst a company of brown moths,' Betty said with a laugh.

'Even now at army reunions, when Cliftie is mentioned, everybody's faces break into smiles.'

My head was full of contradictory images: the gorgeous butterfly of the forties who warmed the world with her smile; the columnist of the sixties who believed in social equity, the dignity and rights of women and men; the mother who had no time to help her daughter shop for her wedding; the talented expatriate writer at the taverna on Hydra in the fifties; the wife who fought tempestuously with her husband; the young London mother who took her children to play in Kensington Gardens; the celebrity in Sydney who tried too hard, drank too much.

The photographs in their envelope were just as confusing. Which one of these was Charmian Clift? Or could she have been all of them?

CHAPTER 13

Four thousand years ago, his/her tongue would be cut out if an adoptee dared to openly say that he/she was not born to his/her parents. And if he/she went further, in search of his/her biological family, he/she would be blinded in punishment.[1]

I had been looking for my mother for two months now. The only ways I could get close to her were through her own words and through other people's eyes.

The complex, many faceted character of Charmian Clift is not easily accessible to the seeker. She is not all of a piece. I felt that I was collecting beads scattered from the broken necklace of her life: beads picked up and kept, sometimes treasured, by those who knew her. Cedric Flower had given me a handful, brilliantly coloured by sun and sea. Mary Andrews had given me a few. Jim Calomeris had given me a

couple. Betty Nunn had given me just one, but that one sparkled like a diamond. Those who never knew her had contributed, too. Nadia Wheatley's multi-coloured gifts would fill a jewel-box. Amongst Garry Kinnane's words I had gathered some more. Were their colours true? Could my collection ever be strung together? The beads didn't seem to match.

Her own words reveal her too. How could they not? By now I had read the four collections of her pieces for the *Sydney Morning Herald* from 1964 to 1969. Her essays. She wrote of a Sydney I had shared with her, a suburb I had shared with her, even a street I had shared with her. But she never knew that. She wrote of a wider world I didn't comprehend clearly then, but—now past her years—understand only too well. As well as her pieces on day-by-day living, which must have caused women to smile with instant recognition, she wrote about issues, minority groups, social justice. She wrote from often unpopular viewpoints. She was not afraid to chide those in authority. She wrote with such life, such sheer human-ness, that on her death letters to the editor expressed opinions like:

> *The warmth, humanity, wit and wisdom of her weekly articles were a joy to read and at times*

> *profoundly moving.*
> *... it was her genuine enthusiasm for all she wrote about that touched us, and her ability to be unafraid of being herself.*
> *... she had a quality that left her readers feeling that they had not so much read an article, as spent a few minutes with a valued friend.*[2]

Her columns read all at once in book form, twenty-odd years later, rather than the way they were intended to be read, week by week when the topics and issues were current, still give the impression of a friend talking just to you. With understanding and compassion. Yet in a programme about his father and mother for Radio Helicon, Martin Johnston had explained that this warm and friendly columnist was a persona adopted for literary reasons. His mother, the woman, had an intensely private aspect.[3]

From Queensland a reply had arrived to the letter I had sent to June Crooke. June had been friendly with my mother in the last years of her life. The artist Russell (Tassie) Drysdale had brought them together when he persuaded Charm to visit his friends, the Crookes, who were living in Cairns. The two women spent some wonderful weeks in Torres Strait, Charmian absorbed in all the big and small human things in their beautiful setting of islands and sea.

June explained:

> *The facts are that for three or four unforeseen, very concentrated and magical weeks in late 1967 I closely shared Charmian's company and confidences in at times quite strange circumstances and places that neither of us had planned or envisaged. It all just happened as if it was meant to be and gave us each—"mothers of three" as Charmian put it—a lift to another plane of living...*

The Crookes had later moved to Sydney and bought a house near the Johnstons.

My letter had been full of questions. One of my biggest mental stumbling blocks was the puzzle of my mother writing those wonderful weekly essays while her life was splintering around her. Had the stories of personal disintegration been exaggerated? June had answered:

> *I think your mother had great powers of perception and great reasoning powers which she delighted in exercising, especially given a good clean uncomplicated chance provided by a weekly press column, and she soon got the captive audience she deserved, because she didn't patronise them or talk down to them. She caused them to exercise their minds too, and they liked that. I know I relished what she wrote—the mark of a great essayist at work is what* I *saw. She began on a high plane, giving readers of her best and if she ever faltered it was hard to detect . . . I have to say there was an insidious loss of self-esteem fed by an increasing amount of alcohol. Her tremendous amount of grey matter could still perform (though it took more and more gritty and difficult endeavours) along the prescribed and* totally hypothetical *lines of her weekly column (which ultimately was an impossible burden to her), but deal with the drastic mounting personal problems with that fine mind she could not. She couldn't face bringing it to bear on the specific problems of health, alcohol and all the various ramifications on the whole family, with, after all, their kids' settling-in problems as well . . .*

According to Kinnane, her oldest friend Toni Burgess often used to sit with her all night 'while she drank and talked out her fear of doing the weekly article'.[4] Was this true?

In a thank-you letter to June Crooke for the Thursday Island holiday which had reinvigorated her, Charmian herself said: '... I would like to go on feeling good, and feeling private too and not public property'.[5]

But it seemed that towards the end, while Charmian Clift, the celebrated columnist, was keeping in the air the bright shiny ball of her public life, her juggler's act could not sustain the pieces of her private life, which were crashing one by one to the ground.

CHAPTER 14

... I expect that people will go on optimistically, year after year, and season after season, getting away from it all. And it all will wait patiently until the traveller returns ...[1]

A whole school term had gone. It was the last week in September, and my life had become divided historically into two periods: B.C. and A.C. (Before Charmian and After Charmian). My life, A.C., was now three-and-a-bit months long.

News from the world outside my obsession had been incredible. Boris Yeltzin had held off the hardliners' coup, Gorbachev had come back to Moscow. The Communist Party was disbanded! Statues of Stalin had been, were being, felled all across the U.S.S.R. Republics had been claiming autonomy. Latvia, Moldavia, Estonia, the Ukraine. There was to be a free market economy. *People power*, it was being called.

I was on the back of Doug's Suzuki 1000 motorbike. He was on the front. His iconic helmet (reminding me of nothing so much as Sidney Nolan's *Ned Kelly* paintings) formed the centre of my present universe. The rest of this universe unrolled from an invisible vanishing point behind the helmet in two streams, one on each side of my visor. The streams were remarkably like Chinese horizontal narrative scrolls. The events and scenes of the future rapidly passed into the present, across my line of vision, to join the rest of the past somewhere down the road behind me.

A striking phenomenon was the way each scroll was divided into three uneven horizontal bands. The bottom strip on each side, the road verge, formed an out of focus blur as it rushed very fast from the future into the past. At the moment it was composed of Naples yellow, burnt umber and yellow ochre stripes, horizontal patches and speed-streaks: drought-burnt roadside grass. The middle band (the widest strip) moved past more slowly. Not quite slowly enough for my eyes to focus on the clumps of desiccated gums, the empty dams, the skeletal cattle, the dried and baked earth, before all these things too became the past. The topmost band, wider than the lowest one, but narrower than the middle, drifted sedately from ahead to behind. Rounded, worn-down ochre hills, sometimes with dotted lines of trees breaking their smooth margins, sometimes grey-green with a covering of scrubby bush, were gradually overtaken by distant indigo mountains: Fred Williams paintings in slow motion.

The brazen cloudless blue bowl of the sky was suspended above me, linking the left landscape to the right, the only still element in the whole scene.

Leaning to the right, I could see my helmeted head reflected just beside Doug's gauntleted hand. In the rectangular frame of the side mirror, the helmet appeared small enough for that hand to take between finger and thumb. If I looked down, my sharply focused leather-booted foot was defined by contrast with the silvery-black blurs of the highway whizzing by about thirty centimetres below it. If I turned around as far as possible, I could just see the leading edge of the little bike-trailer we always towed behind on long trips, and our black shadow flying after us.

One day I will paint this, I thought. *Perspectives from the pillion.*

We were on our way to Murwillumbah, a journey of over a thousand kilometres, to visit Doug's parents. The motorbike was my husband's idea. It was his transport to school every day, and enjoyment for both of us in holiday time. The Suzuki and its trailer were sprayed a matching cheerful cherry-red with gold trim. The I've-been-everywhere stickers on the trailer had been put there by the previous owner. The only sticker we had added was the one that said 'Hug a Tree' on the left pannier. A small black pennant proclaimed our membership of the Ulysses Club. This is a club for geriatric bikers. You need to have turned fifty before you can be granted full membership (the club motto is 'Grow Old Disgracefully'). We had already travelled on the bike to Adelaide and back for the club's Annual General Meeting earlier in the year. Our camping gear was carefully stowed in the trailer, and we fervently hoped the drought would not break while we were on the road.

At speed there was no way to communicate with Doug except by a panicky grab at his waist if he cornered too sharply. Our intercoms only worked at slow speeds, when not overpowered by wind-noise. So there was nothing for the passenger to do on long journeys but become aware of the landscape through which the bike was speeding. All my senses were turned up a couple of notches, and sometimes the hypnotic quality of the unrolling countryside induced a state very like meditation.

I thought a lot.

I had a lot to think about. The previous three months had been unbelievable. Had my dead mother been just any mother, in three months I might have been lucky to have found out a trickle of information. With a mother as public as mine, there had been a tidal wave, at times threatening to drown me. Very conflicting information, too. What a strange thing! I know more about the life of the mother I had never seen than about the life of the mother who brought me up. But whenever I think, *I'm getting somewhere at last. I think I understand this or that about Charmian Clift*, she breaks into facets again.

Perhaps it's all in vain. I know that Nadia has been at her research for many years. How can *I* hope to understand Charmian Clift in a bare three months? After all, do we really understand the people we know best? In everyone there is a private space that we can't hope to breach. Charmian's private space was more carefully guarded than most. When George fictionalised her as Cressida Morley in *Clean Straw For Nothing* he made much of this aspect of her: it filled his alter ego, David Meredith, with frustration and regret that she denied it to him—her unreachable core.

'What a pity Toni Burgess can't be made to appear,' Roseanne had said the last time I saw her. Of all the people who could be expected to know my mother, she surely would know most. She had been her friend from the days in the Bondi flat, and had been the one George called after Charmian's suicide. Roseanne told me that Nadia had tried unsuccessfully to find her. And Nadia told me that she had dedicated *Trouble in Lotus Land*, one of the collections of my mother's *Sydney Morning Herald* pieces she had edited, to Toni hoping that she might get in contact. 'Perhaps she's dead,' Nadia had said.

Strange thing, the universality of human thought. Most of the new people I've met have asked the same questions: 'How has this affected you? Are you coping with all this? Has it changed you?'

At the beginning I had been sure of my answer. I knew it by heart: 'Well I'm nearly fifty, and surely by now I know who I am. If I had found her when we were both in Mosman in the sixties, it might have been a different story. It might have changed my life utterly. As for coping—luckily I have a very supportive family and a network of women friends. There are certainly unanswered questions, probably unanswerable ones, and a great deal of emotional upheaval. But, after all, I am already a formed person.'

I could see a clear picture of the concerned, perceptive expression on Cedric's face as he had warned me, 'You want to be careful that you don't turn into The Daughter of Charmian Clift.'

When I told Doug, he laughed and said, 'Charmian Clift had better be careful that she doesn't turn into The Mother of Sue Chick.'

But the more I struggle through the thickets of my mother's life, the less confident I become. I am still subject to bouts of uncontrollable weeping. I still have sleepless nights. The jabs of insight into three women, myself and both my mothers, that my explorations give me are more often than not extremely painful. True, I have my journal, which lets me strip my soul in private. It helps, but it isn't enough. Everything is still a maelstrom. Is the experience re-forming me? Or un-forming me? Me, the already formed person. Roseanne had suggested counselling.

I came back to the physical world, clutching at Doug's waist instinctively. The distant perspective behind his helmet had moved up close. The bike was heeling as we leaned into the corners. We were climbing into mountain country and it was getting perceptibly cooler. The foreground, middle-ground and background were still moving past at their respective speeds, but all three now had turned blue-green and had strong vertical elements: tall straight timber. The arch of blue above had now receded behind a superimposed tracery of branches. My sense of smell, super-acute on the back of the bike, told me that water was near. With a sense of relief I realised that we were turning off the highway and slowing down on one of the forest's fire trails. If my well-padded backside was numb, Doug's bony one must feel worse, and it was surely time for a mug of morning tea.

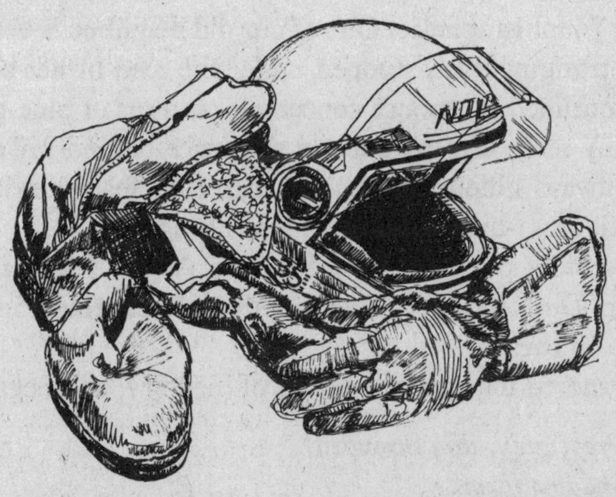

Half an hour later, lying flat on our backs under a giant eucalypt, all was silent except for the lively chatter of the creek over its bed of water-polished stones. Our helmets, socks and boots, leathers and gauntlets lay tumbled in a heap next to the esky, thermos, enamel mugs and plates. Ants were already carrying off their trophies.

'Doug.'

'What, love?'

'Have I ever told you that I used to see auras around people?'

'I don't think so. What brought this on?'

'I've been doing a lot of thinking there behind you. It's amazing your helmet hasn't set up vibrations with the strength of it.'

'I've been wondering what that buzz in my ears was.'

'Well it was me remembering . . . when I was eight or nine I sometimes saw people in a strange way. At least, it seems strange now. It didn't then. I saw them as colours. And haloed by colours. My young brother sometimes seemed to be surrounded by vivid red and yellow flame shapes, like a junior Mephistopheles. One of our old neighbours used to come trudging past, stooped under the load of her shopping, outlined in smooth concentric patterns of blue-grey. And my real, dead parents, in the space behind my eyes, were always silhouettes, leaning forwards, featureless, but shaded, cross-hatched almost, in a strong purple.

'I wrote a poem about them once. When I was about sixteen. Do you want to hear it? I think I can remember it.'

'Go on then.'

I gathered together the skeins of memory, and began.

Grey, grey, dim shrouded
Shadow forms.
Two purple silhouettes against
A rain-washed sky.
Two unknown lives
Unknowing of my life
Yet part of it.

Yours were the screaming shells and bloody beaches,
And death, a carrion crow
Huge, black, menacing.
Yours were the relentless waves
Of childbirth.
And death . . .
Conceived by a serial number,
Born.
Born of a gravestone—somewhere.
And yet you must have had faces.
Met, known, laughed as I do,
Answered the preacher's "Do you take . . .?"
Taken and loved.
But you could not tell me your names
In my prison of flesh.'

'That's when you thought your father and mother had been married and were both dead.'

'Yes. I don't think I realised that Mum and Dad had been lying, or lied to, and that I was probably illegitimate, until I was in my late teens. Isn't it strange that almost everything in that poem turns out to have been wrong? My father wasn't a soldier; my mother didn't die in childbirth and has no gravestone;[2] they weren't married to each other. I hope that the "loved" part is true, at least. And my feelings are true.

'Do you know something else really peculiar? I was talking to Pam. You know how she teaches senior English? Well, they have to analyse poetry the way we art teachers analyse paintings. I showed her that poem and straightaway she fell on the colour purple. To her it was the royal purple, for fame and honour. The fame and honour Charmian achieved. And if I am right about my father, he was well-known in his field, too. And that's how I saw them when I was nine.

'You know what else she said? That I should write a book about all of this. She said that it's obvious I can write and that she would read the drafts for me and help me all she can.'

'God! Do you think you could?'

'I just don't know, Dougal. It'll take a lot of thinking about.'

'Well, think about it on the next leg. Let's wash up and get back into all this gear. Next stop Armidale for lunch, OK?'

The rhythms of the road re-established themselves, curves and counter-curves, and my mind winged away again.

From the beginning, friends had been urging me to write my story. I had always laughed it off: a total impossibility. If I was anything, it was a painter, not a writer.

One of the universal questions that new contacts asked me was, 'What are you going to do with all this?'

Some of these contacts were journalists, or had friends who were media people, and I could see a certain light in their eyes when they asked. Nadia had been most insistent on my keeping the story out of the media. Presumably she knew more about this world than I did, so I had been obediently wary.

Nadia. I was beginning to know her. One of her preoccupations was protecting a Charmian Clift who could no longer protect herself. She had spread her wings over the Johnston/Clift family, and it seemed that I was now included.

So what would happen if I did write a book?

After all it was *my* story. I didn't want anyone else writing about it. I examined the thought. That was interesting. I hadn't realised I felt that way.

But *could* I do it? Could I write at all? The world of authors, editors and publishers was an unknown world. I had never before written anything longer or more demanding than a thesis on the creativity of preschool-age children.

I know that I have unconsciously set up challenges for myself all my life. My pattern is to commit myself foolhardily to large projects before I have any idea of how to achieve them. Once irrevocably involved, I learn as I go along. I am forced to.

Could I do it again? Could I write a book? Did I have more of my mother in me than green eyes and a large mobile mouth? The pressure of this question would be almost unendurable. Did I want to find out the answer? Could I bear it if I failed?

My eyes turned again to the back of Doug's helmet. Its scuff-marked white surface with blue and red decal stripes told me nothing. No answers there.

The curves were straightening out ahead. Doug's leather-encased hand reached back and patted my denim-clothed thigh companionably. I relaxed back against the gear-sack and the rolled-up sleeping bags.

Relaxation. The relaxation of adoption laws in America and Australia has produced a lot of adoption stories. Sad and wonderful stories. From all sides of the adoption triangle. I've been reading every book on the subject I can get my hands on. Some I can only read a page at a time before the tears start. What if she had kept me? No! I've finished with *what ifs*!

What could my story add?

I suppose the different factor is not *me*. It is that my mother was who she was. My story is the incarnation of the first half of the most common childhood fantasy of adoptees:

my mother is really someone famous/beautiful/special. The second half of the fantasy (no longer mine) is: *she will reappear and reclaim me and love me perfectly*.

So, what were my motives? Were they entirely honourable? Was ordinary everyday suburban housewife and teacher Sue, trying to cash in on the myth of her celebrated mother? Or was she trying to claim a birthright she hadn't realised until now was hers? That was one I'd have to examine carefully.

Then again there was the question of my own sanity. Writing a book might drive me to the brink of my technical capabilities, perhaps to the brink of my personal capabilities. But surely I'd have to force myself to codify my experiences, my emotions, my thoughts. To make sense out of them. To know myself. The feeling of being buried under an avalanche, or swept away by a tsunami, or sucked under in a whirlpool, might go. From what I have read, writing is one of the best forms of therapy.

And, in a small way, from my narrow personal viewpoint, I might be able to cast some new light on Charmian Clift.

Could I do it? That was the question.

What would happen to my painting? I was just getting into the swing of it now I had resigned from school. Wouldn't it be better to stick to what I know? Paint my *Charmian and Me* series? The first canvas was well on the way. Or was I setting myself up, using the idea of writing as an excuse for non-achievement in the art world?

Was I getting myself back onto the woman's-guilt roundabout? When I was writing, I would be guilty because I wasn't painting, and when I was painting I would be guilty because I wasn't writing.

We were going to stay with Nadia on our way home from this trip. That was another question mark. How was she going to feel about me turning author? Over the months of letters, phone calls and meetings I had gradually become aware of her feelings about anyone seeing her work or learning her thoughts, or even seeing the Johnston family photographs she is intending to use in her biography. Yet she has been my Greek chorus, running a well-informed commentary on my search. If anyone has given me my mother, it has been her. I owe her so much.

Only a month ago she had sent me a theatre programme from the forties with a little photograph in it of my putative father. The one Cedric had suggested. She, however, seemed to think an American serviceman was much more likely.

I conjured up the scene in Roseanne's terrace house when I had showed her the photograph and told her Nadia's theory. She had strongly disagreed.

'Nonsense,' she said. 'Not unless you were premature. You weren't premature, were you?'

'I've never been told that I was. I weighed seven and a half pounds. I couldn't have been in a humidicrib when Aunt Edna showed me off, all dressed up, to Marjorie. That's if they had such things then. I was taken out of the hospital at three weeks of age, so I shouldn't think so.'

'Well it can't be an American then. They weren't in Sydney until April 1942. You would have been conceived in the third week of March.'

I was impressed.

What the hell was going on! The arms looped around Doug's waist grabbed convulsively as we shot past a red blur, a thundering semi-trailer, the bike screaming up the centre-line of the highway. My God! What did the speedo say? I'd promised Doug that if he ever went over 110 k.p.h. I would get off and catch a train. I started to look out for a railway station. The gauntlet reached back and patted my thigh again. It felt apologetic or at least conciliatory. Language, even that of the body, is limited on a motorbike.

The adrenalin receded, the road straightened out again, the sun blazed out of the thinner atmosphere at this higher altitude, and the wheels began effortlessly to eat the kilometres again. I loosened my grip and leant back.

I had found a picture of myself at thirteen, looking unlike my adult self. I was looking up from under my eyelids at the camera. In exactly the same pose as this possible father in the programme photograph. The resemblance was undeniable. I was convinced that I had found him. If he was my father, it was a better explanation of my talent for painting than through Charmian's sister, Margaret. It had come to me straight from this stage designer. It made sense. And, seeing that it was impossible to prove either way, I decided to make it true by believing it.

Instantly I was back sitting in the sun with Cedric and Wendy at their sunny outdoor table, showing him the photographs.

'Well, that's him all right. I worked with him, you know, painting sets for some show or other.'

'Did he tell you about his affair with Charm?'

'No. He didn't tell me. George did.' He compared the two faces. I distinctly remember his look of concentration.

'He was a dapper man. Yes, dapper's the word. Hmmm. There's certainly something there. But you've grown away from looking like him, to looking like her.'

We were lying on our backs again. This time on hot yellow sand, staring up at mares'-tails of cloud that scudded across a hot blue sky, promising wind. It was the next day. We had stayed overnight in the little town where we had lived and taught for four years, and exchanged the high country crispness for the sultriness of the North Coast. We had been very glad of a chance to stop and swim before we rode inland again to the humidity of Murwillumbah. We had changed from our leathers to swimming costumes with great relief. Changing back with our skins now salty and sweaty was not going to be so much fun and we were putting off the moment. Our eyelids closed. Doug was drifting off to sleep. I was deep in thought.

I was thinking about The Question. The Question I had asked everyone who had ever known my mother. The Question that caused my heart to race in anticipation: *Did she tell you about me?*

Mary Andrews had answered, 'No. We didn't talk about things like that.'

Cedric Flower's reply had been, 'No, but I'm surprised she didn't say something to Pat. They were very good pals.'

Betty Nunn had said, 'No, dear. There was not the slightest whisper of the tragedy in her recent past.'

June Crooke had written, 'No, Sue. I never heard a word from anyone of your existence. It's a wonderful surprise!'

Charmian Clift had given me away, then hidden me away. She had never written about the experience, almost never talked about it, fudged the years around my birth in her writings. When she wrote about her childbirths, it was always about the glamour of the private suite, the flowers, proud George, or about the peasant-style homebirth of Jason. She wrote about her *three* children, or her *only* daughter. In my copies of her books the word *LIAR* is scrawled heavily in the margins.

I knew of only two people who had known about me

directly from Charmian. George Johnston was dead and Toni Burgess could not be found.

Oh, how I longed for a friendly voice to tell me that my mother had loved me, seen me, even held me, had not wanted to give me up.

My anger and longing took me by surprise. More emotion!

I think I will have to write my book.

CHAPTER 15

Genetically, however, adopted children always remain tied to their birth family.[1]

Tara, at Trunkey Creek, was exultant with spring. Shouting even. What glorious sunshine! The paddocks were painted with the most brilliant of brilliant greens behind the iridescent red tips of the photinia hedge. Two black poddy lambs—named Black and Decker by Margo, the youngest Tara daughter—were asleep in the shade, tummies bulging, knobby-kneed legs occasionally twitching. The resident thrush was practising arpeggios as he skimmed low over the lawn, having temporarily abandoned his attack on the wire-gauze of the bathroom fly-screen. For some unknown avian reason, the little blue wrens (little brown blue wrens, not yet in their mating plumage) had taken up where he left off, and a light staccato of tiny beaks made a percussive counterpoint to the thrush's liquid song.

We had arrived at Doug's sister's place the night before, stiff and cold from our second day on the bike trip home from Murwillumbah. The countryside we had ridden through for the first day and a half was in the grip of terrible drought, the normally lush North Coast plains almost white and tinder-dry. No stock in sight, all sold or shot. Dams empty and creek beds cracked mud.

Just east of Gunnedah we had run into a sky-wall of water. Pulling over, we were instantly off the bike and into our wet-weather gear, struggling to thread our boots through the legs of the waterproof pants before our jeans became waterlogged. Fifteen minutes later we were through that boundary curtain of rain and into a different land. Purple splashes of Paterson's curse wove beautiful arabesques on vast green carpets of rye grass and clover. Weddings were literally in the air as we banked into a long aromatic curve and found an unexpected citrus orchard swelling with orange blossom in full flower. Roadside seeding grasses swallowed us up as we tried to take photographs over boundary fences. Dams and creeks were over-

flowing and sheeny; fat, complacent red-and-white Herefords posed as though for calendars; and white kids skipped and leaped heraldically against the green.

I could smell Trunkey Creek long before we arrived. Flowering clover overlaid with cattle.

I was watching Doug and Jeanette, who sat talking in white wooden chairs in front of the green, green backdrop. Brother and sister are extremely tall, both olive-skinned, both with long rectangular faces punctuated by dark hair and large down-sloping dark eyes under thick brows. Hers close to black, his to brown. Both heads of hair have the greying bits in the same place. Brother and sister have very long legs, the extra length in the thigh bone. Both were using similar gestures, angling their over-large hands out at the wrist, playing imaginary pianos on the arm of the chair with their fingertips when making an important conversational point. Their mother does exactly the same. Have they learned or inherited these gestures? Height and body-shape (allowing for gender differences) very like their mother; colouring like their father. Instantly recognisable as brother and sister.

There were equally telling similarities of personality, attitude and ideas. Some like their father, some like their mother. Nothing remarkable in that for most people.

I wasn't most people. I had been adopted. For me it was always remarkable to watch families.

As small children David and I, with our similar colouring and wide-eyed flat faces, looked as though we could be blood brother and sister. From adolescence on we diverged. You would never think of us as siblings now.

Our adoptive family was the only thing we had in common. Out of that charmed circle, even as children, we led totally different lives: the separate lives of boy-child and girl-child in Sydney in the forties and fifties. We were even more disparate than that. We practically spoke different languages. I was the 'good', quiet child, an early and voracious reader, an academic achiever, working on my perfectionism, interested in nature, keeping my own private 'museum', involved in all the arts, making my own fun with friends in theatre and music groups. I had hated sport ever since I came last in the six year olds egg-and-spoon race at Mosman Infants School. I played the dutiful daughter, trailing along with Mum every week to see *her* mother: a long, boring train trip up the North Shore line. I pleased Dad by abiding by most of the rules (most of the time): the rules of the home and school and society and God. I pleased him even more by being involved in his church.

David was the likeable sports-mad rebel. As a little boy he had known how to project a voice that shattered glass and eardrums. He was always being told to cut his voice into ten pieces and put nine of them in his pocket. Stones were made to be thrown at cats or their elderly owners (preferably from behind the concealing virginia-creeper leaves on the top of our pergola), shanghais to kill small birds or shatter street lights, a sister to be chased and branded with a ball (tennis would do, cricket was even better). He organised the two of us into swinging from Mum's fox-fur stole when it was hanging over the high hook on the back of the bedroom door. He dangled from the brush-tail, I clutched (with trepidation) the glassy-eyed head. Our feet traced tentative circles above the Feltex carpet. Both head and tail separated from furry body. Brer Fox never recovered. I was the one who told. The tail thenceforth made a wonderful addition to my brother's Davy Crockett hat, and much later flew from the aerial of the little blue third-hand Morris Minor that Mum bought but we drove.

He shunned church as soon as he was out of short pants and into long arguments. Dad, with his authoritarian breakfast pronouncements, my brother christened the *Sydney Morning Harold.* Although just as intelligent as I was, David perpetually underachieved at school, and was often in trouble. As a teenager he was into everything going. Coming from our teetotal family, of course he took to smoking and drinking. He truanted from North Sydney Boys' High School as often as he dared, especially during exams, when an estimated mark might well be higher than the mark he would have obtained on the test paper... Shawry was a legend. He was part of a group of boys who hanged an effigy of an unpopular master under the stone arch of the bridge at Northbridge. He and his friends made the Guinness Book of Records for the number of people crammed into a phone box. I can remember him setting off for school, waiting around the corner until Mum had left for work, sneaking back home and, after swearing me to silence, taking Dad's car to play golf for the day. I can see him now in his going-out gear: tall and skinny, dark wavy hair slicked back from a good-looking, bony, larrikin's freckled face, mischievous crinkled-up blue eyes, tight black pants, winklepicker black shoes, white shirt, trendy narrow black tie. The latest loud rock music station with its fast-talking American-accented disc jockey was always blasting from his transistor radio. Around him wafted a cloud of illicit smoke.

Home was a hotel he only visited for meals and bed. And to pick up his clean, ironed clothes.

I was the passive, over-protected adoptee mentioned in the literature. David reacted differently.

I used to have a vivid mental picture of his dead pilot father: dashing, brave and rebellious, with a thin black moustache—something like David Niven in a British war film. But of course his father was probably nothing of the sort. His story was lies, too.

After David and I grew up and married, we rarely saw each other, our respective geographies being what they were, yet, when we did, there was a surprisingly strong bond. It is still there. We hold opposing views on many things, but we can always pick up just where we left off. We meet at so few points that there is no need for conflict. I feel very comfortable with my adoptive brother.

As for my natural brothers . . . I had finally sent my carefully composed letter to Jason, knowing his aversion to family business, really expecting to hear no more, but not long afterwards he called me. I had been told of his musical talent, his linguistic ability (he had invented his own language when still a child).

A pleasant baritone voice said: 'Hello. I received your very nice letter.'

The voice matched the photographs I had seen of him. He said yes, he would like to meet me, but not yet. He made his excuses. I babbled like a fool in my excitement, telling him how like *our* mother I look. Or so people say. How strange that sounded! *Our* mother. He told me that he had another box of family photographs, hundreds of them, that I might like to see.

I do hope I will finally meet him, my only surviving close blood relative.

And Martin. Roseanne had lent me a photograph of Martin and Shane from the London days. I laid over Shane's image a photograph of me at the same age. Martin's sensitive child's face, looking out of the picture with unfocused eyes, was much more like mine than it was like that of the sister beside him.

From all accounts he had been a prodigy of a child. George had called him 'the professor', much to Charmian's disgust. Cedric's story of a seven year old correcting his Greek pronunciation ties in well with a small charming portrait of him at about ten by the writer Elizabeth Jane Howard in her novel *The Sea Change*, set partially on Hydra.[2] There are four main adult characters and a young boy, Julius Lawson, who is based on Martin. Julius/Martin speaks with gravity, old-fashioned courtesy and an impossibly large vocabulary. He is the interpreter of Greek language and Greek mores. The organiser of caïques and mules. He is shown walking along, his face buried in a huge book: Wells' *Outline of History*. He stops and waits for one of the other main characters without looking up from his reading. He presents the other characters with lists of topics he would like to discuss, and an elaborate and spirited picture of marine life, which he has drawn in black ink: pictures of the best things in his collection. Fathoms have been marked down the side so that the fish are all swimming at the right depth.

Roseanne had told me that Martin was a fine natural scientist, and that bushwalks with him were a joy of discovery.

At ten, I had read my way through the children's section of the Mosman Library with its bare boards, smell of floor polish and books. You could take out four books at a time and I often finished mine in a day. I sailed through *Mary Poppins*, all the *Doctor Doolittles*, and cried with joy when I discovered that *The Lion, the Witch and the Wardrobe* was the first in a series. I moved on to adult natural science and art books. Mum gave me the big Phaidon *Michaelangelo* for my eleventh birthday. I treasured it then and treasure it now.

By the time I was eleven I had a special friend. A friend

who happened to be a boy. He was a year younger than me, in my brother's class, and had been David's friend first. He had intelligent dark brown eyes, magnified behind thick pebble glasses, and was called Alexander. I was going to Fort Street Opportunity School by ferry every day and the next year he joined me there. A pattern developed. On the ferry he would try to teach me to play chess, after school we would catch the bus up from the wharf to his place where we would become fanatical naturalists. We had butterfly collections (caught with his net), birds' egg collections (from nests in trees climbed in Reid Park), jars full of muddy pond water and microscopic life, other jars full of methylated spirits and little corpses: geckos, frogs, tiny fish, shark eggs. All these desirable items were carefully drawn and labelled. We kept caterpillars of all kinds and watched them pupate, feeding the emerging butterflies on honey and water. We kept silkworms and fed them on mulberry leaves from his backyard, or from down The Deep at my place. We spun their silk.

We had two museums in large cupboards, one at each of our houses. We took turns in displaying our two prize exhibits: a fine Aboriginal stone axe that he had acquired, and an ancient fossilised fish in a huge piece of chalk that had come from England and belonged to my mother. The stone axe we eventually donated to the Museum in the city, and Mum finally demolished the fish by using the chalk to polish the silver.

By then I had grown breasts and outgrown Alexander.

And then there was the matter of coordination. Charmian had been a naturally athletic girl—a strong swimmer and a superb diver who competed to win. David had been talented at all sports that didn't require brawn. I, on the other hand, had failed beanbag throwing. In those days the little square cloth beanbags, filled with heavy beans, were meant to be thrown and caught by those who couldn't quite cope with the rolling qualities of a ball. I also came last in every foot race I was ever forced to enter, even the egg-and-spoon. I was naturally clumsy, spilling and dropping things, stubbing my own toes, treading on other peoples'. This, combined with a stitch in my side and a burning red face that didn't cool down for hours, did not commend the world of sport to me. In my early teenage years Mum organised me into tennis coaching. After only a month, the coach took Mum aside and told her it was hopeless: she was wasting her money. She was upset, thinking of the social opportunities I would miss, all the lovely sporty young men I would never meet. I was overjoyed. Any young man who would be stupid enough to spend a sunny afternoon hitting a small ball against a gut-strung frame would never interest me.

In fact it was only when I discovered that solitary pursuits like galloping over paddocks on horseback or schussing down a ski-slope also counted as sport that I joined the majority of the human race.

With exquisite irony, in my teenage years I was always being asked by boys if I were a dancer. 'You have a dancer's legs,' they would say. Now I know where those legs came from.

When I showed Roseanne the delightful photograph I had printed from Cedric's negatives of Martin with his arm around Shane on the donkey, and commented on how protective he was, she had burst out laughing.

'Protective!' she snorted. 'He's falling off! Shane was the athletic one. He's hanging on to her like grim death! Martin has fallen off anything he's ever tried to ride. Friends refused to allow him on the back of their motorcycles because at the end of the road he would no longer be there.'

Come to think of it, George had much the same to say about him in *Cartload of Clay*, where the character Julian is based on Martin:

> *Julian tripped, spilled things, burnt the bottoms out of saucepans, broke the handles off cups, left lights on, knocked things over, scratched even his most treasured LPs, connected the wrong leads and blew fuses.*[3]

It is a difficult thing to think about my brother as an adult: the poet fulfilling his perceived fate by dying. Roseanne has told me many stories about him: Martin as charming lover, Martin as loving husband, Martin as devoted stepfather, Martin as committed drinker. She has sent me tapes of Martin talking about poetry, copies of his published work. Nadia too had sent me photocopies: the two poems he wrote for Charmian and George.

I carry his poem, 'Letter to Sylvia Plath, *i.m. C.C.*', with me everywhere. Even on the motorbike. He is trying to tell me something important about our mother and I just can't understand him. The poem is so dense with allusion and imagery, so intellectual, so personal and inaccessible that I can only conjure the faintest images from it. Images of a woman hiding in her own skin, her carapace. Charmian Clifts inside Charmian Clifts.

Martin journeyed comprehensively in the land of the intellect. Read any one of his poems and it is immediately apparent that here is a consummate mind-traveller. I understand the siren-call of this foreign country, for it has tugged at me at points in my life. I have not heeded it. My choices have been different.

Like Martin, but five years before him (while he was still a child on Hydra), I gained a Commonwealth Scholarship. I could have used it to enrol in an Arts degree at Sydney University. But my family just couldn't afford my turning down the concurrent offer of a Teachers' College Scholarship with its monetary allowance and the assurance of a teaching position at the end of four years' study. Most seductive of all to my parents was its promise of job security: a lifetime of safety for their adopted daughter. What irony! Charmian's parents had wanted *her* to be a schoolteacher, so she could be safe. But of course safe was the very last thing she wanted to be. Or ever was.

As an art teacher I have needed to constrain my intellectualism and develop my commonsense and compassion. The current mode for teaching art is a practical one. Do first. Theorise later. In country high schools the whole spectrum of the town's adolescent population is gathered in one learning institution, usually in mixed-ability groups. To be understood a teacher must project simplicity of thought. It takes years of honing to realise just how simple that simplicity must be.

I'll never forget trying to explain to a class of fifteen year olds the intricacies of the construction of Gothic cathedrals. I told them that I would be asking questions about the building methods, so they were to listen carefully. We were rapturously soaring into the ribbed vaults where the light, streaming from the rose window set with the newly perfected stained glass, symbolised the metaphysical Light of Heaven, when I noticed that one boy's hand had been waving in the air for minutes.

'Miss, miss!' he called out.

'Just a moment,' I said, as I illustrated on the board the marvellous interplay of pointed arch construction, flying buttress, clustered columns and vastly increased window space. The boy's hand was still waving, but I was processing around the ambulatory, making little forays into the cult of relics, and the cult of the Virgin Mary.

'*Miss*!' the voice was more urgent.

'Well, what can you tell me about the important innovations of the Gothic period?' I asked the class at last.

Some hands shot up and I pointed to the one that had been anxiously trying to attract my attention for so long.

'What can *you* tell me?'

'Miss,' came a strident, just-broken voice, 'my guinea pig died this morning!'

'Intellectual' is a word that could never have been applied to my sister, Shane. Martin had said that she was more intelligent than he was. But she followed a different path. I should imagine a brother like Martin would have been a very difficult act to follow, and neither of her parents seemed too concerned about her academic future. Because she was a girl? Astounding when you consider Charmian's proto-feminist views.

As a young girl in Greece, Shane was very physical (*she* was the one in control of that donkey). She was hedonistic, preferring the exterior to the interior world. Back in Australia, she tried, in the face of her atypical family, to adopt the persona of a typical teenage girl, interested in clothes and boys and pop music and going out. When I look at photographs of her, I see no physical echoes of myself at all. She looks very much the daughter of George Johnston, not Charmian Clift. I have lived with David so I know what it's like to have a brother. I have also had Roseanne to interpret Martin for me, so I feel that I am beginning to know something about him. I can only hope that Jason wants to meet me one day. But I can't imagine what it would be like to have a sister. Shane is an unknown quantity. I haven't found anyone who knew her well. I don't know if I'm ready to think about her yet. It's all too sad.

This search may go on for the rest of my life!

'Suzie,' Doug's bass voice interrupted my thoughts. 'Are we staying with Nadia tomorrow night, or just dropping in?'

'Staying I think. I can't wait to see all the photographs she's got. She said I could borrow them to copy. I'll give her a ring today, and check that we're expected.'

And so on the following day, a cherry-red Suzuki 1000 with rider and pillion passenger, towing a little cherry-red trailer (bottle of white wine in a brown paper bag in the Hug-a-Tree pannier, Mahler blasting from the tape deck), pulled up in the shadow of towering black-green pine trees in the driveway of the house where my mother's biographer lived. Where so many of the mysteries of my mother's life were filed away.

CHAPTER 16

Bloody well soar, why don't you?[1]

Our people-eating lounge beckoned me. We had only been home for a few days, and had finished the long list of chores that always makes you wonder why you bother to take a holiday: collecting the dog from the kennels, the cat from the neighbours and the mail from the post office; watering the half-dead plants in their pots; paying the little boy next door for feeding the birds in the aviary; unpacking everything, airing the smelly camping gear, washing out the esky and the picnic things, packing them all away again; demolishing the mounds of dirty laundry; attacking the jungle of spring weeds and mowing a lawn barely distinguishable from that jungle. The nicest chore, not a chore at all in fact, was walking slowly around my garden, saying hello to my favourites, and lavishly praising our tall liquidambar for its beautiful, newly unfurled tender spring leaves.

Doug looked after the Suzuki: that was his territory.

Now it was time to relax. I sank into the lounge. As usual I had a few books going at once. I had caught this reading habit from Mum. Nadia Wheatley's children's books, *My Place*, *Five Times Dizzy* and *The Blooding*, which she had given me during our recent stay, were on the floor, and George's *Clean Straw for Nothing/Cartload of Clay* was in my hand. It was my second reading. Two boxes of Clift/ Johnston photos lay beside Nadia's books.

The reading lamp defined us: me and Mrs Cat; me stretched out full length, the Siamese cat curled up in the curve of my arm. Outside in the cool moonlight, the corrugated iron roofs of houses, garages and sheds made parallelograms of hammered silver further down the hill. Moonshadows cast by the gum tree branches traced complex patterns on the blue-lit lawn, and in the living room the polished brushbox floor reflected a moonpath as clearly as did the distant bay. Apart from the muffled crunch of breakers on the sand, there was silence.

Suddenly an indefinable sound came from above. Right above the house. A passage of moving air; a change in air pressure. George Johnston's words and the sleeping cat were flung aside as I ran out the door. There, outlined against a waxing moon, was a wedge of black swans in perfect formation, necks thrust before them, wingbeats in unison. In a heartbeat, the pathfinder swan was sharply cut off by the angle of the roof, then the following pair, then all of them, and there was only the moon in the cold sky.

Flight. I had just been reading about it. Icarus and Daedalus. What does George say in *Clean Straw for Nothing*? It is a dialogue between David Meredith and Tom Kiernan (a character based on the artist Sidney Nolan):

> *'I fly with Icarus, not with Daedalus,' said Kiernan.*
>
> *'That's all very well for you. But I'm me, not you.'*

> *'Balls! If you* want *to fly, if you think you* can *fly, then all you've got to do is jump off the twig and bloody well* fly![2]

Charmian had written much the same of Nolan in *Peel Me a Lotus*, her account of their first year on Hydra. Now he was called Henry Treverna, and he was talking to one of their mutual friends, an aspiring writer, who was being philosophical about receiving the latest in a long line of rejection slips:

> *'Ah well,' he says, 'and sometimes you think you can fly.'*
>
> *'Fly then!' says Henry. 'Bloody well soar, why don't you?*[3]

She described viewing in Nolan's studio his entire winter's work: about five hundred oil sketches on thick paper. Most were based on Greek mythology, in particular the recurring theme of the legend of Icarus:

> *The same haunting naked figure soars above fanged rocks and wide, dark seas, sometimes just rising from the ground, sometimes a speck floating high against a burning ball of sun, frail as a dragonfly. And always on the ground, earthbound and staring upwards with sorrowful yearning eyes, is the lonely figure of the Minotaur...*[4]

Nolan gave her one of these sketches for the house by the well that the Johnstons had bought on Hydra. Now Roseanne has the painting, and Icarus wings eternally above the earthbound Minotaur on her cool white wall.

It is a fitting metaphor for Charmian Clift: Icarus. Ever a risk-taker, for a time her spirit soared. Like Icarus, she did not heed her limitations, and plummeted to earth.

In the first painting of my planned *Charmian and Me* series, I had portrayed the two of us against our shared love: the sea. Charmian is a sea-eagle effortlessly planing high above me: in another moment she will have flown right out of the picture. I am a child, playing, imprisoned in a womb-like rock pool.

Perhaps the yearning Minotaur is also a metaphor for me.

The first box of photographs, the ones Roseanne lent me, had already been copied. I had done this before we went away, setting the camera up on the sloping column, cable-release dangling, lights set at forty-five degrees to the baseboard, the sheet of glass meticulously cleaned on both sides, rolls of black and white film piled neatly to one side, photographs on the other. Here were the originals of the prints in Kinnane's biography of Johnston, and some family shots, but in these my mother was deliberately posing. Little Jason was holding on to her leg or tugging at her skirt, while her arm or hand was kept to herself and her eyes looked straight into the lens. She seemed more involved with her audience than with her child. It made me uneasy. I *wanted* to think of her as involved with her children. After all, I was one of them.

I had been delighted to see the photos Nadia had. Here were totally different images of my mother and her other children. I had them with me here. As I picked them up once again, I half expected to see a pattern of tiny holes burnt into them from the beams coming repeatedly from my eyes. In the pool of light from the reading lamp, I picked out three.

A very dark, faded, non-contrasty image. It looks home-processed. From the ages of the children the year would be 1953 or early '54. Charmian is playing with rugged-up five and six year olds in a London park, leaning back on a park bench laughing with her tongue playfully stuck out, long hair drawn back in a tail, crepe paper decorated cocked hat by her side. For soldier Martin? Martin, with childish exuberance, flourishes a toy shortsword and a shield; Shane, looking up at the photographer with a shy expression, drags a doll's pram. A delightful, natural scene. I wonder who took the photograph.

A high quality, professional print. Charmian, in soft white blouse, reading to two just-washed babies in the flat at Bondi. It would be early in 1950. Shane looks to be about eleven or twelve months old, a dear little girl with damp hair and a crumpled face like a pansy. Martin, who must be two and some months, is all bulging forehead and eyes glowing with intelligence as he concentrates on the open pages of the large book she is holding, print on one side, picture on the other, *The Tale of...* I can't make out the rest. I wish I could. Had my adoptive mother read me the same tale on the other side of the harbour? Charmian must be only twenty-six. She is at the height of her beauty. She looks truly lovely, hair pulled back, eyes cast down, winged doll's eyebrows darkly delineated, a smatter of freckles across high cheekbones, the generous mouth just showing slightly uneven bottom teeth. In my other hand is a picture of me, twenty-nine years old, looking down at my first two babies aged ten months and twenty-two months, all bathed and ready for bed. We are piled together in a big black leather chair. My arm is around both of them. My high, freckled cheekbones and dark eyebrows are the frame for cast-down eyes, and my large mouth is smiling wistfully at my round-faced children.

Much later on Hydra in 1960 or '61, Jason, four or five, with a snub nose and wide-spaced eyes is grinning a cheeky, baby-toothed grin at the camera. One of his feet is in

Charmian's lap while she puts his sandal on, and the other foot is attended to by a long-haired Shane. Charm, straw hat on her head, is oblivious to the camera, concentrating on the task, lips pursed, getting her child ready to go out—marketing, perhaps? There is a basket on the floor. Outside sun and vine leaves make a morning chiaroscuro. While this everyday summer scene was being enacted on the island of Hydra, in faraway Sydney, Sue, the eldest daughter, in skirt and home-knitted jumper, drawing board under her arm, would have been getting on the Mosman ferry at Circular Quay; or, despite the cold wind, sitting outside-down-the-back of the boat with a group of chattering friends; or climbing the steps at Mosman Bay in the dark, home from a winter's day at art school.

Just before our bike trip, Kathy, my art school friend, who was also adopted and who is retraining to be a teacher of the blind, had rung to tell me that she was going to meet Barbara Blackman. Barbara is the ex-wife of artist Charles Blackman and the subject of many of his paintings. Barbara is blind. She had moved in the same circles as Charmian and George in Sydney in the sixties, and she lived in my district. Would I like to talk to her? She would certainly like to meet me. The meeting was arranged for Friday afternoon, when Kathy would also be there.

By the creek, against a backdrop of tall wet sclerophyll forest—rainforest, even—Barbara and her partner Marcel have built a remarkable complex of whitewashed mud-brick buildings. Green corrugated iron roofs curve up in subtle assymetrical eastern shapes. The walls are pierced with archways of stone from the site and beautiful stained glass windows. Against the textures of the white interior, peacock-glazed ceramics, huge platters and bowls and

wonderful paintings sing with colour. Rough-hewn furniture on a monumental scale bears witness to the fact that people stay and work here regularly. The property is used as a retreat for study and contemplation weekends. A dozen adults might gather here, while a small tribe of children plays around everyone's feet. The gatehouse, the barn and a hexagon-shaped building down the hill are used for accommodation. The overflow put up tents. Rearing towards the sky, a partly finished tower-like structure, surrounded by builders' mess, is destined to become a library, music-room and theatre.

Kathy had already spent a night and a day here, talking to Barbara about teaching blind children. She met me at the gate, and I hastily asked her if there was any special etiquette for being around blind people.

'Only normal sensitivity,' she said.

Barbara was in the galley-kitchen, behind the massive wooden counter, chopping a veritable mountain of vegetables into a huge stockpot for soup. The closeness of the sharp-edged knife to this blind woman's fingertips caused me to flinch. I needn't have worried. In her own environment, Barbara Blackman is independent and totally competent. I would have been much more likely to cut myself than she was. She turned to greet us, and a face from a Dürer engraving met my eyes. A strong, serene face; long straight hair tied in a knot on top of her head, calm and thoughtful eyes, and a mouth that readily quirks into a humorous smile. An extraordinary woman.

When the vegetables had been chopped and the pot lifted onto the gargantuan black iron range, we retreated with coffee to the stone fireplace, also enormous, where a fire was laid awaiting a match. Kathy applied it, and Rosemary, the present occupant of the hexagon, passed around the cups, telling Barbara that hers was at her right hand. I began to tell my story again. Kathy had heard it all before, but she listened with the same glistening eyes as the first time. I had brought my I-look-like-my-mother photographs, which we described to Barbara. The three listeners interrupted now and again with pertinent questions, and metaphysical reasons for all the coincidences. There was a strong feeling in everyone that Charmian's spirit was guiding my search. I couldn't agree with them.

'When did your parents tell you you were adopted?' Barbara asked.

'I always knew.'

'And they never told you who your mother was? They must have known, living in Mosman at the time she was writing for the *Herald*.'

'They told me that my mother was married and had died having me. I believed them and it stopped me asking any questions. Sometimes, as a child, I even felt it was my fault she'd died, that I'd been a lethal Christmas present. The whole issue was so loaded with unspoken taboos that I just knew it couldn't be discussed. I pushed it deep down.

When I was grown up they told me, unasked, that she had been a Cambridge graduate. To account for my academic leanings I suppose. I was fairly sure I was illegitimate by then. And I've remembered this: when I was having my first baby, just in case the story was true, I asked Mum what had actually killed my mother in childbirth, and whether it was likely to happen to me, too. She answered something soothing about modern medicine being so much better now than it was in 1942.'

'All those lies. It was terrible to tell a child so many lies.'

'I've thought about this a lot. I'm still not sure whether they knew the truth or not. In Dad's family, in his social strata, in his era in fact, there was a strong tradition of evasion, of putting a good face on things, on being devious for other people's good. Protecting other people, especially your loved ones. If your pet canary died, they would buy you another one and sneak it in so that you didn't know the first one had died. Anything rather than let you grieve. So either Dad and Mum knew and were protecting me, adjusting the story to suit, or Matron Shaw was doing the same thing to protect her baby brother Harold, and he genuinely believed what he had been told.'

'But when you were in your twenties, you could have met her. If Matron Shaw knew, how could she *not* have told you?'

'In those days it was the done thing. Especially for her. I wonder how many hundreds, thousands maybe, of illegitimate babies were born at Crown Street? The parted mother and baby were never, ever, in any circumstances to know any identifying details. For everyone's good. Matron Shaw was my godmother and would have been doubly concerned to protect me.

'My brother David's wife just recently told me something very interesting. We were staying with them in

Melbourne—our kids had given us tickets to *The Phantom of the Opera* for our twenty-fifth wedding anniversary. We were talking about all of this, because of course David's adopted too and his wife is very interested to know about his background, even if only to discover where the dark brown eyes of two of their children come from. She told me that back in the sixties when the four of us were newly married and were at some family gathering, Dad's other sister, Ella, had said to her in a conspiratorial way, "If only Sue knew. She has a mother and brothers and sister living quite close."'

'Then your parents *did* know!'

'I'm still not totally convinced. Edna and Ella were very close, and I can see them protecting Harold from emotional concerns in the same way he shielded them from business concerns. If they did know, it makes me very angry. And one of these days I'll let myself feel that anger. To have been so close to meeting my mother!'

I pushed that thought away and changed the subject. 'Anyway Barbara, how well did you know her? Tell me about her.'

She put down her coffee cup. 'Charles and I knew the Johnstons socially during the last year or so of Charmian's life. She was a life-affirmer, with a great quality of personalising immense experiences. My chief memories are of her bubbling over, talking, talking, talking, a glass of wine in her hand. I felt that she and I clicked. We would have been good friends had she lived. I'm sure of it.

'I've only known two people with such a reckless, irreverent, fearless and passionate appetite for life, and that was your mother and the artist Joy Hester. Both beautiful, incautious, physically very strong. They both married men who demanded precedence, and they both left behind them wells of imagery only partially bucketed up to us.

'I blame George for killing Charmian. That book of his, *Clean Straw For Nothing*, was unforgivable. No-one has the right to strip another person bare like that in public. She obviously couldn't stand it. Some people argue that art is always more important than life and that others' pain is immaterial. I don't agree. He should never have published that book. He should have written it, then bottom-drawered it.'

'Apparently she never read it. For his earlier books she had been his sounding-board, but she couldn't bear to read this one. She said she would read it some day when she had earned her own small bundle of clean straw.'[5]

'That was a lovely way to put it,' Barbara said.

'Mmm . . . very Charmian Clift. To me the worst thing about it is not the way he treats her sexuality, but the fact that he doesn't make her a writer. He makes her nothing but a beautiful, desirable woman and a mother. He de-powers her, emasculates her—how strange to have to use that word. He takes away her *raison d'être*, which was not him or the children, but her writing. I wonder if it gave him a measure of control over her that he did not have in real life.'

'I didn't like that man. I will never forget the day after she died. Charles was having an exhibition at Bonython's Gallery to celebrate his fortieth year. There were forty paintings and forty drawings. The opening was to be on Tuesday night, but Charmian didn't want to come in the public crush. She was going to make a leisurely perusal of Charles' show on the Wednesday morning, and then come on to lunch with us and a group of other people. We were seated at the table waiting for them to turn up. It got later and later. Then George was on the phone saying that Charm wouldn't be coming, she was dead. She couldn't make it through the hoops of middle age. "Put the lunch off for a week," he said. "Then I'll come with . . ." Who was it?

Greece and Australia, 1955–1959

41. Charmian and George with Shane and Martin. Kalymnos, 1955.

42

43

44

42. A sunny, happy family scene.
Kalymnos, 1955. (Martin nearly 7, Shane 5.)

43. Dressed up for visitors. Sue (12) and
David (10) on the left, with visiting children. Cremorne, 1955.

44. David (11) the keen fisherman at The Entrance. Harold watching. 1956.

45

6

45. One of many crippled sponge divers. Kalymnos, 1955.

46. Kalymnian fishermen.

47

48

47. Hydra. The harbour, playground of the Johnston children.

48. Mosman Bay, playground of the Shaw children.

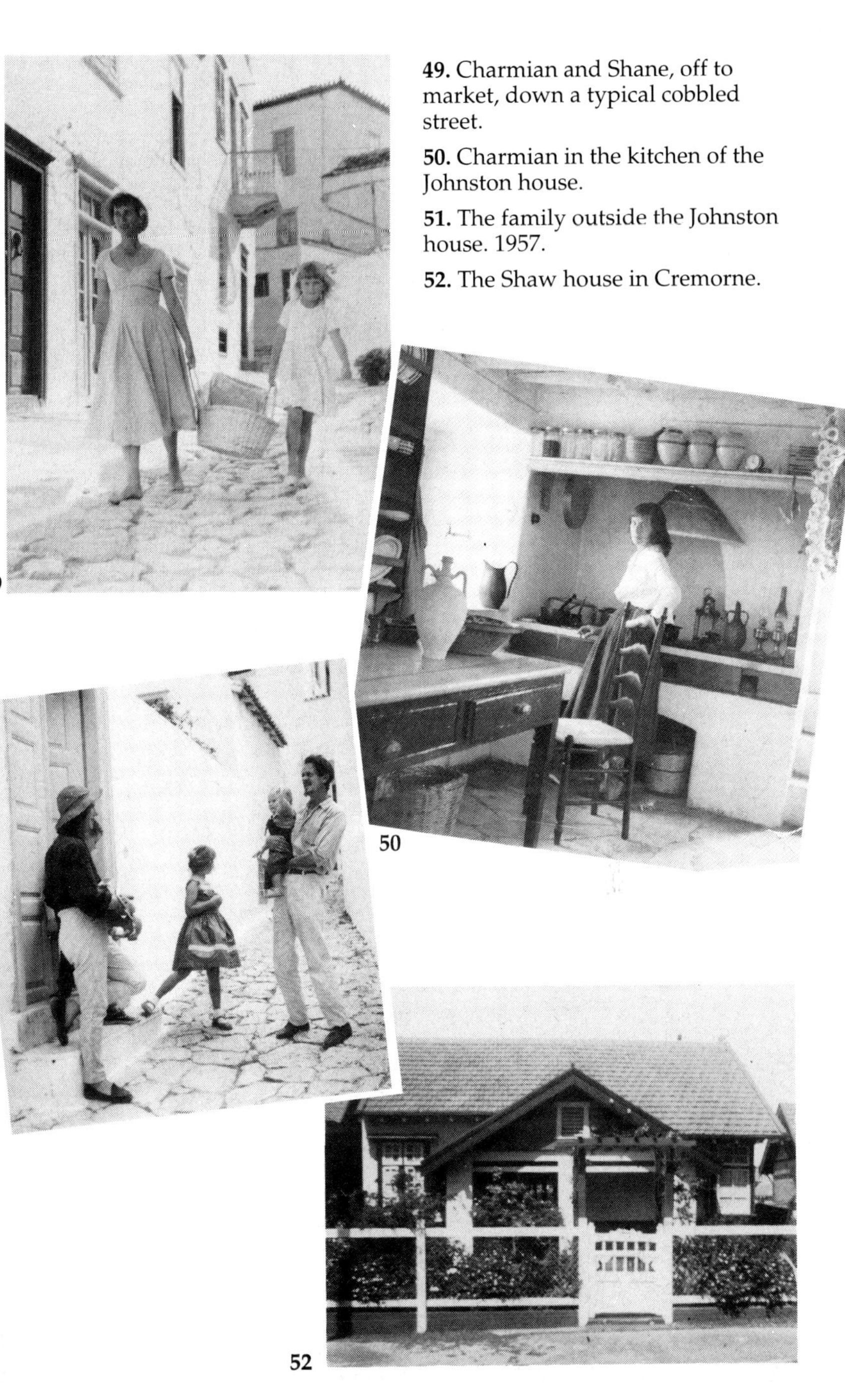

49. Charmian and Shane, off to market, down a typical cobbled street.

50. Charmian in the kitchen of the Johnston house.

51. The family outside the Johnston house. 1957.

52. The Shaw house in Cremorne.

50

52

beach culture - Greece and Australia

53

53. Hydra beach scene. Shane at bottom right. 1957.

54. Australian beach girl: Sue (13) with the newest in inflatable pillows. 1956.

55. The Entrance beach scene. Sandy and Sue (14) with David (12) bottom right. 1957.

56. Balmoral Beach. Sue's friends in typical poses. 1959.

55

54

6

family life

57. A life lived largely out-of-doors. Big sister Shane looks after baby brother Jason. 1957.

58. Charmian, second from left, in the midst of a Greek family celebration.

59. The Shaw family en masse. Sue (16) in centre; Edna, third from right; Marjorie and Harold with heads turned, back row. 1959.

57

58

59

Kalymnos through the eyes of Cedric Flower

60. *Mermaid Singing* coming to life from Charmian's typewriter. Sevasti offers figs while George corrects typescript. 1955.

61. 'I've seen that look on Martin's face many a time. See, his mother has it too.' – Roseanne Bonney.

62. Donkeyback children. 'He's not being protective. He's falling off!' – Roseanne Bonney.

63. Shane and Martin with all the Kalymnian waterfront activities. Ink drawing by Cedric Flower.

64

65

64. 'I thought of her as the chuckling girl from Kiama.' – Cedric Flower.

65. Charmian chooses the best produce.

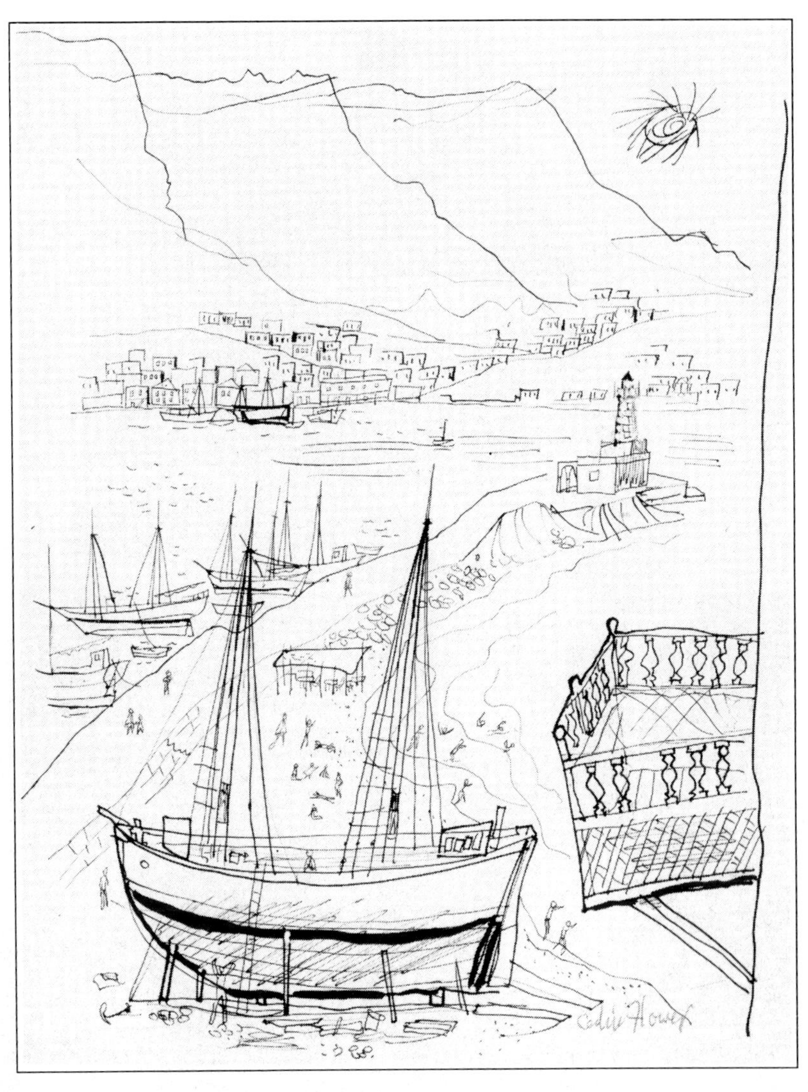

66. The balcony, Kalymnos. Ink drawing by Cedric Flower.

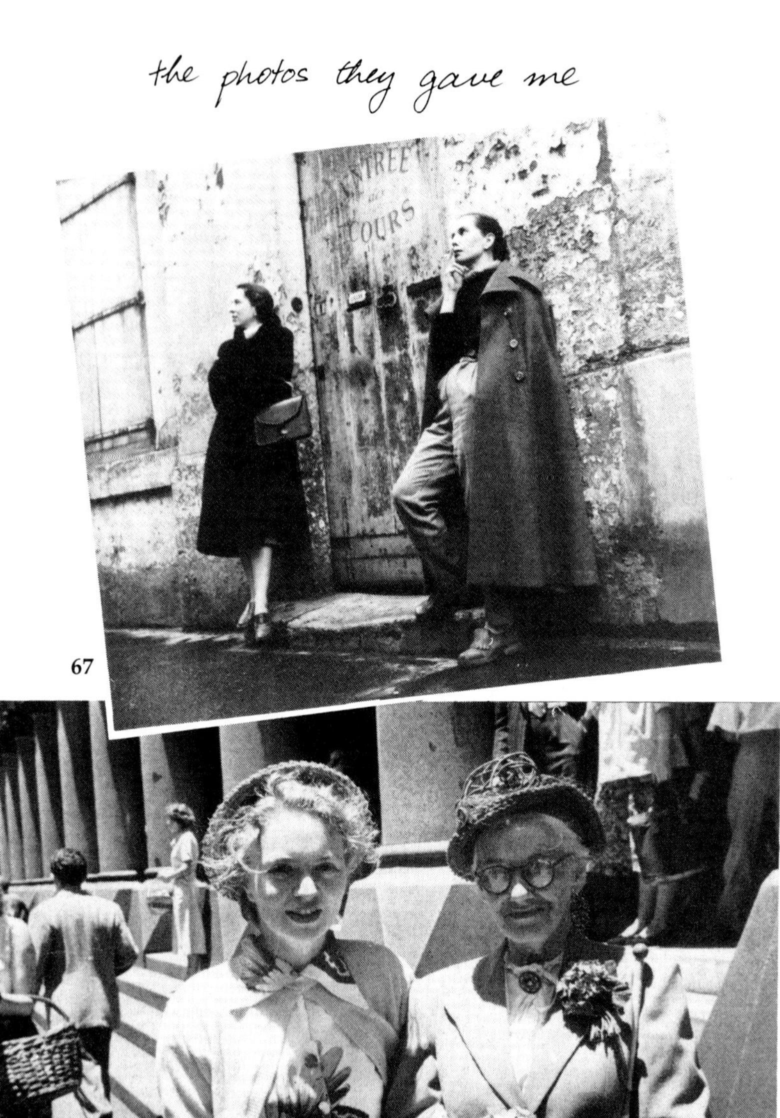

67. Mary Andrews and Charmian, Paris, 1951. 'We didn't have enough money and had to wash dishes.' – Mary Andrews.

68. Toni Burgess and 'Chippy', Charmian's mother, Martin Place, Sydney, early 1950s. 'I think we were going to lunch for her birthday, and I had just bought her flowers from a barrow.' – Toni Burgess.

69. Charmian and George, Athens. 'The reason for the glad rags might have been to attend the Australia Day bash.' – Charles Sriber.

70. An intelligent, beautiful Charmian.

71a

71b

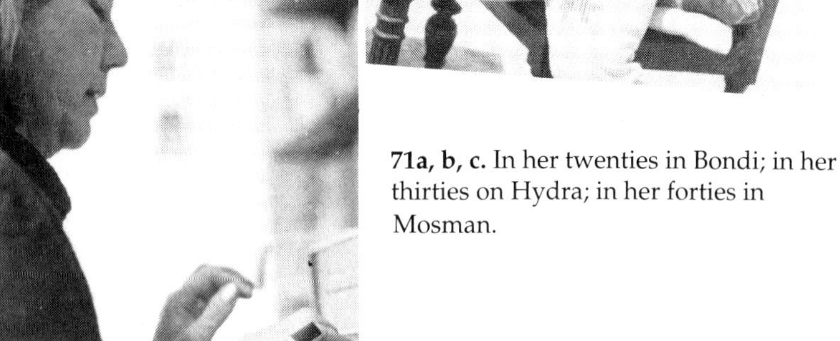

71c

71a, b, c. In her twenties in Bondi; in her thirties on Hydra; in her forties in Mosman.

Yes. Pam Bell. She was a friendly all-rounder we all knew. It smacked of journalistic cold-bloodedness. Couldn't make it through the hoops of middle age indeed!'

'But people do react in strange ways to shock and grief,' I objected.

'Nonsense,' said Barbara. 'You have to remember that these were people who lived with words, who knew exactly what words meant, who made a career of exploring their every emotion. He knew exactly what he was saying. Didn't she leave a note?' she added.

'Yes, apparently Toni Burgess told Kinnane that it said something like, "Please forgive me—I can't bear it any longer, it had all become too much." And a quote from Keats, "I shall cease upon the midnight with no pain".'[6]

'I can remember talk of a note that said, "Why is everyone always angry with me?" Has anyone told you about that?'

'No, I've never heard that,' I said, stretching as I stood up and adding, 'Barbara, I'm standing here now.' She instantly directed her eyes towards the source of the voice. I went on, 'When Charmian Clift died I was often in Mosman, heavily pregnant with her eldest grand-daughter, the one who is so like her: her thirst for life, her love of drama, her lavish embroidery of stories—often out-and-out lies for maximum effect—her general quality of being over the top. She was very relieved to find out who her grandmother was. She said it explained everything.'

'Well,' Barbara said quietly, 'I wonder where Charmian's soul flew to?'

Kathy's and Rosemary's eyes were wide, but Kathy knows my beliefs. They don't include reincarnation.

'I rarely have visions,' Barbara added, 'but I had one on the night of my mother's funeral. It was very clear. My mother was coming towards me with a tiny baby in her arms, pushing through this crowd of people. "How lovely," I thought, "she's found my tiny dead twin." I was born a twin, but the second one lived only a week, you understand. But no, that wasn't the meaning. That very night, my daughter got pregnant. And my daughter's daughter is in some ways an embodiment of Gertrude, my mother.'

Barbara was like the wise woman of the tribe: her power was palpable. Even though I could not agree with all the articles of her faith, a shiver ran down my spine.

I told her then about Charmian and Icarus, and my eldest daughter who had always leapt from the highest possible branch before she had any idea of her wing-power—and flown. In school, love affairs, jobs, life. In her imagination, too, she soared. She once described how, when she was eleven, on a family holiday travelling up the coast of Queensland, she had looked out the car window up into the sky at a brahminy kite sailing effortlessly on the air currents. Her soul, her imagination, her spirit, what you will, left her body and in a twinkling she was looking down on the tiny toy minibus as it followed its earthbound track. She glided above us all for what seemed an hour, until she got scared and instantly was in the back of the van with her sisters. Bereft.

Barbara's response to all this talk of Icarus was to take Kathy and me up her curving staircase, with its highly polished tree-branch handrail, to her own quarters which looked down on the living area on one side and out over a balcony to the massed trees on the other. In one corner of this space was a superb winged figure. Blown in glass by sculptor Warren Langley, it was intended to be an angel, but she had always thought of it as Icarus. Almost life-size, he reached up from a narrow base to gold transparent wings; his face was all contours, ice-coloured, crevasse-coloured, melting at the edges.

Here was my mother-metaphor yet again. Wings uplifted, flying still, but the contours beginning to melt. Too close to the sun.

Later, back at the now crackling fire, Barbara asked about my father. When I told her who I thought it was, she became quite excited.

'But we knew him in London in 1961. He was a lovely warm-hearted, generous-natured man. He was about fifty and had remarried for a second or third time, I can't quite recall, and had a toddler. His new wife was quite young. So you would have another half-brother or sister. More than one, probably. I have a friend over there who might know what has happened to him. I'll see if I can find out for you. Another person you might like to talk to is Maisie Drysdale. George and Tass were close and the Johnstons stayed with the Drysdales often. I ran into her the other day coming out of the theatre in Sydney. I'll see what I can do about that for you, too.'

'Thank you, Barbara, I would be so grateful.'

Rosemary asked me what I was going to do with all this.

'So many people have asked me that question. The answer is that I'm not sure.'

'The sort of people I know are in the journalistic world, and there are some who would love to get their hands on a story like this.'

'Well, I'm not going to give it to the journalistic world. Actually, lots of people have suggested that I should write about it myself. I'd like to. I just don't know if I have the ability or the courage.'

My thoughts snapped back to the present. I was back in the people-eating lounge staring out at the moonpath on the bay.

'I'm going to do it.' The words came out loudly before I could stop them.

'What *are* you shouting about?' Doug's voice came from the kitchen.

'I'm going to do it. I'm going to write a book!' The decision had been made. It was my story and I was going to tell it myself.

CHAPTER 17

... rejection is a possibility ...[1]

Dear Nadia, the letter began.

It was one of my occasional days as a relief teacher. I was sitting in front of an English class of seventeen year olds, who were finally and reluctantly doing the work their regular teacher had left for them. While they were chewing their pens, I was writing a letter. The familiar school smell, sun on plastic blinds, sweaty bodies, stale farts, chalk dust, cheap spray-on deodorant, washed around me. The faces may change but the atmosphere, never.

Now I had decided to write my book, I knew that Nadia would have to be told. During our recent stay she had made it abundantly clear that she was sensitive to other people seeing what she was working on. My impression was that her work was a very private part of her, until she was ready to make it public. Yet she had talked to me very frankly. Although I was fairly certain the liking and respect I had for her were reciprocated, her generosity to me was to Charmian Clift's daughter. I was about to enter a different category: a writer.

From my point of view, one of the most pressing reasons for writing a book was to confirm my status as an adult. I had only recently realised that all adopted people are thought of, and spoken of, as adopted *children*. Even when they are forty-eight years old.

There had been a subtle hint of that adopted-child attitude in my search, too. I went to people as a child seeking her mother. Everyone had been very kind, very generous, but I sometimes felt that I was only being told what was good for me to know. A benevolent censorship was at work, expressed as omissions, or warnings about reading certain books or seeing certain people. At the beginning I had been so grateful for any information that I hadn't noticed, but now the time had come for me to grow up, to actively synthesise what I had discovered and use it as an adult would, rather than passively accepting it like a child.

Nadia's friendship was very important to me. I wonder if a baby at birth experiences a rush of love for the mother whose body she has known so intimately—the corollary of the rush of love the mother feels for her baby. A child who is torn away from her mother cannot express that first love. What I had experienced with the people who were closest to my mother (or, as in Nadia's case, were the powerful ones who knew so much about her) was that rush, forty-eight years too late. It explained my feelings when I first met her on Kiama station.

As a woman, and a woman of my time, connectiveness is at the core of my being. I will go to extraordinary lengths to maintain important connections and in the past would have put relationships before all other considerations. Finding out who I am has given me a new sense that I am important in my own right, not only as the strong connective tissue between other people. The old Sue would have abandoned the idea of writing a book if she had thought any important other would be upset by it. The new Sue needed to write this book, and would accept whatever consequences ensued.

So I wrote my letter. And waited for a reply.

When it came I knew that my worst fears had been realised. I had been excommunicated. A temporary excommunication, until after we had both finished writing. My Greek play would have to finish unfolding without its chorus. I was sad.

I made what concessions I could, sent back a stack of material she had given me, some of it unpublished drafts of my mother's work. I promised that, although I could not unknow what I now knew, I would try not to write anything about my mother that had come to me from Nadia's special knowledge. Any already public material I would feel free to use and, of course, anything that I found out myself. I knew that I may not have met many of the wonderful people who have helped me without Nadia's intervention, but I couldn't roll back time.

I had been invited to a book launch at the new Writers' Centre in the grounds of Rozelle Hospital: the launch of an anthology of children's stories Nadia had edited. That was something else I had never experienced, and I had promised to go. So, with heart in mouth, I went. Would Nadia even want to speak to me?

At the end of all the speeches, she noticed me. Although we hugged and both blurted out something, the atmosphere was uneasy. I tucked the bundle of beautiful images of Charmian that she had lent me into her basket.

Fortunately, Roseanne was there too. We were beyond friends: she was family. We sat side by side on the edge of the wooden verandah in the warm spring sunshine. Children practised leaping from the verandah onto the ground beside us. We talked about Martin, about her and Martin, and she cried as we looked through the photographs I had brought. Angry tears.

'Look at this!' This was a delightful little print of a brother and sister, aged about five and four. 'It's obvious he was as blind as a bat. His eyes aren't focused at all! Anyone with half an eye would have seen it. And the way he used to read with his books right up to his eyes. I'll never forgive them for not noticing! Apparently they thought he was so engrossed in what he was reading that he wanted it right up close. He was quite old, in his teens I think, before he got glasses. He told me that to him it seemed quite normal for the world to be all blurry like that.'

'How on earth did he manage to do so well at school?' I asked.

'He used to go back at recess and stand right in front of the board and read it. Another thing I can't forgive is that she didn't leave a note to the children. Wouldn't you,' she turned towards me, 'if you were going to commit suicide, at least write a letter to your children explaining *why*?'

I had thought about this myself. 'If I was dying of something terminal, and had decided to kill myself, yes, I would write to *everyone*. But if I was in a state of deep depression, had had my self-confidence all but destroyed, had had a horrifying fight with my husband that morning, and been drinking steadily for the rest of the day, well . . .'

I had brought these photographs back because John Tranter was assembling and editing a selection of Martin's poems. It would be Martin Johnston's last book.

At first Roseanne had rung me to say that she needed all the photographs back. I had written in my journal:

> *I hate to see them go. I know I've copied them all, all the family photographs, the most important both as laser prints and by making internegatives. The results are pretty good.*
>
> *But it's not the same. My copies are uniform: all on two sizes of paper, silk-finished, resin-coated. They are spotless. They make two neat stacks. Although their images are ancient history, their substance has no history at all. Not yet. The originals are tattered and creased. Some are pasted onto pulled-out pages of family photograph albums. Some have faded and browned (the photographer on Hydra habitually used his fixer past its wear-out stage, Cedric had told me). There are scraps of writing on the back and sometimes across the front in Charmian's big bold hand—so much like mine. One of her leaning on a lifesaving reel—it must be Bondi beach—has scrawled across the front a misquote from Yeats: 'When I am old and grey and full of sleep . . .'*

> *I can see only too clearly the young romantic girl writing that across her beautiful image to look back on in old age. But of course, she never did grow old.*
>
> *Hand. There's the important word. Her hands have flicked through these over the years. Her hands have put drawing pins or sticky tape in the corners to display them—where? Her hands have packed them to travel from Bondi to London, from London to Kalymnos, from Kalymnos to Hydra, from Hydra to Mosman, Sydney. Some might even have come with her from Kiama to Kings Cross when she was only a girl. Or did those early ones come into her keeping on the death of her mother? Is it always women who are the guardians of the family icons?*

Faded photographs. Charmian referred to them being stored in 'the portable attic', a rusted tin trunk that had accompanied the family on their travels, full of the memorabilia of the years. She wrote:

> *Perhaps we've really been hoarding all this stuff to form the nucleus of a permanent attic for the amusement, edification—and possibly the mystification—of our grandchildren and great-grandchildren . . .*[2]

Ah, Charmian. You have no great-grandchildren yet. But three of your grandchildren have seen part of your portable attic. And did you ever imagine that the baby girl you called Jennifer, and had to give away, would one day be leafing through the same photographs, staring intently at every one for traces of you?

CHAPTER 18

But what are the rules for girls now? Who makes them? The Church?[1]

I was committed. I had committed myself. I would have to write a book.

Wendy Flower had given me good advice: 'I should wait at least six months before you begin, maybe a year, so that you can get things into perspective.'

It had been just over four months. There was no way I could get my natural mother into perspective yet. My own perspectives were straightening out a little. The Sue I had always known had moved closer to the Sue who might have been. A passionate, life-loving woman had left her print on me. And more and more often now, I was able to see it.

Spring had overtaken my garden. Drunk with perfume, I was picking purple and pink sweet peas from the vines I had been tying up when the world had stopped for me. The bulbs I had planted in the new terracotta pot were now a mass of gold on green. Daffodils in bloom. The tiny green feather-dusters on the liquidambar had opened into tender young leaves. Underneath the sometimes frantic pace, the elation and despair of the previous four months, the earth had been turning.

To write, to write, to write. How could I even begin? The feeling of a blank white canvas was one I knew well. But a blank white page?

Everything I had done so far had subconsciously led to this. The non-stop reading of all her books. The late night journal that charted the temperature of my ups and downs. The accounts of conversations with interesting people who had known my mother. The letters I had written. The letters I had received. The photographs of her. Of my brothers and sister. The photographs of me.

The photographs of me. I was not yet ready to start writing my book. But couldn't I try to understand myself better? After all, the raw material was to hand. Come to think of it, there was archival material, too. I had more than photographs to talk to me across the gulf of years. I had my own voice.

From its secret hiding place—a dilapidated leather document case, embossed in gold with the initials H.A.D.S. (Harold Augustus Druitt Shaw)—I unearthed a tattered yellowing school exercise book. It no longer had a cover,

and linen threads and dried glue were all that was left of the spine. Silverfish had gnawed away at its margins, interrupting the complicated drawings of faces and eyes and swirling hair doodled there. The faint blue ruled lines were covered with large handwriting in blue ink. My writing, first penned when I was sixteen and continued over the years.

The book had started off as a troubled record of nightly bible study:

> *Proverbs 4: 18–19*
>
> *The path of the just is as a shining light, that shineth more and more unto the perfect day. The way of the wicked is as darkness: they know not at what they stumble.*
>
> *Prayer:*
>
> *Me. Work Thy will in me. So often, Lord I ask this, so often I fall away. Oh God, why can't I surrender myself? I would like to. I would really like to live close to Thee, day by day, hand in hand with Thee. I really would. But I cannot seem to do it.*

Gradually observations about the outside world began to creep in. At first impersonal scraps. One about a fellow Sunday School teacher:

> *This morning Patsy Barraclough looked remarkably like a turtle angrily sticking its neck out of its shell, when she was scolding some little boys.*

Then, in the expanding spaces at the end of each day's shrinking bible passage, appeared little scraps of diary entries, homing in ever closer to my inner feelings and secret longings. Mainly for the object of my unrequited love.

I had chosen him three years before, when he was nearly a man, a charismatic man going about his manly business, and I was only a child. How safe it was to have an unrequited love. How safe and how agonising. One winter, when I was fourteen and my wings were fluttering, urging me to be off, the agony had been so great that I had tried to drown myself in our fish pond. *I'll show him. I'll show them all!* The water was only six inches deep and, in my dripping water-hyacinth-draped nightgown, I had run out into the suburban night. Howling at the city-stained sky, I had thrown myself down in long grass to rage and sob. *I'll catch pneumonia, then they'll be sorry!* But of course no-one was ever sorry. No-one ever knew.

And here he was again through my sixteen-year-old eyes. My acutely seeing eyes.

> *His eyes are strange. Light blue eyes surrounded by short, stiff, jet-black lashes should belong to a sinister, cold, Nazi villain from a war movie. And his eyes can be cold, but also they can have depth and tenderness. In the dark, dancing, his eyes have that depth. And he always looks right into your eyes. Never slides away. When I draw my eyebrows up in the middle and pout just a little and wrinkle my brow and look pathetic, he does the same, quite unconsciously.*
>
> *He is shaped like the German language. Solid but satisfying. It's a very neat language, with no straggling ends and everything comfortably fitted between the beginning and the end of each sentence. No awkward pauses. That's what his body is like.*

Until God all but disappeared, to be ultimately replaced by me.

Tuesday 17th November, 1959
To myself in 10 years. Age 26 years 11 months.
Dear older Suzanne,

I have nearly finished with school. Only two more exams. Just think. Do you remember how it felt? Happy and sad? Happy at your freedom and sad at leaving your friends and your last link with childhood.

He has made me so unhappy. His tender pale blue eyes have grown cold again, he has begun to behave in a hearty bluff manner, like a total stranger.

Who are you with now? No doubt you're married and have children. Treat them, my older friend, the way you were brought up, with a lot of love. But try to accept them for what they are. Don't try to live your life through them. Let them make their own mistakes.

Hoping you are strong in the faith,
Your young adviser,
Suzanne (age 16 years 11 months)

Here it was. The first record of my independent voice. 1959. For me, a milestone year.

CHAPTER 19

I've always thought it a difficult business to be a young female.[1]

1959. Two incomes were keeping the Shaws up with the Joneses. Marjorie was working longer hours and contributing more money now her teenage children didn't need her to be home at three-thirty every day. Out of habit, Harold had opposed her most ambitious project, enlarging the tiny back verandah into a sunroom, but now it was finished he spent most of his time there. It was a comfortable informal space for meals, hobbies, and doing homework. The broad expanse of sliding windows gave a sweeping view of red and green: Mosman's tiled Federation roofs patchworked with eucalypts and jacarandas. At night, smart white plastic venetian blinds closed out the Sydney fairyland of lights.

In the kitchen and bathroom hot water came directly out of the taps, and in the laundry under the house a washing machine with mangle had replaced the gas copper.

The ancient, finger-picked cabinet radio had gone to the Salvation Army, and a new radiogram stood against one wall of the sunroom. In it long-playing 33⅓ r.p.m. records of musical comedies like *Oklahoma!* and *Carousel* rubbed shoulders with extended plays like *Caruso's Greatest Hits* and 45 r.p.m. singles like Elvis Presley's 'Heartbreak Hotel'. Marjorie loved that one, and embarrassed Sue and David immensely by playing it in front of their friends and singing along.

In the lounge room every evening a marvel of modern technology kept everyone riveted to the big old horsehair-stuffed three-piece lounge suite. Harold had been unable to resist the lure of the TV set. In its shiny veneered cabinet, supported by splayed legs with metal tips, it stood at an angle beside the standard lamp with the pink and green silk shade that Marjorie had made at evening classes. A rabbit's-ear aerial stood on top of the set next to a grotesquely fat, highly polished brass Buddha that Marjorie's mother had brought back from her world tour in the thirties.

Oh, how the children loved the flickering black and white pictures. No more listening to radio serials, radio quiz shows. Goodbye to the Argonauts. Goodbye to Phidias and Mr Melody Man and the Muddle-Headed Wombat. They were too old for all that.

It was the Johnstons' fifth year in Greece. Charmian had urged the move, although the blocking of George's career ambitions in London had been the catalyst. She had high hopes. Perhaps a simple lifestyle amongst an elemental people would help them recapture something of the heart that had bound them together in the early part of their relationship. She was drawn by a country with echoes of her sun-drenched childhood beside the sea. A country with an irresistible attraction for a writer: a country from whose soil western civilisation had sprung.

They had rejected the dull suburban safety of post-war Sydney and the financial rewards of London's journalistic treadmill in favour of the life of the individual spirit.

> *It had seemed a glad thing to declare against all that; to declare for individuality, for risks instead of safety, for living instead of existing, for faith in one's own ability to build a good rich life from the raw materials of the man, the woman, the children, and the talents we could muster up between us.*[2]

She and George had been prepared to work hard at their writing, hoping for financial as well as artistic success. At least they would be their own masters. George in particular was a prolific writer, but none of their books was bringing in much money. Although it was possible to live very cheaply, if very simply, in Greece, they were anxious that the poverty might not be temporary. After all there were the needs of the children to be considered, and George's health was deteriorating. His lungs were under assault, leaving him open to any infection that happened to be floating by. He was also almost impotent. 'A one time a year man,'[3] he called himself.

Still, the lovely old eighteenth-century sea captain's house where the family lived was their own. For Hydra, it had a very modern water supply. In the rains, water from the upper terrace rushed down to fill the cavernous cistern cut into the rock at basement level. A galvanised water tank was fixed thirty feet above this and George had to pump one ton of water by hand whenever the tank needed filling. This water enabled the bathroom to function. (Most of the villagers simply drew their water from wells like the one in the square outside the Johnston house.) Sweet drinking water was delivered in cans by mule and emptied into an enormous ribbed stone jar in the white-washed kitchen that was the centre of the house.

They had bought some good old furniture in Athens to add to the gifts from their Greek friends and neighbours, and the walls glowed with paintings given to them by artist friends such as Sidney Nolan and Cedric Flower. Greek heroes of the War of Independence glared from their passe-partout frames. Books piled on the window ledges and shelves were interspersed with shells, an ancient amphora and a beautiful model of a caïque. Lovely Greek rugs were thrown over beds or on the stone-flagged floor. The house by the well was cool and spacious, but warm with atmosphere.

George and Charmian's lives were complicated by the tensions amongst the small, but growing, expatriate community on the island. To aggravate the situation even more, over the last couple of years there had been a seasonal summer stream of visitors. And the stream now threatened to become a flood. Hydra was in the process of being 'discovered'.

In later years, Charmian harked back to this time:

> *... winter after winter and summer after summer others came drifting in, buying houses and there began to be established a foreign colony ... a foreign colony composed of people who wanted to write and people who wanted to paint, drifters and exiles from all over the world. I think practically every country, every nationality was represented there. And it was a weird sort of way to live ...* [4]

and:

> *... the regular morning steamer from Piraeus would disgorge Oxford or Cambridge students with rucksacks, maiden aunts with sketchbooks, various distressing people of the type known as 'fringe',*

> *earnest academics, city men out of uniform, the old Chelsea guard with aberrations at the ready, used-car salesmen, minor aristocrats, pasty poets, debs and debs' delights, useful relatives, discarded nannies and old retainers, all of whom beat an eager and purposeful pathway to our door and knocked there until admitted . . .*[5]
>
> *Poets and painters and potters and novelists. I remember these better, because I connote them with long early-morning sessions over the kitchen table, cups of coffee, making up spare beds, the lonely, the lost, the desperate, the raging dreamers, the sick and the desolate, the stifled, the suffocating.*[6]
>
> *. . . how many visits to tavernas that mere tourists never found, how many times we must have related the history of our long island sojourn, explained again about the children's education, conducted tours of our house . . . farewelled steamers at afternoon or dawn . . . Surely we must have needed those strange people in some way or we would never have gone to so much trouble . . . needed them momentarily, I mean, perhaps to convince ourselves that our lives were as meaningful as we had hoped they were, or, perhaps, selfishly, to preserve a reputation for hospitality of which we were proud.*[7]

Not far below the surface of the Johnston marriage smouldered embers of resentment and jealousy, embers ready to be fanned into flame. A private life was almost impossible to achieve. Against the backdrop of the burgeoning foreign colony the drama was acted out, as Greek drama had always been, in public: public rows, public drunkenness, public accusations.

*

In Cremorne, the sanctity and privacy of the family behind its closed suburban glass-panelled door was all important to Harold and Marjorie. Breaks in family routine were rare. Occasionally Marjorie's mother and stepfather would drive down to Sunday lunch. A baked dinner. Or one of Harold's brothers or sisters would come at teatime. A baked dinner. '*Merde alors*' would issue from the pokey kitchen as Marjorie spilled the roast (or the dessert) on the grey and yellow lino.

'Quick, Sue,' she would hiss, 'close that kitchen door and come and help me scoop up the gravy (or the ice-cream). What they don't see can't hurt them.'

She hated entertaining as much as she hated meaningless politeness.

'Would you like peas?' she asked one of Harold's brothers.

'Just a couple,' he answered.

So that's what he got. Two peas.

That winter, a guest speaker at the church men's club was invited to tea. He was an American lay preacher and held Sue and David spellbound with his stories of the dating habits of girls and boys much younger than they were. Harold harrumphed his disapproval of foreign morals.

Dinner table debate was not encouraged. Expressing an opinion was, to Harold, argument. He preferred the sound of chewing jaws behind closed lips. Marjorie, however, when roused, tried to goad her husband into a row, like an unsuccessful picador at a bullfight. However she shot the darts of the Irish potato famine, the Church Missionary Society, or Robert Menzies, her target turned an impervious shoulder and the missiles fell unremarked. Her anger simmered and David and Sue knew to keep out of her way until she had sneaked half a dozen cigarettes, flung two Bex powders onto the back of her tongue and made herself a cup of strong tea.

Sometimes she directed darts against her daughter's thin unprotected skin. These darts were labelled 'niggers', or 'your common friends', or 'the youth of today', or 'get some commonsense'. Sue learnt from her father to take the hits with an expressionless face and a flat toneless voice. David dealt with the barbs that came his way with nervous laughter, and by staying out of the house until the bullfight was over.

On the Hydra waterfront, crowds of summer tourists were landed from the daily steamer. The exhausting round began again. Visitors trekking to the door, overnight guests, guests for a week, guests for more than a week. Friends, acquaintances and acquaintances of acquaintances. For Charmian, the added burdens of making up spare beds, cooking and making ends meet. The steady drinking around taverna tables. The picnics to the jewelled bay called Bisti. The parties. The admiring glances of interesting men from a world apart from the island. And George impotent and getting steadily more and more ill. But still holding court. Afternoons of conversation, argument and alcohol. Nights of more alcohol, conversation and argument. King of the Island at the taverna table, surrounded by courtiers leaning forward to hear every word.

The arguments could turn inwards, and become blazing rows. Or perhaps Charmian had heard his every word too many times. Martin would sometimes try to sleep with a pillow stuffed over his head, to block out the shouts and accusations that moved from room to room long into the night, ending in the next bedroom.

Charmian had to face the tyranny of time. Youth was passing. She was thirty-five and had been a writer all her adult life, trying to juggle this with her various other selves: beautiful woman, mother, cook and housekeeper, stretcher of the budget, hospitable Greek neighbour, loyal friend, good hostess, wife to George the man, sounding-board for George the author. A slow and private writer, she was trying to uncouple her literary reputation from that of her husband. Her two solo books about the family's life in Greece, *Mermaid Singing* and *Peel Me a Lotus*, were documentaries, and now she was waiting for news of the fate of *Walk to the Paradise Gardens*, her first novel.

George had always been possessively jealous of his much younger wife, fearful that, having won her, he would not be able to keep her. Despite her evident loyalty over the years, he neurotically feared the worst. And the summer before, under the influence of the growing foreign colony with its 'summer indolence' and 'moral laxity',[8] and perhaps fuelled by his own pessimistic expectation, that worst had happened. A passing affair with a physically beautiful, existentialist, French artist. She must have known what she was getting. She had, after all, already seen the seduction technique of Jean-Claude Maurice with other women, and had already described him:

> *Not Dionysos after all, the fleet, the free, the beautiful, the ever-young—but only a little curly dog in season, whose imperative it is to sniff after any and every lady dog.*[9]

As George's health deteriorated, he struggled with his writing of a partially autobiographical novel, published as *Closer to the Sun.* It was a new departure for him. In it his alter ego David Meredith made his first appearance. There was more than a hint of revenge and self-flagellation in this book, as George picked publicly at the old wounds of Charmian's affair with Maurice. But in May the steamer from Piraeus brought wonderful news with the mail. *Walk to the Paradise Gardens* had been accepted by the American publisher, Harper, with an excellent advance and good royalty rates.[10] For the moment, at least, their financial worries were over.

The Johnstons were riding a seesaw. And Charmian Clift's end was on the way up.

'I am immoderately happy,' she wrote to her British agent in May 1959, and writing again in July she declared: 'I have all sorts of writing plans and will probably go on producing a novel a year for many years to come.'[11] In the spirit of public professional loyalty that each always showed to the other, George wrote: 'Charmian's beginning to do very nicely under her own steam, isn't she? I'm overjoyed.'[12]

But in the way of seesaws, when one end is going up, the other must be going down. An attack of Asian flu had left

George weak, and his heavy smoking and drinking was catching up with him. His weight had dropped dramatically by over three stone, and he was coughing constantly and bringing up blood. Despite all Charmian's urging, he kept putting off the visit to the doctor in Athens. Perhaps he feared cancer.

Despite all the undercurrents, the illness and the distractions, both of them tried to be as professional as possible about their writing routine. In the morning, after Martin and Shane had run up the stone steps to their primary school, and Charmian had hurried to the waterfront to buy whatever fresh produce the market boats had brought from the mainland, husband and wife would retreat upstairs to their long studio, looking out over the Peloponnesus.[13] A fug of blue cigarette smoke and a clacking of typewriter keys would fill the morning air.

Perhaps, as she typed, into Charmian's mind slipped the satisfying knowledge that at the moment the family was surviving on *her* money, the advance of one thousand five hundred U.S. dollars for her first novel, set in the remembered sunshine of thousands of miles away—the Kiama of her youth.

Thousands of miles away, a fresh wind of cultural change was blowing through Sydney. On Bennelong Point, excavations for the fabulous dream-like sails of Utzon's Opera House had begun. *The Summer of the Seventeenth Doll* had been made into a film, which was showing in the city. Home-grown culture was beginning to find a voice.

In Cremorne, Marjorie's French lessons at adult evening classes had resulted in a whole series of orange-covered school notebooks crammed with exercises and translations, and editions of Simenon, Colette and Simone de Beauvoir in their original language. Sue, who was also learning French as well as German and Latin at her selective girls' high school, dipped into them too. Marjorie tended to translate her favourite swear words literally:

'Rang en rang des derrières des cochons!,' she would yell when her Singer sewing machine, or the spotted mirror in her bedroom, destroyed yet another dream. 'Pig's bum' was her favourite expletive. 'Rows and rows of pigs' bums' was saved for particularly dire occasions.

A framed Dufy print of four scribbled horses on a splotched green ground had been Sue's present to her mother for her fifty-sixth birthday in April. It now hung in the hall, in place of the Chinese junks in the sunset. The cultural shake-up of Harold was a pair of jazzy modern socks with matching tie, neither of which he ever wore.

Over the past few years, Marjorie had taken Sue to matinees of the entire season of Shakespeare, the Borovansky Ballet, the d'Oyley Carte Gilbert and Sullivan performances and, at the Elizabethan Theatre at Newtown, the Opera Company productions. A ferry and train trip, a short walk from the station through what seemed like a foreign country, then a steep climb to the cheapest seats in the gods brought delight and a permanent love affair. At the Cremorne Orpheum, Shakespeare's *Julius Caesar* was shown with oh-so-British, oh-so-handsome, brown-eyed, chocolate-voiced James Mason, and another sort of love affair ensued.

Fragments of beauty embedded themselves in the young girl's soul. A sculpture by Gaudier-Breska, a simplified marble evocation of the human form, crying out to be caressed, seen in an art book. A Byrd motet, sung with the school madrigal group in the choir gallery of St Mary's Cathedral, the pure, separate lines of *Hodie Christus Natus Est* floating in woven strands out into the vast vaulted space. The imagined scent of pine forests while the Sydney Symphony Orchestra was playing Sibelius' tone poem, *Finlandia*, at a youth concert in the Town Hall. She would never forget them.

Sue's brothers and sister were growing like wildflowers on their rocky island. As children do, they had adapted to the Greek rhythms of life better than their father and mother. They spoke Greek fluently.

Shane, ten in February, now had long hair, not quite as sun-bleached as it had been, and a sturdy muscular body. Martin was eleven, a serious, studious boy with brownish-blond hair cropped as short as that of the island boys, and a fine-boned, sensitive face. He charmed visitors, male and female alike.

Only their blue eyes and fair hair distinguished them from their Greek classmates as they marched proudly along the flag-decked waterfront at the *Oxi* Day celebration. This national day commemorates Metaxas' historic answer '*No*' to Mussolini's demand that Greece put up no resistance to his invasion. The schoolchildren marched in separate squadrons of boys and girls. The boys were dressed in their best white shirts and dark shorts, faces and shoes shining. The girls were arrayed in newly washed uniforms of pleated skirts and long-sleeved tops with starched white sailor collars and cuffs, decorated with braid. Fiercely starched white bows perched on their heads like oversized butterflies. Patriotic rosettes were pinned above each heart.

Out of school, Shane ran barefoot and as wild as any peasant boy. At home both children spoke English and Martin, in particular, read from books that their parents had sent out to them from England.

Often they looked after their baby brother. Jason, the

first foreign baby to be born on Hydra, was now three years old, with his father's down-sloping eyes and his mother's wide-boned face. Cared for by Greek women, notably Zoë, as well as by his mother, his first language was Greek.

In August Charmian had her thirty-sixth birthday. She was no longer a girl, but she was beautiful still and very attractive to men. Her long, slightly wavy brown hair was pulled back from a straight forehead, scarcely lined, slanted green eyes reflected her moods, full ripe lips pursed thoughtfully or lifted from large square teeth in a long curling smile. Her broad-shouldered body, although thickened around the waist from four pregnancies, was still admirable, and her legs and arms shapely and tanned.

In October Charmian, friends and reason triumphed. George travelled to Athens for X-rays. The feared lung cancer turned out to be tuberculosis. Fearful enough, but the disease was at a fairly early stage, and controllable, even curable, with drugs and a drastic change in lifestyle. He was to stay with a friend in Athens for three months[14], away from all stress, receiving regular injections, and giving up smoking and drinking. He lasted six weeks. He could not give up the habits of a lifetime, and his jealous fantasies were running riot over his wife's imagined activities on Hydra.

Later, recalling and probably exaggerating this time in *Clean Straw for Nothing*, he has a character called Clarissa, visiting David Meredith in Athens, say: 'They're leaping around from bed to bed like fleas on a blanket.'[15]

George came back to the island. Charm then added 'nurse' to her list of personae, and monitored his health (for which he held her responsible), giving him regular injections of antibiotics. And as for a change of lifestyle: the heavy smoking, the drinking, the fights continued. He raged against his illness.

'He was, of course, affronted and outraged by the corruption working in his lungs.'[16] And he raged against Charm because she was whole and healthy and still sexually attractive.

'I do not like to think much on those years because we almost foundered,'[17] she was later to write.

Harold was sixty-one and, because of a succession of illnesses and operations over the years, had never expected to live long enough to see Sue and David finish primary school. Now, increasingly bemused, he was having to cope with two teenagers.

The daughter he adopted as a baby often felt too large for her skin, as if she must either suppress herself, squeeze herself small, or burst out. Whichever of these things she did, she felt guilty. Guilt, to her, felt like sin. She was torn between her innate questioning rationalism and the blind faith that her religion demanded. If she questioned, she felt she was sinning against her faith. If she accepted blindly, unease followed. She did not yet know that the unease signified the worst of sins, the sin against the self. A naturally assertive girl, she tried to soften herself into the submissive femininity that society, and especially evangelical Christianity, rewarded. Disquiet followed. The conflict between the private, introspective girl and the public, extroverted one was never resolved.

With her father, Sue could be sullen and withdrawn. She had an intense desire for a secret life, apart from her family, and felt a great sense of power in withholding herself from them as much as possible.

'Where are you going, Sue?'

'Nowhere,' in a flat expressionless voice.

'What are you doing?'

'Nothing.'

Marjorie was allowed to be supportive of school ventures, but was coldly rebuffed whenever she wanted to enter Sue's separate space. Marjorie responded with black Irish rages and vicious slashes of her razor-sharp tongue. But both mother and adoptive daughter were always very careful to stop short of saying the unforgivable:

'You're not my real mother. Why did you adopt me if you didn't want me?'

'You're not my real daughter, and I bloody well wish I hadn't!'

But all the same, the thoughts hung in the air.

Love of beauty, guilt, and fear of flying. These were threads that had been woven inextricably into the warp of her life.

From the time she was a tiny child, Sue had always been terrified of the next life-step. Perhaps that first abandonment had made her cling to whatever security she had. On the first day at a new school she would vomit with fright. She had never slept a night away from her family, never even been to the school camps where her friends had so much fun. Looking ever backwards, she dug her fingers and toes into the safety of what she knew.

All her out of school life centred around the church. In suburban Sydney in 1959, a place of single-sex schools whose task was solely academic, where else was there to go? Sunday School teaching, Church Fellowship, Friday night choir practice and singing contralto in St Clements' choir twice on Sundays were made exciting by the presence of those mysterious and desirable creatures—boys.

At sixteen, sexual desire shimmered like haloes around all but the most puritanical boys and girls. Untutored, innocent and naive, Sue had only recently been kissed for the first time. Her best friend Sandy, on the other hand, found it hard to avoid being kissed. Her thick waist-length gold-red hair, classically boned face and impressive bust measurement, combined with a beguiling smile, a low English voice and a demurely provocative manner (modelled on Doris Day and Sandra Dee) proved irresistible to droves of boys. And a problem for Sue. Scared of diving into this new world, she nevertheless suffered agonies of jealousy towards the friend who was swimming in it with such style and confidence.

To make matters worse, Sandy also had a clear soprano voice which earned her leading roles in the musical comedies for which the Fellowship was becoming renowned. Sue's strong mezzo-soprano and her organising skills inevitably saw her leader of the chorus, painter of the sets, or rehearsal accompanist. Challenging and rewarding, but never glamorous. Jealousy was a hard guilt to conquer.

Other guilts were impossible to surmount, for they were guilts about her very being.

It was a Saturday night in winter. The gang was at a twenty-first birthday party in the pine-lined rumpus room of a wealthy family in the water's-edge suburb of Fairlight. Against the teachings of the church, the record player was belting out a stack of the favourite rock singles of the day: Buddy Holly's 'Rave On' and 'That'll Be The Day', Bill Haley and the Comets' 'Rock Around the Clock', Little Richard's 'Good Golly, Miss Molly', Gene Vincent's 'Be-Bop-A-Lula' and Sue's song 'Wake Up Little Susie'. And they were dancing. Dancing to the driving beat of rock'n'roll.

Sue was wearing a dress she had finished sewing that afternoon on the Singer treadle machine. A low scooped neck in a tight bodice that hugged her figure to below the hip. Then a very full skirt gathered onto the hipline. The fabric was a cotton patterned in overlapping scale-shapes, sea colours, blues, greens and purples. Underneath were two petticoats, one of stiffened net under another of starched white cotton edged with rope.

She was dancing with the older boy she had long secretly loved. In her mind's eye she looked like an animated mermaid in her undersea dress as her legs flashed out the step, twirl and kick rhythms. Forgetting for the moment all restraint, her sixteen-year-old body delivered her up to the primitive beat. Hair flying, skirts flying, petticoats flying. Hip-throw, shoulder-throw. Rock'n'roll. Face flushed, laughing mouth. *Wake up little Suzie. Wake up little Suzie.*

A lifetime, a second later, the music ended and the secretly-loved one put his arm in a fraternal way around her shoulders and walked her to the drinks table. Soft drinks only. They were Christians, after all. One of the boys who had been leaning against the wall, watching the dancers, leant across her partner and said:

'That was disgusting! No Christian girl should make an exhibition of herself like that. You should pray for your soul!'

Her soul shrivelled with shame and guilt and inexpressible anger.

In November, in the gathering heat of a Sydney summer, squeezed safely back into her schoolgirl skin, Sue was studying hard for the Leaving Certificate. Night after night, the light in her little box of a bedroom burned late.

In November, as the northern hemisphere turned away from the sun into winter, Martin turned twelve.

At last it was Christmas. Seventeen years since the birth of Charmian Clift's first child.

CHAPTER 20

I was of an age when the male of the species haunted my feverish dreams . . .[1]

There were more word-pictures in the tattered yellowing book. Words written by a slightly older girl in 4B pencil. And to emphasise the single-mindedness of the pencil's attack upon the page, there was not a single doodle in the margin.

> *He doesn't raise a flutter in me any more. Now I have found the real thing. Peter put his arm around me in the car coming home from the dance, went to the beach with me and has asked me to an all-day yacht picnic. Peter almost fills the aching void in myself. He is young, silly and very good looking. His eyes crinkle up in the most delightful way and he has the* nicest *eyes. Dark brown under strong black brows and black wavy hair. This afternoon we both lay on our backs in the dappled sun outside the zoo wall, watching two escaped chipmunks and a willy wagtail.*

My first real boyfriend. Not a fantasy, or a boy-on-a-pedestal, but flesh and blood. There he was, twenty forever, in my pencilled scrawls on the yellowing pages.

The memories flooded back. Memories of the long summer holidays when I turned seventeen. The holidays that signalled the end of my childhood.

January had begun with jubilation when the Leaving Certificate results were published. I had come third in the state in art, in the first one hundred in English, had A's for all my languages and a B for biology! Mum and Dad planned a celebration party as my reward.

Set modestly back from the still green water of Mosman Bay was a hall used mainly by the Mosman Sea Scouts. It had a wooden floor, scuffed walls and large glass windows overlooking the water. The entrance was through barred, paint-peeling double-doors, set flush with the building. They decided to hire it. I had wanted the Mosman Rowing Club, two doors down, much more glamorous with small tables and a terrace. But reality won.

It was ours for a Saturday afternoon and night in January. Lugging decorations, Pops for the floor, crockery and cutlery in boxes, and borrowed dance records in stacks, we staggered down the path to Mosman Bay, negotiating the endless steps carefully. Then we set about preparations. Over the wooden floor, Dad and David sprinkled the Pops, a white substance that made the floor slippery enough to dance on. They blew up balloons while I cut coloured crepe paper into streamers and Mum arranged glasses and plates and cups and saucers and checked out the urn and the power points and moved chairs and set up trestle tables for supper. She had already been cooking for a week.

Dad's precious Christmas lights were strung above the entrance.

The party was a huge success. Rock'n'roll music thumped out across the water, competing with the laughter of young voices. The boys shed their coats and rolled up their sleeves, and the girls' full skirts over stiff petticoats swung in multicoloured arcs as the dancing hotted up. Ties and ponytails were flying.

It was getting close to supper-time, but where was Mum?

Three-quarters of an hour later, she reappeared behind the supper table, handing out hot goodies to hungry guests. On closer inspection it was obvious that she wasn't as ebullient as she had been. In fact her face was deathly white, and if you looked below the table you could see her shin wrapped in enough crepe bandage to entomb Tutankhamen. And a bedroom slipper on her foot. And blood oozing out of the bandage down her ankle into the slipper.

We forced her to sit down but she would not stop serving the party-goers, and we did not wring the story out of her until much later. And then only reluctantly.

Running back up the stairs in the dark to ring up a guest who had not arrived, she had slipped on the shiny Moreton Bay fig leaves that littered the path. She fell and cut her leg deeply. Cut into an artery. Lying bleeding copiously on the stairs, she had been stepped over by passers-by, who must have thought she was drunk. Eventually she had pulled herself up by the rail and hand over hand dragged herself home. There she had fainted, regained consciousness, stood in the bath with her finger pressed over the artery until the blood stopped spurting. She had packed the gash, wound her leg in bandage, rung up the non-arrival, made herself a cup of tea, smoked two cigarettes and taken a Bex powder, then limped back down the steep path again to slip into the hall and carry on as though nothing had happened.

She was tired, pale and very irritable for the rest of the summer holidays, but had refused all along to see a doctor. In the selfish manner of the young, we kept out of her way and went about our own affairs.

Those holidays were an end and a beginning.

When I started going to art school, Peter and I caught the same morning and evening ferry. He worked at Circular Quay. I was learning my craft at East Sydney Technical College in Taylor Square. He always looked handsome, immaculate and very British. I tried hard to be feminine, grew my hair, wore skirts and blouses to art school, never slacks. Peter had very strong views on girls wearing trousers in the city.

My black-haired boy asked me to parties, picnics and balls. Or I asked him. He drove me home from choir practice and church. The long way round. Via Balmoral Beach in the moonlight. Under the deep shadow of the fig trees our lips would melt, our faces grow hot, our eyes languid. As the months went on, we would leave a party two hours after we arrived so that he could get me home sometime before two o'clock in the morning.

What was Mum thinking as she lay awake listening for the car? If she knew the truth about my origins was she thinking: *Is the other mother claiming her? Like mother, like daughter? Will the bad blood, the illegitimate blood, come out? Will she come to a bad end?*

Coming to a bad end had only one meaning in those days. But once again whatever she might have thought, she never said it.

'That is never going to happen again!' I would wail in a guilt-stricken voice as I did up my strapless bra and tried to smooth out the creases in my velvet party dress. 'What'll I say to Mum? She's always awake. She always asks what time I got in.'

'Always tell people the truth,' he laughed. 'She'll never believe it.'

Guilt would have me home early for the next two weekends. Then it would happen again. In the end we would set out for the party and not arrive at all. To save the creases in my velvet dress I would take it right off. His pinwale corduroy trousers would soon join it. The back seat of his little car was cramped, but by the time the windows had fogged up we no longer noticed. For me, it was the first-time of man-flesh pressed to woman-flesh, hard to soft. Lips to lips, noses squashed sideways. Tongues and teeth. Eyes a blurred gleam in the darkness. All sensation focused in the quivering beam of a hand's passage, or a single finger: strong man-hands and gentle woman-hands.

He was my sex education. Now I knew that it was pronounced 'pea-nis', not 'pennis'. Now I knew what 'erection' meant. And 'French letter'. And 'mutual masturbation'. Now I knew what my mother had meant when she had warned my eleven-year-old self not to get changed in my friend Alexander's bedroom when Alexander was there.

Peter and I tortured ourselves on and off for four long years. All through my years of art school and Teachers' College. The two o'clock became three o'clock, sometimes four o'clock. But we always woke up in our own beds in our own rooms in our parents' houses.

Finally it was over. I was twenty-one, and before I went out to the country, teaching, I wanted to give Peter a farewell present. After all that had passed between us, my virginity, technical though it was, seemed the perfect gift. I had already given him everything else.

He was sick in bed. I was visiting him in his room at the top of his mother's big old house, empty that night except for us. It seemed a good opportunity. At the penultimate moment, as we awkwardly positioned ourselves on his childhood bed, there was the ominous click of a key in the front door.

'God! Mum's home! What'll we do?' All desire had fled.

'Pretend you're not here,' I whispered.

'I can't. She knows I'm here, sick. Get up, quick! What'll I tell her?'

'Tell her the truth,' I snapped as I feverishly dragged on my clothes. 'She'll never believe it.'

CHAPTER 21

Bunches of little children would burst through the side door like ragged posies, raggedly chanting the ritual Christmas carol, interminably long and interminably boring, but profitable in reward of drachmas, nuts, sweets, and fizzy gasoza.[1]

The phone was ringing as I got out of the car. Scrabbling with the front door key, I took the stairs two at a time and was out of breath when I picked up the receiver. It was Barbara Blackman. As she had promised, she had contacted Maisie Drysdale, who with her famous husband, artist Russell Drysdale, had been close friends of the Johnstons in their Mosman days. Maisie had been about to leave for Paris for six weeks or so, so it would be impossible for me to meet her at the moment.

'I asked her whether she had known about you,' said

Barbara. 'Apparently Charmian had rambled on in her cups about giving up a baby, but Maisie hadn't taken much notice. Thought she'd made it up. "She always was a drama queen." That's how she put it.'

Just like my eldest daughter. The thought popped into my mind. 'Well, thank you very much anyway for asking on my behalf. Perhaps we can organise something when she comes back?'

'That will be getting very close to Christmas. You know what that's like for everyone. I'll certainly be tied up. We're having a Christmas party and grand opening for our new building, a combination of theatre, music room and library. It's nearly finished. It's going to be the spiritual outgrowth of this place... the wings. But, of course, I'm forgetting. You've seen it, haven't you?'

'Unfinished, yes. It was builders' chaos when I was there.'

'Would you and your husband, what was his name...?'

'Doug.'

'Would you and Doug like to come? I'll make sure that you're sent an invitation.'

'Thanks, Barbara, we would.'

I put down the phone and went back out to the car. Christmas, our half cocker spaniel, half who-knows-what, circled round and round me, a stick in her mouth and a foolish hopeful expression on her face. The groceries and the library books were deposited on the table. More books on adoption.

It had been five months now since I had opened the envelope containing my birth certificate, and my appetite for reading about the subject was insatiable. The inter-library loan section of the town library had been kept busy on my behalf.

With the inevitable cup of Earl Grey tea and the latest

pile of books I climbed the stairs to the gallery sunroom. Where to start? This one looked interesting. *Dear Birthmother, Thank You For Our Baby*. I started to skim.

The 4 Myths of Adoption:
1. The birthmother obviously doesn't care about her child or she wouldn't have given him away.
2. Secrecy in every phase of the adoption process is necessary to protect all parties.
3. Both the birthmother and birthfather will forget about their unwanted child.
4. If the adoptee really loved his adoptive family, he would not have to search for his birthparents.[2]

'Hmmm, what happens next?' I was full of intellectual curiosity. My eyes flew over the lines of type and independently my brain thought its thoughts: 'Oh, it debunks each of the myths . . . and here are letters written by mothers to the children they had to give up.'

So I started to read the letters. I got through the first one, full of the love and pain and longing of the young mother, and I burst into tears as rending as the ones I had cried on the very first day.

'Oh God, oh God, why am I doing this? What is happening to me? I've known for months now. I've been fine.'

I put the book face down and my head in my hands and tried to think it through. But the snowstorm-in-the-dome erupted, blotting out all rational thought. My left brain was out of commission. Whenever I got close to the wellspring of this issue my powers of logic deserted me. This was something I just had to *feel*.

Gradually I calmed down and tried another letter. This time I did not even make it to the end before the splots of salty water fell onto the page. If I went on at this rate, this was going to be the longest book I had ever read.

Half an hour passed while I made myself watch a flock of rainbow lorikeets land on the deck outside the window and begin to drink at the birdbath. Soon water was splashing in a fountain of light as the brilliantly coloured, quarrelsome clowns started to bathe.

I picked up the book again. With exactly the same result. I could only read a few pages at a time before I broke down. My cascades matched the ones outside the window.

The book lay, spine broken, on the floor.

Doing something ordinary might be the answer. I had forgotten to feed the birds in the aviary. I wish I did not have them captive, but they are aviary-bred and would die in the free sky. They are the descendants of several pairs that had belonged to our daughters. At least their large, planted, split-level aviary gives them room for flight.

There was a tiny dot of fluff on the aviary floor. A just-fledged zebra finch. I picked it up. It was totally unafraid, sitting in the palm of my hand, weightless. I put it onto my forefinger and jiggled it up and down. Tiny wings flapped for balance. I did it again and there was a brief whirr of flight—straight back to me. I tried again. And again. And again. There seemed to be no anxious parent birds hovering near, so I placed it high on a branch and watched from outside the wire netting. Still no obvious parents. I hurried back to my kitchen to make up a baby finch feeding mixture, but when I took it back into the aviary I could no longer see one baby.

Now there were a dozen babies, intermingled with the adults, their dark beaks and minuscule tails distinguishing them from their elders. There was a commotion of whirring wings as the little ones made tiny flights from branch to branch, sidestepped to the end, then took off again. Their parents made *zit-zit* calls of encouragement from an ever higher branch.

It is easier to fly down than up, but they must fly up or their parents will not feed them. Fly or die.

Into my head there sprang a summer's day when Doug and I were newly married. We were with his younger brother at an airfield outside Newcastle to try gliding. Malcolm was a keen glider pilot, working to become an instructor while waiting to join the air force.

Doug went first while I waited, terrified for him, on the ground. Then it was my turn. Even more terrified now, I sat behind the instructor as the perspex bubble closed over us. A truck with a winch towed us at ever-faster speeds along the ground. Then, suddenly, we were casting a racing shadow on the blur of close-mown grass, on the stippling of treetops, and we were free—sky-borne. There was no noise except a thrumming of air. Far below our shadow sped across a patchwork of ochre summer paddocks, emerald lucerne crops, dark pine forests and earth-green bush embroidered with winding roads and light-catching creeks, starred here and there with the silver of dams and ponds. Our racing earthly counterpart overtook a slowly sailing cloud-shadow, then another. I forgot to be afraid. I had the feeling that we could soar so high that we would cast our shadow on the cloud tops, on the sphere of the earth itself.

I thought again of Malcolm, who had lived to fly, and had died, flaming, when his Mirage fighter plunged into the ground. Yet again my eyes overflowed.

After this day of emotional storms there came a hiatus, a welcome respite.

Late spring merged imperceptibly into summer. The bright green leaves on the liquidambar grew larger and darker. The primulas faded, the petunias bloomed. A beautiful red-headed, charcoal-grey male gang-gang began to spend hours in our casuarina trees with his mate and young one. When startled, the cockatoo family would take off in their typically drunken flight, calling to each other with strange cries like so many creaking doors. Galahs and rosellas and lorikeets began to bring their just-fledged babies to the deck. The air was full of the demanding honks and wheezes of scruffy-looking fledglings.

It was the best time of summer, before the refugees from the city started to arrive in their thousands. The bay put on its summer spangles and the beach became an irresistible magnet. Christmas the dog took me for long walks along curving white sand beaches where the bush grew right down to the high tide mark. Here wind-twisted banksias overhung tumbled formations of sandstone, fretworked by the sea. Dolphins often paralleled our course to seaward, while above us the ever-patrolling sea-eagle traced effortless circles in the high blue sky.

The black and white dog had a strong retriever instinct and loved nothing better than to swim out after a flung stick. She was an accomplished surfer and could judge to a nicety the breaking curl of a wave. Up and over she would jump with half her body out of the water on her way out through the waves, slide her jaws around the stick without swallowing any water then, with head high and tail acting like a rudder, ride the breaking face of the wave back into the sand, shake herself all over me and ask to have the stick thrown again.

So we would make our way around the coastline, a middle-aged woman and a dog: the woman walking slowly, bent over beside the tide-line of wrack, looking for whatever might turn up; the dog running around her in hysterical circles.

It was December and Christmas was approaching. I had never lost my childish excitement at the festive season, and I flung myself into preparations with even more enthusiasm than usual. The four paintings that I had been working on for weeks as special presents for the most important people in my life were at the stage where a tiny touch of vermilion or cerulean was all that was needed. My weeks were full of friends and parties and thinking of family and just the right present and Christmas trees and coloured lights and the traditional joy of singing carols.

Sandy and Sue had decided to go carol singing the Christmas Eve before Sue's fifteenth birthday. They both had good voices and often practised together, Sandy's sweet voice singing the melody, Sue's low voice weaving a harmony around it. They waited for dark and with two fat white candles in candlesticks filched from Sue's place, they started out. At house after house they stopped and sang.

Windows were flung open, heads popped out, money and sweets were thrown. Together they sang their way down dark lanes, up lighted streets, along pathways, up steps and into stairwells. Doors opened and men and women, old and young, singly, in family groups or in parties, asked them in. They drank glasses of lemonade, ate pieces of Christmas cake, accepted coins and notes and sang again.

At about eleven o'clock their voices were getting strained and it seemed time to be going home. They had walked further than they had realised and home seemed a long way. Together they rounded the corner of Sue's street to find both sets of parents out on the footpath in a panic, about to ring up the police.

'Where on earth have you been?' Furious faces, angry voices. Arms were yanked, shoulders shaken. Money flew out onto the footpath. 'Where did that money come from? Don't you know you can't just take money from people? Don't ever do anything so silly and dangerous again. Anything could have happened to you! You could have come to a bad end.'

Everyone in my family plays at least one musical instrument and when our daughters were younger one of our Christmas traditions was to sing carols as a family around the streets that wind up from the bay. Flute, clarinet, bassoon, guitar, recorders and voices in four-part harmony—we could ring the changes. We would work out a programme from the *Oxford Book of Carols* at home and practise for a while, then off we would go. There were no spare hands for candles, so we would stop under streetlights in front of houses with silver Christmas trees blinking, houses with lit-up front rooms full of the sounds of clinking glasses and babbling voices, houses dark except for a blue rectangular glow. As our music became more confident and the children's harmonies soared above my voice, windows and doors would open, figures appear on front balconies, chatter cease, lights switch on.

We wish you a merry Christmas. We wish you a merry Christmas. We wish you a merry Christmas, and a happy New Year. We would swing into our finale.

'Thank you! That was lovely! A merry Christmas to you!'

'Merry Christmas!' The figures would wave and shout, and our little band would move on into the soft warm night.

This year the music would be much more professional. With my group, the Lydian Singers, I was to sing a service of carols, medieval to modern, in a church that would be packed to the gallery. The acoustics were wonderful and our voices had been well-trained to blend, whether whisperingly soft or full, rich and joyous. To be one inseparable thread of that close-woven sound raised the hairs on the back of my neck.

Doug and I went to Barbara Blackman's Christmas party. Their new hall was to be opened with a concert, followed by dancing and feasting. The car headlights picked out the rutted dirt road through the stock gate as we turned off the bitumen. Through quiet paddocks, beside regenerated rainforest, across a tree fern lined creek, up a hill and we were there. Gusts of music and laughter greeted us as we climbed out of the car. Light streamed out of open doors and stained-glass windows, slicing swathes and bars and coloured patches out of the world of dark, towering eucalypts beyond.

In the open house, groups of people formed and re-formed in overlapping pools of brightness. The vivid colours of Charles Blackman's paintings under their individual spotlights sprang to life on the dark walls behind them. Barbara was the centre of one admiring group. I worked my way through the circle and introduced Doug, warning her, as he put out his hand, that his voice would be coming from way above her. Before long we were being introduced to a friend of Barbara's, a vivacious bubbling woman with springing blonde hair and bright, dark eyes. Shirley Fenton-Huie came from the neighbouring property. She already knew about me and asked if I minded being introduced as the daughter of Charmian Clift. She had someone she would like me to tell about my discovery. The someone was a Melbourne couple who listened to the story, polished by now to an art-form, in interested silence. The husband was obviously waiting for me to finish. He had his little piece of information to contribute.

'I knew your father's older brother. He's dead now, but his widow lives just out of Melbourne. If you like, I'll try and find out for you if your father is still alive and where he is. I can tell you this much. Their father was a vicar of the Anglican Church.'

If this man *was* my father, then both my fathers had been born in rectories, and two of my four grandfathers were men of the cloth.

Shirley also had some information, and an invitation.

'We have a friend, a journalist called Charlie Sriber, who was friends with the Johnstons on Hydra. He stays with us sometimes for weekends. Apparently Charmian told him about your existence. He certainly knew about her illegitimate baby. Next time he comes down would you and Doug like to join us for brunch and meet him?'

CHAPTER 22

... they sent their friends, or friends of their friends... and their names too are written into my old red book.[1]

The new year was rung in. For me, a new year indeed.

We were duly invited to brunch with the journalist who had known about Charmian's illegitimate baby. It was a cold, grey day, unusual for January. We drove along the by now familiar road towards Barbara Blackman's place. This time we stopped at the first place through the stock gate, a brown mud-brick and wood house with smoke lazily curling from its chimney, set in an acre of mown grass. Shirley and her partner Denis opened the door to us on a warm family scene. A long wooden table was set with fruit, flowers, breads, jugs and glasses. A pot-bellied stove puffed importantly behind it, and standing around the stove were two young people, a fair boy and a dark girl, and a small white-haired man with a neat white beard.

'Welcome, welcome!' Shirley's rich voice embraced us as

we kissed cheeks and Denis shook hands. 'Let me introduce you. These are my children, and this is our friend, Charlie Sriber.'

The small man shook my hand with brief pressure and a brief 'Hello' in an American accent. He did not look particularly glad to see me.

Over croissants and bacon and fruit and coffee, conversation ranged across general topics: the additions to this farmhouse, which could be seen glowing with polished wood through the open doorway; Shirley's time living in Indonesia, and how she was going back shortly with a group of Dutch women; Denis's collection of old tools; the growing influence of Japan in Australia, and whether we were likely to become the 'white coolies of Asia'.

'No, Denis. I'm not saying that we *are*. I'm saying that some people are frightened that we are going to be...'

'But that's ridiculous. We need them and they need us. What we have to do is set up . . .'

'Yes, I know all that. But . . .'

And so it moved on—to the state of education in New South Wales. Now Doug and I grew heated.

'This Harvard Business School, New Right philosophy is ridiculous when applied to education . . .'

'School principals are now so busy being financial managers . . .'

Our voices overlapped. We were well away.

'You know,' I said, catching Charles watching me intently, 'country high schools are a fascinating social phenomenon . . .'

Around the long table, the others caught the conversational ball and threw it back and forth.

'School uniforms . . .'

'. . . on democratic principles . . .'

'But everything ends up a compromise . . .'

Talk moved on to Aboriginal education. We had found common ground and the words grew passionate. Charles was still watching me as the discussion went around and around. There was no mention at all of Charmian Clift.

We finished eating, and Shirley turned to Charles and asked, 'Well? What do you think? Do you think she's like Charmian?'

I could still feel a cool scrutiny that was making me nervous. *He is making judgments. He is sitting here looking at me, listening to me talk, and somewhere in other times and places he has sat opposite my mother and looked at her and heard her passionate opinions.*

He took his time in answering. 'Yes,' he said. 'I can see the resemblance.'

By this time Barbara had arrived, been given coffee and

seated near the pot-belly, which was puffing away ever more strenuously.

'Did you bring your photos?' Shirley asked me.

Of course I had. They were passed around the table. Charles found one of my mother in front of a Greek windmill.

'I took that one. I remember the occasion well,' he said. 'We were hot and I asked her what she'd like to drink. She had a citrus juice. She wasn't always the heavy drinker people make her out to be . . . I took quite a few photographs on Hydra. The negatives and some little contact prints are somewhere in my files. Would they be of interest to you? Perhaps you could have them copied.'

'Would they be of interest? They'd be wonderful! I've got my own darkroom, so I could print them up and send them back to you. I'd love to borrow them,' I said.

'Tell Charles how you came to be adopted,' said Shirley.

So once more the history was told: the matron and the dressed-up baby girl; Marjorie and Harold in their middle age becoming parents practically overnight; the baby brother brought home in a cardboard box in the back of the car; the myth of the dead father and the mother dying in childbirth.

Everyone including Charles was leaning forward in the attitudes of rapt attention I had come to expect.

'I didn't know that about your brother,' said Barbara, although I had told the same tale to her before. 'I must have missed that the first time.'

'Your adoptive parents must have been remarkable people,' said Shirley.

'Actually they were the opposite to Charmian Clift. They were very conservative, especially my father, very respectable, and although my mother was a bit of an eccentric, my father was entirely suburban and conventional. But they had the most necessary qualification. They loved us.'

'How must Charmian have felt when she gave you up?'

'Yes, that's the question, isn't it? I think about that all the time. She was the same age as my youngest daughter is now, and it seems so very young. All that I've read suggests that women who relinquish a child never get over it. They were told to forget all about it, to put it behind them and get on with their lives. But it's worse than the death of a baby. They always wonder. Some manage to repress it completely, but a number of them turn to drugs or alcohol, or have mental breakdowns. Some contemplate suicide.'

'I can understand that,' said Shirley. 'When you go to sleep at night you do think of all your babies, the living ones, the ones you've lost. You look around for them and gather them around you.'

Prompted again by Shirley, Charles told the story of Charmian, in her cups, weeping and weeping in her kitchen and telling him how she'd been a bad girl and had a baby long before she met George—a girl, whom she'd had to give up.

'What else? What did you say? What did she say?' The women sat on the edges of their seats, vitally and femalely interested.

'Nothing,' he replied. 'I comforted her, patted her on the shoulder, and listened. She just needed to talk.'

Charles told us that he was very much aware that the Clift family, especially Charm's sister Margaret, dead now, had been upset by some of the things he had said in Kinnane's biography, but that he could only tell what he knew as he knew it. Which is all anyone can or should do.

'Charles,' I said, 'You don't have to censor what you say on my account.' This exchange seemed to break the ice, and he opened up with a series of anecdotes and vignettes of George and Charmian.

*

Sydney, 1949. He knew George quite well, but Charmian hardly at all. A chance sighting. Charm, pregnant with Shane, glowingly beautiful, walking hand in hand with George down a city street. Heads turning to watch their passage.

The waterfront at Hydra. Charles had just arrived on a cheap weekend excursion from Athens. The unofficial mayor of Hydra (called Creon in *Peel Me A Lotus*) heard his accent and said: 'You're Australian, aren't you? You must know the Johnstons then. Sit down! Sit down! Have a coffee. I'll go and get them!'

There they were walking along the waterfront towards him, arms outstretched in welcome.

'Charles! Charlie!'

'Who? Me?' looking around him.

They took him home and gave him lunch. When they found out that he had a wife and two children, Charmian immediately said: 'Next time you come, you must bring your family and stay.'

Martin added, 'Bring the boy!'

Shane, 'Bring the girl!'

A story of his little daughter, Cleo, then three. The Sribers had been staying with the Johnstons and in the morning, as sometimes happened after a night of too much drinking, too much smoking and too much talking, George had lost his voice. When they went home to Athens, Cleo would only speak in a tiny lost-voice whisper. They took her to a doctor who had to bend low and cup his ear to hear her. He couldn't do anything for her, and she kept it up and wouldn't speak normally.

Some weeks later, Charm was visiting them in Athens and said to the little girl: 'I know what's happened, Cleo.

You've left your voice on Hydra. I'll tell you what. Next time I come, I'll bring it back for you.'

And she did. In a box, wrapped and tied. Cleo opened the box with wide eyes.

If this story had had its proper ending Cleo would have been cured. But she kept up her whispering for about seven weeks, until one day she snapped out of it herself.

Easter on Hydra. *Carnivale*. It means literally 'Farewell to meat'. Following it was Clean Monday, when you cleared all the meat out of your cupboards for the long Lenten fast ahead. But for this night it was a carnival. Greek style. Charles dressed as a pirate—an egg-slice in his belt instead of a sword, a mouldy old stuffed bird nailed to his shoulder. George dressed as an Edwardian beau; Charm in hooped skirt and homemade pantaloons, beribboned like a Brighton belle, danced and danced with total self-confidence while the Greeks looked on amazed.

Easter Sunday morning. A white church. *Christos Anesti! Christos Anesti!* Christ is risen! Christ is risen! The chanting priest came out from behind the altar-screen with a lighted candle. Everyone in the congregation had a candle ready. The people all pressed forward, candles held high. From the priest's candle one other was lit, then another then another. These candles lit others beside and behind, until the light spread like a fan of flame to the back of the church.

You then took the candle back to your house and, under the eave of the door, you inscribed a cross with the soot.

Christ is risen indeed.

The best times with Charm were when he and she were washing up in the beamed kitchen of the house on Hydra.

They would tell stories and sing songs together. He had strong recollections of her singing the chorus of the old Cockney music hall number:

Oh, me baby 'as gorn dahn the plug'ole.
Me baby 'as gorn dahn the plug.
The poor little thing,
Was so terribly thin,
'E should 'ave been bathed in a jug.

George, holding court at the taverna table. He talked and others listened. George was a great raconteur. They were wonderful stories the first time you heard them. Charm knew the script, took her cues and fed him back the right lines when needed. They were the King and Queen of Hydra.

George didn't sleep with other women on the island. Charles knew a few women who'd tried and been knocked back.

'Well he was practically impotent, wasn't he? At least that's what I've heard.' More than one person had told me this.

'One night when I was sleeping there, she and George had a very noisy session in the room right next to mine. Unless they had pre-recorded it, to impress visitors, George was definitely not impotent,' Charles replied. 'But of course Charm always had all sorts of men interested in her. She seemed to need their admiration and their company.'

'According to Roseanne, George used to say that she had more faggots around her feet than Joan of Arc.'

Everyone burst out laughing. I could immediately see the Hydra waterfront, George and Charm and a circle of friends around a table, retsina flowing, and a roar of laughter greeting his epigram.

'Ruth asked me once if I loved Charmian. "Yes," I told her, "I do. But not in that way. Not in the way you're thinking." It was impossible *not* to love her.'

Into my mind came Cedric Flower, sitting with his wife and his sister around our table, wine glass in hand.

'You know, Cedric was in love with Charmian Clift,' his sister told me in a stage whisper.

'No, my dear,' said Cedric, who was meant to hear. 'Not *in* love. I loved her. You couldn't help but love her.'

What was this quality in my mother that inspired love?

'How did you part company with the Johnstons?' I knew that the friendship had not been continued in Sydney in the sixties.

The *Bulletin* had published a short story by Charles called 'We'll Never Go Back', or something like that, he couldn't remember the exact title, about a couple living on a Greek island. A couple with some connection with radio, and relying too heavily on alcohol. He had based this couple partly on himself and Ruth, his first wife, and partly on the Johnstons. It had ended with the female character saying something like: 'People think we're escapists, and now we'll never go home again.'

George was furious. 'I'll never speak to Charlie Sriber again,' he said. Neither he nor Charmian ever did.

We began to talk about the people I had met and the things I had discovered about my mother. The name of Toni Burgess came up.

'She's the one I would *really* like to meet, if she's still alive,' I said. 'From all accounts she was Charmian's closest friend.'

'Well, she was certainly alive eighteen months ago,' Charles said. 'I'm in contact with her nephew, so I'll see if I can get her number for you.'

'That would be wonderful, Charles.' I was extremely excited. This could be what I had been looking for from the very beginning. A friend very close to my mother who might have shared some of her secrets. Who might even have known something about my birth.

'Have you heard of the Hazel de Berg collection?' Barbara asked me.

'No. What is it?'

She told me it was the largest oral history collection in Australia: over a thousand interviews, made over a period of twenty-seven years or so. Hazel de Berg started off making talking books for the blind, and went on to do taped interviews with well-known Australian writers and artists. In the collection was an interview with Charmian. Would I like to hear it?

Barbara organised us: 'So what are we all going to do for you? Write this all down, so that none of us forgets. I'm going to contact the National Library and have you put on a priority for the taped interview that your mother did for the Hazel de Berg collection. Charles, what are you going to do?'

'I'm going to look out my files and send Sue the negatives from Hydra so that she can print them. And I'm going to contact Toni Burgess for her, if I can.'

'And I,' I put in, 'am going to go home and do nothing and wait for all of you to do it all! You're marvellous. I can't thank you enough.'

As we left, I gave Barbara and Shirley a hug, and a big thankyou for organising this for me. Charles got a hug and a kiss too.

'I'm so glad I've met you,' I said.

'After all the terrible things you no doubt heard about me?' he said with a twinkle in his eye.

I told him I preferred to make my own judgments.

A week later, a fat envelope arrived. A letter addressed to Sue Chick (alias Jennifer Clift) and some large-format negatives and contact prints of my mother on Hydra. The last paragraph of the letter made my heart leap.

> *The good news is that Toni Burgess is still very much alive. I have just phoned her, had a long talk, told her about you and she would be very happy to meet you and fill you in on any part of the saga to which she could contribute. She was amazed at the sequence of events and that you had established an identity to which she could relate. She first knew Charmian when she was 19 and, as I think I told you, was associated with her right up to the time of her death. Her address is . . . and the phone number . . .*
>
> *I hope this is all helpful. I certainly enjoyed meeting you and your husband. Do keep in touch.*
>
> *Sincerely*
> *Charles Sriber*

CHAPTER 23

I never walked into my friend's sitting room but with a sense of refreshment and ease. It was that sort of room.[1]

In an inner city suburb, a narrow street rose sharply from the arterial road below. It was lined with small weatherboard workers' cottages, each separated from the footpath by a metre of lawn then a metre of verandah. Some of the lawns were just that—lawns. Some were flourishing gardens. Some of the verandahs were bare. Some were falling down. Some were draped in flowering vines. Some houses had visible letterboxes, and on some of those the house numbers were clearly displayed.

The number I was looking for belonged to a house of the flourishing vine persuasion. In fact it was hard to see the fence, verandah or house for the riot of greenery. I found a steeply sloping parking space opposite, pulled on the handbrake with all my strength, and hoped no big truck was going to want to get up the street.

Stumbling over my own feet, I gathered myself, my bag, my portfolio of photographs, my birth certificate and a bunch of white baby chrysanthemums, and got out of the car. She was waiting at the gate for me: a short woman in her sixties wearing a full, black and white patterned skirt and a dainty white shirt over a pretty chemise top. I had time to study her as I crossed the road, and she to study me. This was the woman I had long wanted to meet, my mother's closest friend. Toni Burgess.

'They're her eyes. You've got Charm's green eyes.' She held me at arm's length and looked closely into my face, then hugged me to her as the tears rolled down both our cheeks.

'Hello, darling.' She had the loveliest voice, middle-range and musical. 'You know you look *so* like her. I had the strangest sensation just then. As though part of her had come back. Well, come in, come in. No, get *down* Sam!' as a large and boisterous German shepherd-cross came pelting out of the front door and threatened to bowl us over. 'Do you drink?'

'Not much. That's one way I'm not like my mother.'

'Nor am I usually, but we both need some champagne. I know I do.'

She was right. The champagne did help. I gave her the flowers and she found a large white jug with a broken handle to put them in. Just at that moment the doorbell rang.

'I'll fix the flowers,' I called, and began to cut down their stems and arrange them in the jug.

'My God! She gave me that jug! Charmian's daughter arranging flowers in Charmian's white jug.' Toni had come back into the room and was watching me.

We sat in a sunny little room at the back of the house, in well-used white wicker chairs that showed signs of frequent

dog occupation. Bright ultramarine-blue glassware stood translucent on the window ledge. A little spray of cumquat—glossy dark green leaves, tiny orange fruit—zinged with colour against a blue and white tiled coffee table, where a single red tomato sang its own discord.

On one wall was a large noticeboard covered with memorabilia, and a single photograph of Charmian Clift with a little envelope pinned beside it. On the back of the envelope in fading ink a big bold hand had written:

Because
I love you for yourself alone,
Not for your yellow hair.

Noticing the direction of my glance, she explained, 'It's a quote from Yeats. She used to say to me: "I've got the legs, darling. You've got the hair."'

I tried not to look at this best friend of my mother too inquisitively, but it was difficult not to stare at her wide-spaced eyes in the heart-shaped face, the long thick fair hair piled on top of her head, and the eyebrows which had a life of their own, rising up into her hairline with every question mark. How many hundreds, thousands of times had those eyebrows shot up at something my mother had said?

Toni had obviously prepared herself mentally for my visit and said, 'Perhaps it will be best, darling, if you just ask me what you want to know.'

Having said that she proceeded to ask me questions. 'You must have always been very curious about who your mother was. What made you decide to find out?'

I started to tell her a confused version of the adoption story, starting from the middle, but corrected myself and told it again properly, in the third person, from the very beginning. When I got to the baby-brother-in-a-box bit she said: 'But what *nice* people they must have been.'

As we talked, the sun moved slowly around behind a tall golden robinia in her back garden, filling the room with its gold-and-green light and changing all the blues to green-blues. We sipped our second glass of tingling champagne and I got out my photographs.

'Oh, my God! It's extraordinary. You're so like your . . .' She hesitated. 'I don't know what to call her.'

'Call her my mother. She was.'

'You're so like your mother, then. Turn sideways a moment. Hmmm . . . your nose is quite different. It turns up. And you have much thicker hair.'

'Perhaps I got those things from my father,' I said.

Toni had turned back to the photographs. 'Look at this one with you and your babies—especially in this one. It's extraordinary. You're much more like her than her other children.' She looked up. 'Would you mind leaving these with me? I'd love to show them to my daughters. They both knew the Johnstons well. They were always in and out of their Mosman house. Roie was a very good friend of Shane's. I know they'd love to see these. I told them about seeing you today.'

She lit a cigarette, pushed the inquisitive dog's nose away from her lap, ordered him outside, and began the story of meeting Charmian for the first time at a Saturday night party at the flat in Bondi.

'You have to remember in all of this that I'm biased. She was my friend, not him. Not George. They held open house, you know. My father, who was a journalist, took me. I was only twenty-one. She was about twenty-four. She was lovely. Alive and glowing. Absolutely beautiful with a figure like Venus. And charming. Her name was just right for her. We got on well straightaway. We were both newly married. It was terribly hard to find anywhere to live in those years after the war, and when the caretaker's flat in her block became vacant, she arranged for me to have it. It was a poky little place attached to the laundry out the back.

'We were young girls together. We sewed clothes, read poetry, minded babies and loved each other deeply. It was a kind of symbiotic relationship. We painted our toenails amongst the nasturtiums. We dressed up. You know the sort of thing. Went out wearing straw boaters. Mine was a little French number. Charm suggested we be outrageous so we stole the geraniums from the garden of a horrible neighbour and put them in our hats, sticking straight up at the front. We'd go to the Hotel Australia for afternoon tea, wearing little white gloves, with a spare pair each in our bags for when the first pair grew dirty. We'd roll around in hysterical laughter. We were just a pair of young girls.'

I took a deep breath, dug my fingernails into my palms, and asked The Question: 'Did she ever tell you anything about having me?'

She leaned her head back, drew deeply on her cigarette, closed her eyes and let the smoke out in a rush. The words came out very slowly after it.

'One Christmas, when Martin was just a baby, asleep in his bassinette, I came into her flat to find her in tears. She was sitting at her typewriter with the tears flowing down her face. I asked her what was the matter. For an answer she handed me what she had been writing. "Here," she said. "Read this."

'So I started to read it. It was a radio script for the A.B.C.—a Christmas piece about the baby in the manger. I read it, but I was more concerned for Charm. "Yes," I said, handing it back. "It's lovely. But what's the matter with you?"

' "I didn't really write it about the babe in the manger at all," she said.' Toni stopped and drew at her cigarette. 'Now let me remember this right. *When* were you born?'

'Christmas Day,' I told her.

'That's what I thought. She said, "I wrote it about *my* baby. My baby who is out there somewhere!" And she told me about it. "Chippy," that was her nickname for her mother "wouldn't let me keep her. I'll never forgive her for that. Never! She said that she couldn't afford to support me, and that I couldn't support a baby. So I had to give her up." She felt so guilty, so terribly guilty.'

There was a long silence. Tissues were busied at two pairs of eyes. We took another sip from our glasses.

'Where did she stay while she was pregnant? Have you any idea? It couldn't have been in Kiama. They could never have kept it a secret in a little country town.'

'I don't know.'

'I suppose she could have stayed with her sister Margaret at Kings Cross, though Margaret apparently denied my existence to various people.'

'Oh, she knew. The family all knew.'

At this moment Sam, the young shepherd-cross, came bounding into the room followed by Etsi, the old red kelpie.

'Out, you dogs. Get out!' Toni pointed to the open door without much effect. Sam wanted some attention. After putting his forepaws on Toni's lap and trying to lick her face, he consented to sit at her feet. The old kelpie flopped contentedly on the floor.

Then I asked the other, secondary question: 'Toni, do you have any idea who my father might be?'

She thought again, eyes half-closed, eyebrows raised, then said: 'It could very well have been . . . um . . .' She named the set designer suggested by Cedric Flower. 'Charm had an affair with him while she was working at the Minerva Theatre.'

So I showed her my little photo of him, and the one of thirteen-year-old me that looked like him. We talked about him and his marriages. Was he still alive? She didn't know.

'She never forgot you, you know,' Toni returned to my first question. 'Later in her life, when she was very depressed about things, I presented her with the old bromide—you know the one—your bottle of wine is either half-empty or half-full. It's all in the way you look at it. You have all these blessings not to mention your three children. "*Four* children," she came straight back at me. "Don't forget I have *four* children."'

Another aspect of my mother had puzzled me. 'For such an autobiographical writer, she hid me very successfully. Very few people knew about my existence and I haven't been able to find a hint of it in her work.'

'Oh, yes. You were the only thing in her life she didn't exploit that way. Although many people won't believe this, for all her unconventionality she was inculcated with the correct forms. As a girl in her insular family she learnt the right way to do things—you know: "this is the way the Clifts do things". And when she had an illegitimate baby, she did the right thing for the time.'

'And suffered for it.'

'Yes, that's true. She did. But then she went on to do the other things society expected of women. She married. She had children. Women were expected to marry, to breed and to be good mothers. When the marriage turned bad, she stayed with it.'

'It might have been much better for her if she'd just lived with George and never had children.'

'It would have been better if she'd never met him. She should have married that fellow she was engaged to, but she was carried away by the golden-boy war correspondent. "Stick with me kid, and I'll show you the world." That's what George offered her. She wasn't going to dribble her life away in the suburbs, thank you very much. She wanted an exciting, glamorous life.'

'Don't you think she loved him, even then?'

'I think she was in love with love.'

'I don't know, Toni. I've seen photos of the two of them together in those very early days, and they look to be truly in love. Not a posed man-and-woman-in-love either, but the real, blazing thing.'

'Well, perhaps it was, *then*. But she mucked up her life. She was much more fragile than anyone realised. She wasn't equipped to cope with her life—with him, with being a mother, with the writing.'

As though to shake off sad ghosts, Toni got up and walked into the tiny kitchen. 'Come on, let's have lunch. Take your glass and the bottle out onto the balcony.'

Over lunch she talked about how she had never wanted to visit Charm in Greece, how she couldn't have borne to be part of the scene that Hydra eventually became. They had corresponded over the years, but Toni had destroyed all the letters much later. She had needed a life-threatening operation and had tidied up so that if the worst happened her friend's letters wouldn't fall into grasping hands.

'It was obvious from her letters that she wasn't happy with George. He was mean-spirited. Mean-spirited. He had convinced her that *she* was the cause of his illness. If she'd behaved herself, he wouldn't have got ill.'

'But she didn't leave him,' I said.

'No. Towards the end when she was desperately unhappy I said to her: "For God's sake, leave him!" But she couldn't. Her guilt was too strong. She said to me once—I think these are the words: "I couldn't stand *that* guilt, as well." Meaning as well as the guilt about giving you away.

'Once, in Mosman, I had had a fight with Bill, my second husband, and I went round to Charm in a fury. "I'm going to leave him! I'm going to pack up and leave him!" I announced to her. She looked at me in horror. "But you can't do that again! You've done that to one husband already."'

I asked her about my mother's death. The suicide of one's mother is a terrible thing.

So she told me. She told me about the week of my mother's death, early in July 1969. On Monday night a distraught Charmian had come round to Toni's place in a black depression, weeping inconsolably, and begged her to go away with her, to Fiji or Honolulu—somewhere. Right now. She couldn't bear it any more.

Toni felt deeply for her friend's distress but, naturally enough, couldn't drop everything and leave at that moment. Charmian stayed late into the night, drinking and weeping, while Toni tried to comfort her. She wouldn't be comforted.

'"Everyone loves Charmian Clift. You're the only one who loves *me*!"'

Toni smiled a wry smile. 'She meant it at the time, but she was always a great exaggerator.'

On Wednesday morning Toni arrived late to work at Wally Summon's bookshop in the city. As well as being Toni's employer and friend, he was also a friend of Charmian's. He and Toni had a kind of running gag about her lateness. When she came in late she would say something jokey like: 'I didn't notice the time. I was watching a white peacock in the fountain.'

This morning she came in late and Wally was behind the counter at the little window that opened into his office.

'Toni,' he said. 'Charm's dead!'

She leant on the counter and came back at him: 'Not this early in the morning,' thinking it was part of their running being-late joke. But she saw the colour of his face as she heard him say: 'Toni—No! Charm *is* dead. George has just rung. He wants you to go over straightaway.'

Somehow she kept from falling apart while Wally rang a taxi.

When Toni got there Charmian was lying on the bed in her studio, head pillowed on her hands, hair tied up with a black shoelace, looking asleep. She had taken an overdose of barbiturates and left a note, ending with a quote from Keats, 'I shall cease upon the midnight with no pain'.

Toni went into the room to take off her friend's wedding ring, then back outside to get George to ring the doctor.

'George told me that they had had a terribly vicious fight the day before, and told me some of the rending things he had said. She had been drinking very heavily. Later on, when he had more control of himself, he was angry with me, probably because he'd told me too much. Then I had to ring up the Drysdales and tell them. They had come down and were staying in a motel. They were all going to have lunch with a group of friends.'

She looked away at the distant Sydney skyline for a moment, then turned back. 'I was furious with her for leaving me. And so guilty. If only I had gone away with her it mightn't have happened. I went grey after she died, you know. It was unbelievable that she was dead. She was so *alive*! So full of life! She loved the sun, she loved the day, she loved the sounds, she loved everything.' Toni gestured towards the sunlight dappling through the feathery robinia leaves. The sounds of children playing in the next backyard floated in to us.

'We'd planned to be eccentric old women together, dye our hair red, wear purple and stick a stuffed parrot each on our shoulders. I'll never do it now.

'But, you know, there's something left of her. You got the best of Charm. She gave you the best in her. Somehow the whole thing has now turned full circle. I've got something I want to show you. It's been put away in a drawer. I couldn't bear to look at it. Wait, I'll get it.'

She came back with a little pencil sketch. 'Bill did this of her at a lunch in the last bad year, and I've never been able to put it up on the wall. But now I'm going to get that drawing framed. Somehow, you turning up has made it all right. A circle has been closed.'

A few days later, as we were leaving Sydney, Doug and I called back to collect the photographs I had left with Toni. We rang the doorbell and a frenzy of barking and thundering paws came closer and closer up the hallway. The door opened and the familiar dog-eruption exploded all around us.

'Down Sam! Down Etsi! Wretched animals! It's like a zoo around here. Etsi's my own dog, but Sam's a stray. I couldn't turn him away.'

I had the feeling that not many strays were turned away from Toni's door.

As we walked through the lounge room I noticed something on the wall.

'Is that...?'

'Yes, it's a Rembrandt etching. Charm sent it to me from London. She bought two of them. "So we can both have a Rembrandt in our kitchens," she wrote.'

The baby chrysanthemums I had put into Charmian's white jug on Wednesday were still shining modestly in their corner next to the vivid blue of the glass collection. The green-gold of the feathery robinia overhanging the tiny wooden balcony cast its hues, dappled and cool, over the room.

We were only going to stay for a minute, perhaps for a cup of coffee, but once we were sitting down Toni started to fascinate Doug with the story. She is a natural actress and her expressive face and voice brought all the characters to life. I watched Doug, his face so alive and interested, his long legs stretched out under the table, one arm draped along the back of the cane lounge, one hand restraining an importunate dog. I felt proud to have this large, kind husband to show to my mother's dearest friend. It was as if I were bringing her the gift I would have liked to have brought Charmian: the gift of my own good life, changed but undamaged (as far as I can tell) by her relinquishment.

'You know, my darling,' Toni said to me when Doug had taken the dogs out for a moment, 'you have what she really wanted at the end.'

I was taken aback. 'What? A small safe life? I would have thought that was the last thing she would ever have wanted.'

'No, of course not. Never that. She never wanted to be safe. No. Love. You have love. A man you love, who loves you.'

Ah, that.

CHAPTER 24

Somewhere between galaxies and electrons there is an eloquence that begins with tick and ends with tock and that's the sort of time that suits me just fine. In fact I think that's the only sort of time I could possibly cope with.[1]

Meeting my mother's best friend had, for me too, closed some kind of circle. She was what I had been waiting for. I came home on fire. Ready to start writing my story. It was as though talking to her had provided a catharsis for my emotions, in particular the powerful emotion I had experienced reading the letters in *Dear Birthmother*. I felt as though my mother had left a letter for me, and that letter was Toni.

At home in the study, the blank basilisk eye of the computer screen glared at me. It was even more intimidating than a blank white canvas, and quite different to a blank white page. I typed the words *Chapter 1.* Terrifying! The words typed on the keyboard appeared on the screen instantaneously with the unalterable quality of holy writ. *Holy writ!* I did not mean to write that, but there it was, unalterable. Educated in the pen-and-paper age, how was I going to teach myself to regard this screen full of beautifully typed words as a rough draft only, the equivalent of scribbled notes? I typed *Merde alors! Scheisse! Shit! GARBAGE, GARBAGE, GARBAGE!* There! Now I'd have to alter, delete and edit. That was the key. I had to give myself permission to write whatever came into my head, garbage included, and then let the word processor do its job: process words. Heaven knows, what I wanted to say was all there in my head. I'd been thinking about it deeply, obsessively even, for seven months. As for writing it down, what was that aphorism about writing? Writing is merely a matter of getting the right words in the right order.

On the occasions when the computer screen overwhelmed me, I set up my darkroom. The last time I had been in Sydney, Roseanne, Doug and I had sat on cushions on a cool tiled floor, looking through an old briefcase and a cardboard box crammed with Johnston family memories: the portable attic. Crumpled, higgledy-piggledy, photographs, negatives, slides in broken glass mounts, drawings. Rescued from total disintegration by Roseanne when they were in Martin's possession, they had been passed on to Jason. Now they were here, under my hands. Out they came: Jason as a baby, a festival in Greece, caïques, Charmian in the sixties with a beautiful vintage Rolls Royce, Charmian on Hydra, Shane and Martin, Charmian again. Groups around tables on the terrace or on the waterfront. A colour print of George at the well surrounded by a gaggle of *gorgonas* (old Greek women), on the back in his handwriting a reminder to Charmian of what it was like when she had a man around the house (a bitter reference to his impotence, perhaps?). A single sheet of typescript from *Clean Straw For Nothing*. A sketch, presumably by George, of an eight or nine-year-old Shane and her little Greek girlfriend, blonde against dark, pencil lines confident in the girls' faces, hesitant about their arms—the sketch of a man of unpractised ability.

The negatives were in terrible condition. Most were scratched and torn, cut into singles and thrown into the box anyhow, some in little paper envelopes, some in strips, twisted and coiled around each other. I offered to take them home, clean them up as best I could, flatten them out, print them up while they were still printable, put them in files.

What a massive task! But how fascinating! The little transparent envelopes contained some stunning images: a shepherd playing a primitive bagpipe made of a rough sheepskin; a sponge caïque with its bounty threaded on the rigging; the haunted, powerful Poseidon face of a crippled sponge diver wheeling himself in his homemade billycart, an out of focus caïque, in which he would never again sail, behind him; a pilgrimage or festival with hundreds of people thronging up the mountainside; ancient battlements looking out over islands springing up out of the Aegean.

Who took these? A whole series of delightful pastoral simplicity. Under a dapple of vine leaves a very fair naked baby stares at, then reaches out to, a little tortoise. A beautiful Greek girl watches with the slight triangular smile one sees on archaic korai (maiden) figures. Jason and Zoë. One can imagine her running form on the side of an amphora, draperies trailing, chased by a satyr, stylised grape vines over their heads.

This young girl's expression as she guides the baby's hand to the tortoise's rounded shell is remote and mysterious. The pure curve of Jason's baby-boy back repeats the shape of the little animal's shell. At any moment he and his tortoise could metamorphise into the base supporting a Hellenistic sculpture of Apollo.

Series after series of Charmian. One series: in full skirt and white blouse, hair loose and short-fringed, posing on a sofa covered by a beautiful woven rug. On a deep ledge is the shipwright's model of an Aegean caïque which now adorns Roseanne's balcony, and an ancient barnacle-encrusted amphora. Another series: unposed, unflattering, forehead creased, her arms raised to knot up her hair. Yet another: Charmian on a rock platform above their bathing spot, with a smiling young man in shorts and loose jersey. She is in shorts, posing happily, playing the fool for the camera. *Will this do?* she seems to be saying as she spreads her arms wide. *Or this?* weight on one bare leg, the other resting on pointed toes. Her smile is wide and delighted.

Who is her companion? Who took the photos? More mysteries.

Charmian in dark denim shirt, striped fisherman's pants and floppy hat, posing in front of a windmill, walking down a cobbled street. Charmian in dark pants, striped shirt and fringed straw hat, posing on the waterfront, beside a large anchor and in an old dinghy. These look like one of the series Charlie Sriber took. A few unposed shots around a waterfront table with George in hideous moustache and straggling beard holding court, Charmian quietly playing with baby Jason on her knee.

Never, apart from media stars, has a woman been more photographed, yet I couldn't get enough. I devoured them all and looked for more. Each little silver ghost represented one two-hundred-and-fiftieth of a second of my mother's life. That tiny fraction of time lives on. I could share it with her.

How strange time is. How relative. Toni had commented on it when my visit plunged her back into her own life as a twenty-one-year-old girl and a forty-year-old woman. Time speeds up, slows down, expands, contracts and folds back on itself in the most extraordinary way. Three months before her death, Charmian had written about time in what, to my mind, is one of her best essays, 'On Tick and Tock':

> *How can we use 'now' to throw a beam onto the future, or to illuminate the past? If our consciousness is only a torchlight moving along a back alley, what is the use of it? Did we invent time to explain change and succession, the irreversibility of events, the ageing process, the 'moving finger writes and, having writ, moves on' bit, or does it really exist . . . as another dimension . . .?*[2]

For me, past time was looping both forwards and backwards as present time began to race. A wealth of data from the distant past was only just reaching me, like the light from distant stars, at the same time as I was writing about things that had happened only seven months ago. But the things that had happened seven months ago concerned other events from sixty years, forty-eight years, twenty-three years before that. Taking advantage of my temporal difficulties, present time—the tick and tock sort—took the bit between its teeth and stretched out at full gallop, dragging me with it. I would sit down in front of the computer screen as Doug left for work in the morning, and after what seemed to me like only two or three hours, I would hear the sound of his music, then his motorbike, coming back up the drive. The day would be over.

The world was turning too, and the days of late summer,

humid and stickily hot, were relieved by the occasional crisp breath of the cooler autumn days to come.

The magnetic trace of a voice from twenty-seven years back in time reached me. The National Library had sent me the tape of Hazel de Berg's interview with Charmian Clift: thirty minutes of her voice, sometimes hesitant, always melodious. I already had the transcription in David Foster's *Self-Portraits* to follow. The hairs rose on the back of my neck as I listened. She was talking about her teenage years:

> *I came to Sydney on the search for glamour. This is a country girl's search. I think country girls always dream of the big bad city and glamour in that sense. So I did a little bit of modelling around the place. I got a job as a theatre usherette at the Minerva Theatre, which was then a straight theatre, and I hung around backstage, and all that was marvellously exciting too. Then because of a series of things, I went back home for a while, and then . . .*[3]

Written down, the words have meaning. Listened to, the intonation and the spaces between the words have added meaning. The last sentence sounded like this:

> *Um . . . then because of a series of things* (two seconds pause) *I went* (pause) *back home* (voice trails off on an upward note, then pause) *for a while* (brief pause) *and then . . .* (continues in confident rhythm).

Of course, her pregnancy and my birth were the series of things that had culminated in her going back home, womb and hands empty. What was she seeing in her mind as she paused? I could well imagine her face setting in that staring-into-space, tears-close-behind-the-eyes look, represented so well in Hal Missingham's much-reproduced photograph. The very photograph I was looking at in Foster's book.

How incredible that I should be able to listen to my mother's voice, her hesitancies even, and be able to read meaning into her pauses.

Down in the study, in tick tock time, Chapter 1 grew into Chapter 2, and I gave them to a friend who has spent years in the publishing trade.

'You'll do,' she said.

A playwright with a grant from the Playbox Theatre in Melbourne rang me. She was doing research into Charmian Clift for a play she was writing. Could she come down and speak to me?

I had premonitions about future time.

I took a bundle of the photographs I had printed from the Johnston negatives, and re-read *Mermaid Singing* and *Peel Me a Lotus*, pencil in hand. Here were images from Kalymnos and Hydra. The words she had written added meaning to the images: the images added meaning to the words. Here, on Kalymnos: the sponge diver's haunt, Skeftarios' taverna, with the divers themselves around their table, plates oily with fish, copper beakers and tumblers full of retsina, and cigarette packets on the black-checked tablecloth. Here are Captain Miches; Mikailis ('with the pure, austere beauty of a face on an old coin'[4]); other divers of the Olympian breed; the mayor and the cousin of Golden Anna, their voices raised in song. Through the kitchen window is the aproned back of Golden Anna working over the primus stove. Behind the divers is 'a Pan-faced shepherd from the mountains who often plays the *tsabuna* (a primitive Greek form of the bagpipes)'.[5] In fact here is the scene, here are the people, exactly as it was in 1955. Exactly as she described it:

> *The* tsabuna *squeals, the brown fingers of Pan flicker across the horn of olive root. All the sea boots beneath the tables are thumping out the rhythm against the wooden floor.*[6]

Time came snaking from the past into the present.

To tease the past from its lair again, I took the same photographs, together with those from Charlie Sriber, with me to Cedric and Wendy Flower's place. He seized on a series of three that showed a crowd climbing up a rocky mountainside to its summit, where some kind of icon surmounted by a Greek flag was surrounded by masses of people in their best clothes.

'I remember that,' he said, as we sat at the sun-drenched table facing the purpling escarpment. 'I can't quite remember what the festival was. Something to do with earthquakes, I think. But I do remember that Charm was wildly enthusiastic about it. She made us all climb the wretched mountain. We spent all night crouched among the sage bushes and the rocks, with nowhere to pee. Wait a moment, I did a sketch of that icon. I'll show you.'

He returned with a series of sketchbooks, opened one and showed me a charming little watercolour sketch of the flag, the bell and the icon. The icon had a big pot of basil underneath it.

'Of course, Basil was the patron saint of Greece,' he told me.

'Are those almond blossoms in the photograph?' I asked.

'Hardly likely,' he replied bitterly. 'Nothing flowered on Kalymnos.'

I showed him a photograph of Charmian in her kitchen. Which kitchen, Kalymnos or Hydra, I did not know. Cedric was not sure either.

'That dreadful kitchen!' he said, remembering the Kalymnian one.

'Oh, I think it's quite beautiful. Why do you say that?'

'Well, Pat and I were guests, and of course we liked to make ourselves useful. George and Charm would hurry off to their typewriters after a meal and we would be left with the washing-up. Plates cold and slippery with olive oil in a dreadful sink. Marble.' He turned to Wendy. 'You know how marble goes? Covered in algae. And only some green

Greek soap to wash up with. Oh look. There are the hurricane lamps. When we were there, there was limited electricity. On a Tuesday, for instance, the other side of the island had electricity. They needed those hurricane lamps.'

He was equally unimpressed by a shot of boys jumping from the rigging of a boat.

'Those horrible boys! We watched one throw a kitten into the harbour and pelt it with rocks.'

The impression I had gained from previous occasions, that Cedric did not share Charmian's romantic vision of the raw primitivism of Kalymnos, was reinforced.

'There was one hotel on the waterfront. The *Oxi* hotel. It means "No" in Greek, from the answer Metaxas gave the Italians in the war, when they wished to overrun Greece. It was the No Hotel all right. Anything you wanted, the answer was "No".'

Despite his avowed feelings about the island, his sketches and watercolours showed another response entirely. He had the original line drawings that were used to illustrate *Mermaid Singing*, lyrical in their simplicity. In the sketchbooks were charming watercolours of the houses clustered around their harbour, and a delightful painting of the coifed heads of two large-eyed Greek women sailing, disembodied, on the surface of that harbour. Charmian had described how they swam in full-length shifts, their head-coverings still in place. And here they were, transmuted through Cedric's eye. There were also little donkeys lugging burdens: goats in panniers bleating all the way to the slaughterhouse. There were paintings of a small Greek boy carrying a string of fishes and a girl carrying an icon; paintings of deserted Byzantine churches crammed with religious images. There was a drawing that spoke directly to me. On one page of a sketchbook were all the activities of the waterfront: women carrying water jars, priests patting the heads of toddlers, caiques being unloaded. At the bottom of the drawing were the heads of two small blond children: Martin and Shane. It was beautiful.

Cedric couldn't fool me. The fruit of his eye contradicted the words of his mouth.

Back at the computer I attempted to make my words say exactly what I wished them to say. The chapters marched or crawled across the screen, sometimes with rhythm, sometimes haltingly.

Present time was turning its cyclical wheel. A dearly loved uncle of Doug's died, aged eighty-four. We had thought he would live forever. Somehow he had never seemed an old man and his death was a shock. His whole family, wife, sister, brother-in-law, children, nephews, niece, their wives and husband and all their children, including one unborn great-grandchild curled in its dark, warm place—four generations of family—wept unashamedly at the funeral. Yes, the great slow wheel of life was turning. My generation was moving inexorably to its leading edge.

There were phone calls back and forth between Toni Burgess and me. During one I could hardly hear her for the barking of dogs in the background. She had been looking out over her garden and talking to Charm's memory.

'Charm, my girl, you've done something good,' she said. 'You didn't get the good thing, but you've given it to me.

'When are you coming to Sydney again, darling?'

The good thing, the darling—me—felt warm to the very centre of her being.

So back I went to Sydney to see Toni again. As I rang the doorbell, I was greeted with the usual cacophonous barking interspersed with muffled cries of 'Down Sam! Down Etsi! Now stop it!' Out they hurtled—one young part German shepherd, one middle-aged red kelpie and, bringing up the rear, slowly and painfully, one very old golden labrador.

'It's my daughter's. She's in Greece and I'm looking after all her things. Come in, darling. Don't mind me. I've always said I intended to be an eccentric old lady one day.'

'What do you mean *one day*,' I said.

As I jostled with the stream of animals down the narrow hall I was instantly aware of a new picture on Toni's wall. It was the little sketch her husband had made of Charmian. It had been beautifully mounted and framed. The circle had been closed. Toni had done exactly what she said she would do.

'Yes, I could finally bear to do it. I loved them both, you see. Bill who drew it, and Charm who was it. After she had come back to Sydney, the film of D. H. Lawrence's *Women in Love* was being shown. After it someone made the suggestion that she and I were having it off with each other. Charm laughed her head off at that. "I love you better than a sister," she said, "but I certainly don't fancy you. Give me a man to go to bed with any time."

'Bill used to get furious sometimes at the amount of time I spent with her. Sometimes, when George was in hospital and she was drinking heavily, I used to arrive at breakfast-time to drink beer with her so she wouldn't drink whisky. "Why don't you fucking marry her!" Bill would rage. But, of course she was my dear friend.'

We were sitting in the cane chairs, with the doors open to the sun-dapple. Her mug of coffee was getting cold, her cigarette burning back to the filter as she talked.

I asked another of the important questions. I already

knew the answer—I'd certainly been told, but I didn't want to believe it.

'Toni, is it true about her drinking?'

'Yes, it's true.'

'So how did it start—the heavy drinking?'

She sipped her coffee, drew on the cigarette. I could sense her marshalling her thoughts. She began slowly as usual, eyebrows on the way up.

'Strangely enough, when we were young she hardly drank at all. We got tiddly on home brew once, thinking it was something like ginger beer.'

'So it all started in Greece?'

'Yes, as I told you, she wanted to go to Greece to get back to the grass roots of civilisation, and of themselves . . . It was all right for a while, but then the fights and the drinking started.'

'Was it an inescapable part of the life there?'

'Oh, yes. I've been there, done that, too. It's lovely sitting in the heavenly sunshine at a taverna table on the waterfront, drinking wine and talking. If you're feeling miserable, you know, the wine makes you feel all right again. But when you're trapped there, year after year . . . a lot of the time they didn't have enough money even to get to Athens. When she came back I asked her, "How could you bear to leave the island, Charm, and that beautiful house? It must have been paradise."

' "Yes," she said to me, "it was paradise, but it was a prison in paradise." '

'So was the booze an escape?'

'Partially. Your mother was very good at escapes. She escaped into arms, into beds, into bottles. But I largely blame George. Charmian had a great generosity of spirit and a deep-rooted honesty. Her honesty and reality made him insecure. He didn't have it himself, and it made him feel less than he wanted to feel. *Her* sins were large sins. Human sins. *His* were mean and petty. He constantly undermined her.'

'But, surely, he was always so loyal. I'm always hearing and reading about the loyalty they had for each other.'

'That was in public. Privately he was forever needling her, slicing her up with his tongue, killing her with small bites. She had lost her beauty. It was gone. No man would ever love her now. Once the two of them were at our place at Cremorne Point. They'd both had too much to drink. Charm was leaning back against the mantelpiece.

' "Look at her!" George said. "Standing there like some fucking great praying mantis."

'Intimating, you know, that she'd gobbled her mate. After attacks like this, she would break down and weep and then reach for the bottle again.'

Toni looked thoughtful. 'I shouldn't blame George. I used to feel very bitter—savage—towards him. But with the passage of time I see it differently. It was her fault too. After all, we are our own executioners. We make our own choices. She could have left him. But she didn't. She chose to stay.'

I thought of Martin's words on tape, ghosts from the past that they were. He had considered that, right to the end, his parents had found each other tremendously stimulating. Frequently exasperating and maddening as well, but that they had needed each other above all else. It had been a difficult marriage, but one that neither of them could do without.[7] Martin had been in his twenty-second year when his mother died. Toni had been three years younger than her friend. How very differently the young son and the middle-aged friend saw this woman, Charmian Clift.

I turned my attention back to Toni. She was saying: 'When Charm first came back in 1964, she was furious with me because I'd done nothing more with my talents than use them to write advertising copy. She lashed out at Bill, because she considered he'd let me bury my talents. But later in private, she said to me, "Antonia, you sacrificed ambition for love. I sacrificed love for ambition."'

CHAPTER 25

There is a sort of dreamlike quality in returning to a place where one was young. Memory is as tricky as a flawed window glass that distorts the view beyond according to the way one turns one's head.[1]

Typically, Sue started to vomit the night before she had to leave.

Marjorie, wrapped in her chenille dressing gown, listened to the retching behind the bathroom door with anxiously clenched fists.

'Is there anything I can do, darling?'

There was nothing she could do. Harold also got out of bed and offered to make them all a cup of tea, but it was useless Sue trying to drink anything. The tiniest sip of water came straight back up again.

'Thanks, Dad,' she gasped. 'I'll be all right. Go back to bed. Really, I'll be all right.'

All the bags were packed. The sewing had all been done:

new summer dresses, two pairs of shortie pyjamas, a checked cotton brunch coat. New underclothes had been purchased. The portable sewing machine, her parents' twenty-first birthday present to her, was there in the hallway next to the suitcases. They were driving her out to the country, where she was going to be a teacher. She had actually applied for this western country town, when most of the final year students would have done anything, anything, to be posted to a city school. But she knew that if she didn't force herself out of the nest now, she might never fly.

It was January, 1964. Tomorrow she was leaving home.

George Johnston was coming home. *My Brother Jack* had been a great success in England, and now it was about to take the Australian literary world by storm. He was coming home to a feeding frenzy of publicity.[2] George had become that hero most beloved of the media: the local boy made good. He was ill, emaciated, and emotionally battered, but his self-analytical novel, a work of integrity, set as it was in a real Australia, had turned the tide. At last he was riding high.

Charmian Clift was staying behind. During the past years she had written letters to her friend Toni; occasionally about the dark side of her life in Greece. She had been anxious to know about the prospects of work for her if she were to come back to Australia without George. Toni's letters back had been guarded because she knew that George read them. As fate would have it, it was George who left.

Up until now it seemed that while they could not live with each other, neither could they live without each other. Emotionally they had torn each other apart over the last few years. And physically, too, if the gossip was to be believed.

During one quarrel, she had cut his face with a broken glass; during another, he had gone berserk in a drunken rage and spent the night in the Hydra prison cell.[3] The Hydra experience had become a destructive thing for the Johnstons. It had turned into something like the hydra of the Greek legends, a many-headed serpent which could only be killed by amputation and cauterisation.

Despite the bitterness and resentment that had developed between them, Charmian had still exhibited all her deep-seated loyalty in supporting George during his illness-racked writing of *My Brother Jack*. She had made herself available to read and talk about the manuscript as it was wrenched from his typewriter. Her critical contributions had helped him reshape his youth and early life. And this despite the fact that she had her own novel, *Honour's Mimic*, on the boil. Five years later she wrote about this part of her relationship with George:

> *He needs a constant presence, an ear, a sounding-board, an audience . . . I sat on the step by his desk every day for seven months so that I would be there when I was wanted for discussion or suggestion or maybe only to listen.*[4]

George was leaving. Alone. Charmian and the children were to stay on Hydra while George made his triumph and his reconnaissance of the new Australia.

They would follow later. Perhaps.

Martin and Shane had totally opposing views. Shane, now fifteen, did not want to leave what she felt was *her* country. She had been only five when she first came to Greece and it suited her wild spirit, so like one aspect of her mother as a girl. Her friends were all there: the girlfriends who, in the sanctity of her room, giggled while they tried on each others' clothes and the make-up that was frowned on by the Orthodox priest. More importantly, she was in love and had promised to marry, but had to wait while her Greek boyfriend finished his military training.[5] She didn't want to go. Sixteen-year-old Martin's intellectual curiosity made him want to see the land where he had been born, and about which he had heard so much. Jason, nearly eight, had been born and baptised a Hydriot.

Charmian did not want to leave Greece.[6] Quite simply it had become her home. She resonated to the warmth, simplicity and honesty of the people; to the sun, the open blue skies and the ever-present sea, so reminiscent of her childhood. At the same time she was tied to George Johnston by many chains. Fetters of loyalty, similar ideas and values, a parallel work, a life shared so closely that for the last nine years they had spent most of each day together, remembered love, three children, and her own guilt. Woman's guilt. She had abandoned a baby. She had loved her other children, but had given her writing, not their needs, the major share of her attention. She had caused George's illness. He had convinced her of it. She could not leave him.

For herself she was apprehensive. George had an assured future in Australia. But what would be waiting for Charmian Clift?

She saw him off at the airport in Athens in the last week of February. Qantas Airways flew George out of a Greek winter into the height of an Australian summer.

The temperature was over a hundred degrees Fahrenheit. A red dust cloud threatened the town. From the window of the women's staffroom, Sue could see it rolling over the distant bleached hills, blotting out the paddocks, the poplars and willows of the park, the steeply sloping street that came up from the town.

'Quick. Help me shut the windows,' one of the more experienced teachers yelled to her over the increasing roar of the wind. 'It'll be a bugger when it hits.'

Perspiration running down between her breasts, soaking the elastic waistband of her half-slip, teeth gritty with dust, Sue bent her head to the class lists. She only had another five minutes before the bell would send her back to the iron-roofed portable classroom in the hollow of the playground where the furnace of air swirled like a living thing. She had to get these lists made. And it would take her a good four minutes to hobble down there. She looked down at her right leg, encased below the knee in clean white plaster.

Only last week the young maths teacher, the extremely tall thin one with the brown eyes and the funny crew cut dark hair, had asked her out for a swim after school. The opaquely brown, swiftly flowing Murrumbidgee was the only place to go, apart from the chlorinated, urinated, town pool.

How she hated being away from the sea! She had never imagined it could feel like this, the land pressing in on her from all sides. No edge to it. No distant background rhythm to life.

At least the river was tree-shaded, and the water cool in the relentless heat that never let up, not even at night.

The first night she had been here, in the hotel with her parents, the atmosphere had been stifling. After dinner she had pushed open the gold-engraved glass doors to walk out onto the street. To get a breath of cool night air. A blast straight from the fierce desert heartland had sent her, edge-of-the-land, edge-of-the-sea creature that she was, scurrying back into the hotel.

Never could she get used to it, the heat, the dust, the encircling land, hundreds and hundreds of miles of ancient, worn-down, bleached-bone white summer land pressing in on her from all directions, separating her from the sea.

But he had asked her out to the river bank for a swim. Her. *The new girl with the proud breasts.* That was how he had thought of her as she walked into the staff meeting on the very first day of school.

They had taken a picnic tea, and a blanket and a transistor radio in his old bomb of a car. Diving in from the high grassy bank, they had struck out across the current to the other side. He showed her how to aim for a spit of land further downstream than she would have chosen. Then they walked a surprisingly long way upstream and swam again for their picnic spot. He was a strong swimmer and positioned himself downstream of her, just in case the current was too strong. It was a bit like swimming in the surf, across the rip, not against it. Swimming with her own personal lifesaver.

They had climbed out and eaten their picnic, deliberately not drying themselves to keep the lovely cool feeling. The tall young maths teacher had put his arm behind her and she had leant into him. He was nice. Funny and nice. Other girls who had been in this town for a year or two had warned her off him. 'He's strange,' they said. 'He drinks too much,' they said. 'He always looks scruffy. He doesn't clean his teeth. I wouldn't go out with him.' But Sue liked him.

'Let's dance, Suzie.' He switched on the radio and it was playing good music. 'Can you rock'n'roll?'

'Can I rock'n'roll? I practically invented it.'

So in the hot river bank evening, they danced. They danced like crazy people, like people possessed. This was something from home. This was something she knew. Rock'n'rolling back and forth, flung over his hip, back and forth, swept between his legs, back and forth, legs wrapped around his waist, back arched and her hair sweeping the ground. He was a wonderful dancer.

'Game to try a shoulder-throw?' he panted.

'Sure. Why not?'

Out-two, in-two, out-two, then his arms lifting her, lifting her always with the beat. And... over.

And... down.

But he did not catch her straight. Their dance floor was too uneven. She hit her head on his knee, and her bare foot thudded into a tree-root.

In the casualty department at the base hospital, they told him that he would have to carry her out to the car. The plaster was not yet dry. Her big toe was broken and she had concussion. She would be in plaster for the next eight to ten weeks.

And as he had carried her, his face so worried and apologetic, Sue had known that she was going to marry Doug.

*

The bell rang, and she gathered up her mark-book and her keys to begin the hobble down to the art room. She was going to be late.

'Sink or swim' was the edict given by hard-shelled old-time teachers to the vulnerable new young ones. And that was just what it amounted to. A first-year-out teacher was thrown into a turbulent sea without a life-jacket. She dived under giant waves again and again. She would just manage to catch her breath when a huge dumper would grind her under. Occasionally, a long, smooth curler would take her on an exhilarating ride. And just when she thought she was swimming in smoother water at last, the dumpers would crash over her head again.

The first two terms seemed to go on forever. Sue felt nauseous every Sunday night, wondering if she could survive another week.

It was in the first years of a big educational shake-up called the Wyndham Scheme. One of its provisions was that a certain number of hours of art would be compulsory up to Fourth Form. The philosophy behind this was excellent: all children had the right to a basic creative education. But the practical results were classes full of resentful adolescent boys, large and loud, who saw no reason why they should be forced to do such sissy things when their older brothers had not. As the perceived enforcer of the new scheme she was the nearest object of attack.

There was little money in the school and the art store-room was practically bare. Butcher's paper had to be scrounged to eke out the supplies sent by the Department of Education. The supplied Brenex tinned paint became mil-dewed in a week and a reek of death arose whenever a lid was prised off. There was no kiln, no clay, no sculpture or printmaking equipment. She purchased materials out of her own money to make lessons more interesting.

This town and this school were a culture shock. Her whole upbringing had been sheltered and middle class. This was the first time she had ever had contact with working-class values. Her selective girls' school had fostered ideas of intellectual elitism and feminism of a sort. It was hard to come to grips with the fact that the majority of the population thought quite differently.

Even her Mosman accent was a drawback. Until now she had not known that she had such a thing. When she said words like 'dance' and 'France' with a long *a*, the students did not understand what she was talking about. Before too long her speech became nasal in self-defence.

She was saved by three things. Firstly, there were two other art teachers, slightly older and slightly more experienced than she was. Secondly she was in love with a certain maths teacher, and he with her. Thirdly there was her own grim determination not to crash. She was flying... just.

The August school holidays came just in time. At three twenty-five on the last afternoon of school, an unbelievable scene occurred, like the start of a Le Mans race. Most of the teachers were young and single and longing to get away, away back to their cities. The cars were off and racing down the main street before the echoes of the bell had died.

Sue and Doug took it in turns to drive the ten-hour trip to Sydney. It was a time of reunions. Sandy was home from her country school. Vanda and Kathy were living and teaching in Sydney. They exchanged atrocity stories and Sue felt better. It was not just her. Everyone was having a hard time.

Doug was quite happy talking to pretty girls and they all liked him. He had always had a good manner with older women too, but did not make much headway with Marjorie.

Greek son, Australian daughter

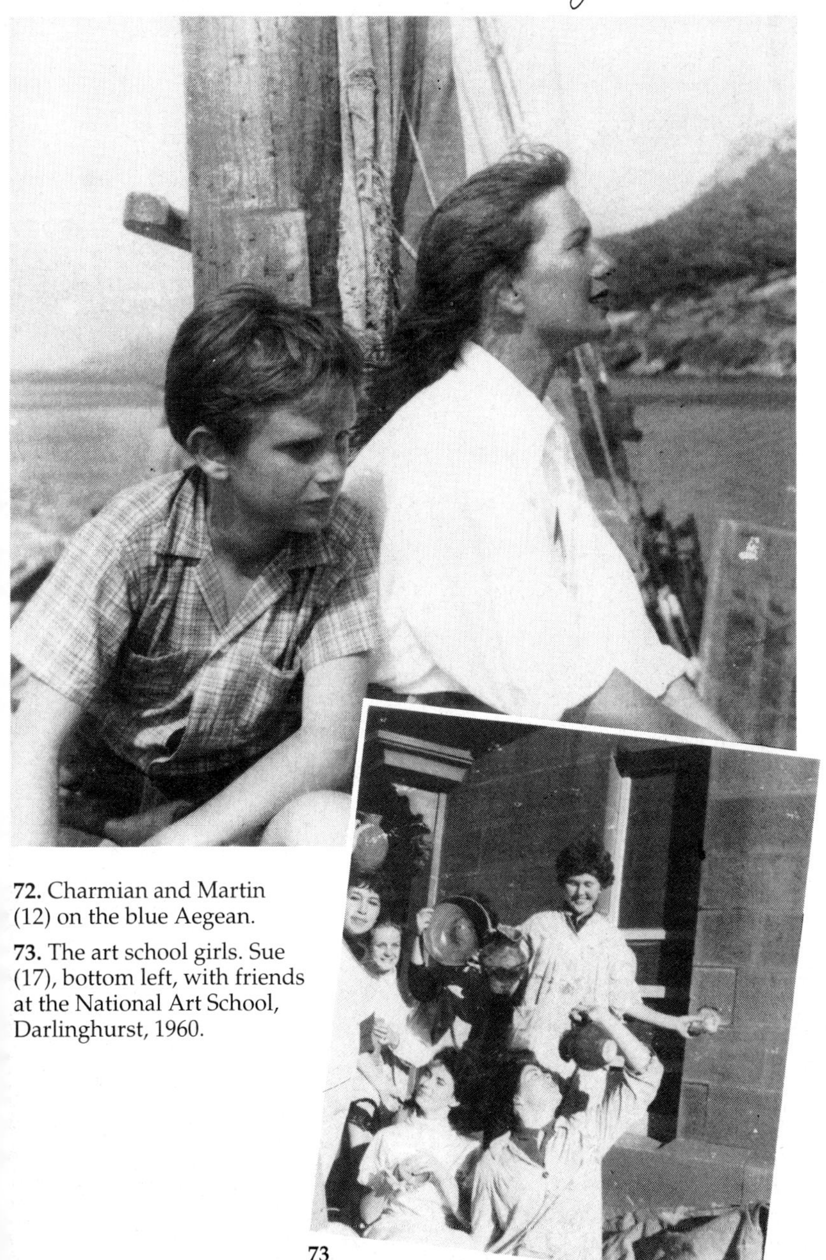

72. Charmian and Martin (12) on the blue Aegean.

73. The art school girls. Sue (17), bottom left, with friends at the National Art School, Darlinghurst, 1960.

Hydra and Sydney
1962, 1963

74

76

74. Shane (13) with friends dressed up for a national festivity, Hydra.

75. Sue with Kathy, Vanda and Sandy, dressed up for a twenty-first birthday, Sydney, 1963.

76. The Johnstons posing on the waterfront, Hydra, 1963.

77. Sue (19) posing at an Art Students' Ball. The Trocadero, Sydney, 1962.

78

coming home

79

leaving home

78. Farewell to the Greek Charmian, 1964.

79. Hail to the Australian Charmian, columnist, 1964.

80. Miss Shaw, art teacher. Sue (21) hangs a student's work. 1964.

girl meets boy

81

82

83

84

81, 82. Sue and Doug on the banks of the Murrumbidgee amongst the Paterson's curse.

83. Between them they owned a black-and-tan kelpie pup and a grey-and-white Persian kitten.

84. A fancy-dress affair.

85. The new Mr and Mrs Chick outside St Clement's Church, Raglan Street, Mosman. December 1965.

86. Harold and Marjorie nearly burst with pride.

for better or worse

mini skirts, legs ar
body language

87

88

87. Charmian and Shane on the back deck of the Raglan Street house. Late 1960s.

88. Sue and Doug at his graduation. University of New England, 1968.

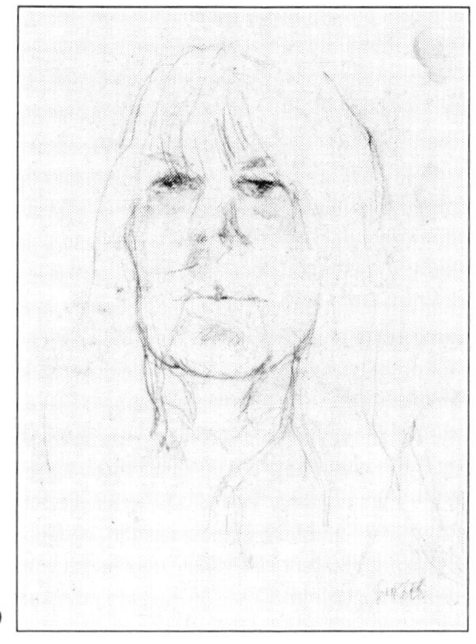

her last year

89. Charmian in her last months. Quick sketch by Bill Burgess, 1969.

90. The Johnston family, 1969.

for Sue, it was one baby, two babies

95

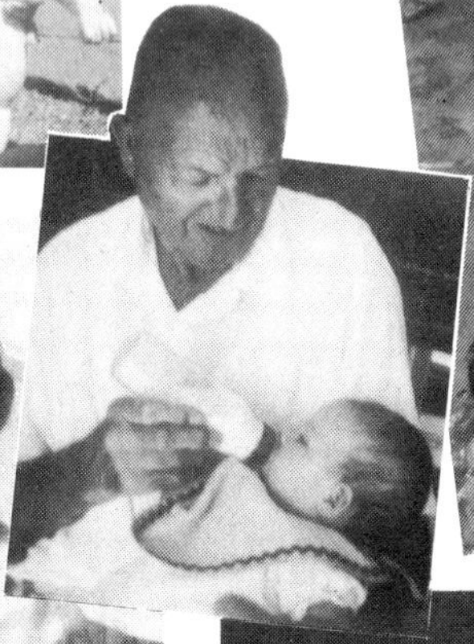

91

92

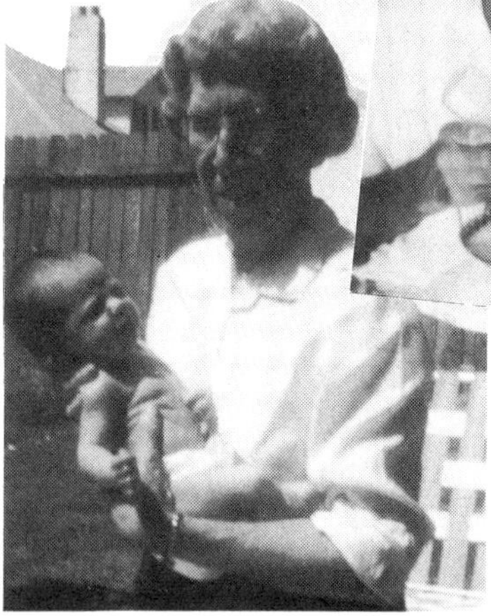

93

94

96

91-100. Daughters Gina, Danielle and Kristin. Born 1969, 1970, 1972.

three

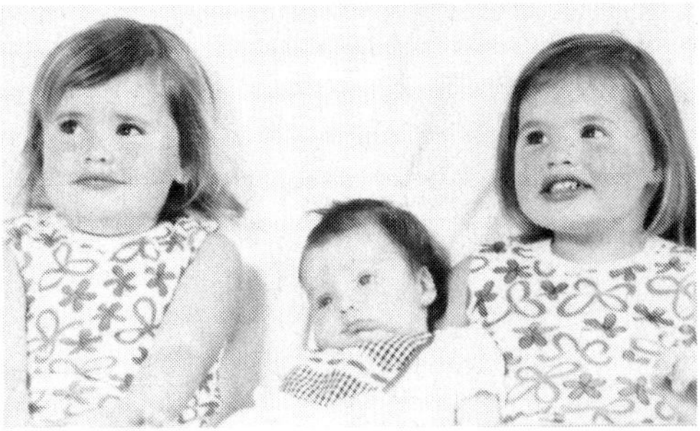

97

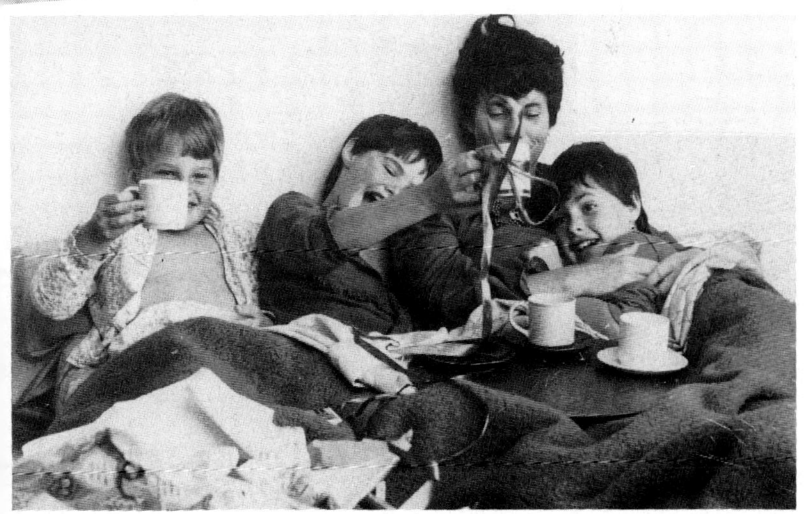

she bought a guitar and taught herself to play

101

101. Sue, the entertainer (of small children), 1973.

102, 103. Producer and musical director of school rock opera, with students and colleagues, 1974.

104. The all-singing, all-dancing Sue with fellow performer Stuart Hearne, 1974.

103

102

The
TROUBADO
OLD TIME

old family

105

105. Harold and Marjorie at the gate of the house they had lived in for over forty years, 1984.

106. Cousin Diana Bradshaw, Barré's daughter. Fresh flowers on the grave of grandfather Syd Clift, 1992.

107. Sister-in-law Roseanne Bonney with Toni Burgess and Sue, studying the Michelin guide to Greece, 1993.

108a, b. Niece Rebecca O'Connor, Shane's daughter. Love affair with a cheetah.

new family

106

7

108a

108b

to the future

109. Doug and Sue with her fiftieth birthday present: a season at the opera. 1992.

110, 111. Charmian Clift's grand-daughters Kristin, Gina and Danielle, 1993.

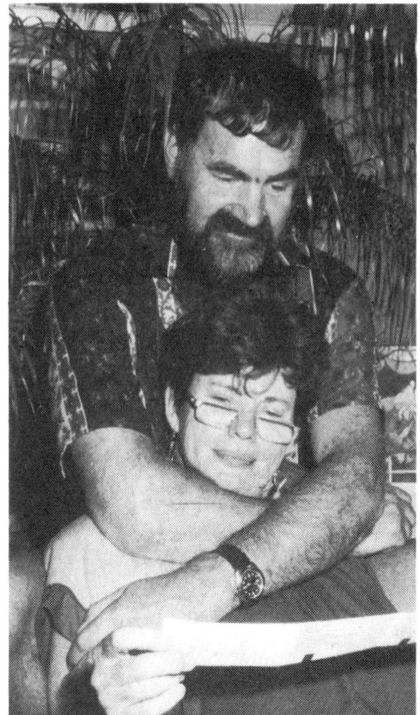

109

110

111

She objected to his large, dirty bare feet, his tight black jeans with the seams split at the narrow bottoms to get his feet through, his coat with the buttons held on by copper wire, his occasional lack of a shirt at the meal table and the way he held his cup with his hand wrapped around it instead of holding it by the handle.

'But Mum, be fair!' Sue defended him, 'Look at the size of his fingers. He can't *fit* them through the handle.' It was true.

She took him to an evening service at St Clement's Church in Raglan Street. She took him to Balmoral Beach. She took him to the zoo. She showed him off at parties. She took him one fresh day by ferry to Circular Quay. They were going to walk up Macquarie Street and across the Domain to the Art Gallery. As the ferry, the *Lady Denman*, passed Bennelong Point with its embryo Opera House, skeletal shell arches thrusting up to the sky, they happened to glance across to the overseas terminal. A large white passenger ship flying a blue and white flag was moored there. The wharf was empty. A few small figures were moving around the upper deck of the ship with the Greek name. Sue and Doug exchanged a few desultory words about immigrants in general and were beginning to wonder about the motivations and destinations of these departed immigrants in particular, when the clanging of bells and the change of note in the engines indicated that the ferry was slowing down. They forgot the Greek migrants, stood up, wrapped their coats around them more firmly in the crisp August air and prepared to walk down the gangplank to Number Four Wharf.

*

At the tail-end of August, on a wild night, 'with the lights of Sydney Harbour blazing away like a festival of coloured candles',[7] a Greek migrant ship, the *Ellenis*, docked in Sydney. The ship was packed with more than a thousand people:

> *families of English migrants, Greek proxy brides, be-shawled and bemused grandmothers shrouded in shapeless black and already wailing ritually, and young Greek labourers with the sturdiness and aggressiveness of Cretan bulls.*[8]

Among the polyglot and excited crowd waiting in the rain on the wharf were a middle-aged man in his good suit and a fourteen-year-old girl wearing her best red dress and a new pair of shoes. Charmian's brother, Barré, and his daughter Diana had driven up from Wollongong through dark and fog and driving rain. They waited and waited. The flood of people streaming off the ship dried to a trickle, but no Charmian appeared. Diana begged her father to go and ask after her, but he shook his head, turned away sadly, climbed back into his old car and began the long drive home.

In Charmian's cabin, meanwhile, a party was raging.

> *It was a queer feeling to be part of a nomadic horde—more than a thousand souls . . .*
>
> *In a special sense it seemed actually miraculous to arrive. 'I can't believe we're here,' was a literal statement. Australia did in fact exist, and we were one family under one roof again. Our windows, as ever, looked out on the water. Only the water was not the blue of the Aegean, but the blue of the Pacific . . . It is, after all, so terribly* big. *More than all the weeks of travelling this view of the Pacific makes me realise how far away Australia is from the world we have left.*[9]

She wrote this not long after her arrival, when she and the children were first back with George, the Johnston family together again in a big old rented house with views through the heads. It was in the only straight stretch of a typically hilly, twisty Mosman street, not far from Balmoral Beach.

There had been a welcome-home party in this house. George had gathered a crowd of old friends. Some, like the Nolans and Cedric and Pat Flower, had visited her on Kalymnos or Hydra. Some, like Toni Burgess, had not seen her since she left thirteen years before.

When Charmian first opened the door to her friend Toni, her appearance was a terrible shock. She had changed. Her once confident demeanour had gone. Frightened green eyes looked defensively out of a ravaged, sun-damaged, drink-damaged face. Her once strong white teeth were discoloured and decayed. Her hair was dry and thin. Across the bridge of her once-straight nose was a scar, a break-line.

The beautiful young woman of style and flair, who had left Sydney in triumph, had returned middle-aged and apprehensive. She was close to her forty-first birthday, but it was more than this—she had been wrenched from an environment where she felt assured. On top of the inexorable processes of ageing (for her friends had undoubtedly aged too), the physical difficulties and dilemmas of the spirit during the last years of life on Hydra had left their mark. After all she had lived a life not so very different in some aspects from the lives of the peasants: day by day under a harsh sun, without medical or dental facilities, often without money for more than necessities, without the softnesses of Australian urban life. With too many cigarettes and too many tavernas. For years now she and George had been like a country living through an unwinnable civil war, torn and battered, yet one country still.

'Antonia! My God!' Charmian said. 'You've still got your beautiful yellow hair.'

Toni did not know what to say. She just hugged and hugged her.

Later that evening, Charmian led her friend into the bedroom. She sat her down in a chair facing the mirror, and leant her chin on the top of Toni's blonde head. She gazed at their two reflections for long moments, then without saying a word, covered her face with her hands.

'You haven't changed at all.' The words finally came from behind the hands.

'Come off it, Sis,' Toni replied. 'We've both changed.'

One thing that was unchanged was her lovely low, slow voice.

'We can't really talk now,' she said to her friend. 'Come around and have breakfast with me tomorrow after everyone's gone.'

Breakfast was another shock. In her insecurity, Charm's breakfast was whisky. To make her comfortable, Toni had a beer. George and the children were out, and the two friends had a chance to talk. They were in the kitchen. Charm turned on the taps and let the water run.

'You know, Antonia, people talk about what they would take to a desert island. Shakespeare . . . the great writers . . . I know what I'd take. I'd take hot water. Look at it. Just running out of the taps. I can't believe it!'

After what she called the 'donkey-amble' of Hydra, she had to adjust to 'the screaming blast of city pace'.[10] The house with its sea view and surrounding bushland must have seemed like an oasis at times.

As a first priority, the children had to be enrolled in schools. The two elder children were accepted by North Sydney Boys' and North Sydney Girls' high schools. The gymnasium or high school on Hydra had given them a solid, no-frills classical education and Martin, in particular, had kept up his English reading.

As they set off for their first day at an Australian school, Martin in college grey with maroon and gold school colours, Shane in bottle green and navy, they too had great adjustments to make. Added to their understandable apprehensions were memories of the Secondary Modern School they had attended briefly and very unhappily in Winchcombe, England, three years before. As they caught the School Special bus in Military Road, they must have wondered how they were going to adapt.

Charmian was soon caught up in the city pace. Like George, she too was feted by the media. *Honour's Mimic* had come out in July to good reviews, and there were two overseas enquiries for film rights. The editor of the *Sydney Morning Herald*, J. D. Pringle, offered her the chance to write a weekly column for the women's pages. The subject matter could be her own choice. She also took over the scripting of the television adaptation of *My Brother Jack* when George (busy on other projects) was not interested in doing this himself. She turned out to be a natural writer for this medium, which was totally new to her. The spectre of playing second fiddle to George faded. There was work aplenty for both of them, and it looked as if the days of poverty were over.

> *Safety, plenty, prosperity, jobs for all, a television in every lounge room, a car in every garage, steak for breakfast, youth-worship with its attendant permissiveness... What a fabulous, Utopian land it is.*[11]

This is how she first saw the outwardly observable Sydney, so different from the dreary city of post-war austerities that she had left.

A question of even greater concern was whether Australia had yet built for itself a cultural identity. Its absence was one of the factors that had sent so many artists and writers and musicians and film-makers flocking overseas in the years following the war.

> *... what I have been really looking for is evidence of a spiritual change—a burgeoning and a bursting of the image qualities into a real cultural and social flowering, spiky and wild and refreshing and strange and unquestionably rooted in native soil.*[12]

It was not long before Martin and Shane were quarrelling over which programme to watch on television, ringing up their new friends, planning their weekends, practising Twist and Shake to full-volume music and behaving, in superficial ways at least, like Australian teenagers.[13] But at their core, behind the patina laid on them by Australia, was Greece.

On 10 November, Prime Minister Menzies announced the re-introduction of National Service, starting in July 1965. Twenty year olds were to be selected by a birthday lottery for two years' full-time service. Conscripts would be liable to serve anywhere in the world.

'Harold, what do you think about Nashos being re-introduced?' Marjorie sounded worried.

'Do 'em good,' replied her husband. 'Make men of them. A bit of discipline is just what some of these young louts need.'

'But what about David? He seems so settled in the bank. I'd hate his life to be disrupted.'

'Nonsense! It would do him the world of good. But I don't think it's going to apply to him anyway. After all, it was two months ago that he turned twenty. He'll be too old.'

'I don't know about that. He turned twenty in the year leading up to July next year, when it starts. His birthday might come up. It's awful doing it by lottery this way. It's betting with boys' lives.'

When Martin turned seventeen in November, he and Shane gave a party. While the girls in their frills and ruffles and the boys in their tight pants and winklepicker shoes partied uninhibitedly, the adults discussed the conscription issue with some heat. The idea of a lottery was repugnant. It was dishonourable to take two years from a young man's life by a mere chance. Australia had never lacked volunteers to go and fight for good causes. Compulsion, by lottery, seemed degrading.

Martin and his friends made an attempt at cynicism. But for them twenty was a long way off, three years or more, and the odds were in their favour, anyway.[14] In the meantime, there were six or seven more weeks of school to be got through and then there was the prospect of the long Christmas holidays.

It was the Tuesday before Christmas. It was going to be another hot day. Bushfires in the Royal National Park had left the city sky stained with smoke haze. In dressing-gown and slippers, Marjorie padded out to the gate to pick up the morning paper. The kettle was boiling on the stove as she quietly closed the front screen door. In this, the best time of the day, she liked to make herself a quick cup of tea before anyone else woke up. With Sue home for Christmas the house seemed full again. Thank heavens that tall skinny disreputable-looking maths teacher of hers had only stayed a few nights before driving home five hundred miles or so to his own family. She took her tea and the paper to the sunroom, its view capped by a skyline of newly raised home units next to the three cabbage tree palms. The steam from the cup curled upwards and she yearned for a cigarette, but she had given up smoking again and there were none hidden in the house.

After glancing at the headlines, she opened the women's section of the *Sydney Morning Herald*. Usually in the paper on Thursday, it had been published early this week, presumably so the ads could have their maximum effect on shoppers before Christmas Eve. For several weeks now she had been turning to a column by a new woman writer. She enjoyed the writing, which was sometimes controversial and always alive. It felt as though the writer was sitting across the table and chatting. She would not miss it for the world. This week's piece was titled 'Novelist Charmian Clift on Christmas', and underneath, 'We Took Santa Claus to Greece'. As she sipped the first scalding mouthful, she began to read: 'It is really rather strange to be having a hot Christmas again.'[15]

There is a photograph of Sue taken this Christmas. A little square Kodak Instamatic print with rounded corners and a silk finish. In colour. It was taken in the Shaw family's dining room on Christmas Day. By whom is uncertain. Certainly someone who was no photographer.

They are all in it. Two-thirds of the photo is taken up by background. To the right is the white-painted cedar mantelpiece with the chiming clock in the centre, a clock that has marked out in quarter hours the lives of everyone who has lived in this house. It has just finished the three-quarter hour chime. Christmas cards are ranged symmetrically on each side of the clock, with one balanced precariously on its curved top. Harold's foxed and spotted watercolour of Westminster Cathedral's pulpit hangs on the chartreuse wall above it. The window, which when open looks out on nothing but the neighbour's side wall six feet away, is decently clothed in three layers. First there is a venetian blind, slats closed. This can be glimpsed through a sheer gathered curtain of white nylon. This in turn is flanked by autumn-toned cretonne drapes, home-sewn. At the bottom of the picture, hardly visible, is the festive table. There is just a suggestion of best white lace tablecloth, red-candle-and-coloured-balls centrepiece (looking uncomfortably phallic), chicken bones on the rose-patterned plates, the best crystal, and (can this be true?) a bottle of champagne on the table.

Jackie, Marjorie's stepfather, and the only grandfather Sue and David have ever known, is formal in white shirt and tie. His party hat is on the table. He will not put it on. He is a dignified old man and hates to look ridiculous. His gnarled hand is curled around his glass, ready to raise it.

Harold is drinking from his glass in a toast. *Happy days and many of them.* His benign blue eyes are smiling over the rim of the glass. On top of his shiny high forehead is a shiny blue party hat with orange spots. He is wearing a white shirt but, uncharacteristically, no tie.

Sue is in an expensive dress that she bought for six pounds five shillings out of her twenty pounds a week salary as a first-year-out teacher. It has a low scooped neck with a round collar and cut-away shoulders and is made of a pretty pink floral silk. She is wearing it with a suntan and a big smile. Her funny hat is green and is perched on top of caught-up dark hair. She is holding up her glass to join the toast.

David, next to Sue at the round table, has a silly look on his face, his expressive black eyebrows raised. His hat, shiny red with a yellow tassel, sits jauntily on his short black hair. His glass is obscured, but one dark red shirt sleeve can be seen. It looks to be made of knitted cotton.

Of Marjorie, only a narrow strip of horsy face is visible. Her forehead in profile, with a wavy fringe of grey hair, her bumpy nose, part of her glasses and part of her self-conscious smile. She hates having her picture taken and won't look at the photographer. She too is holding up her glass in a salute.

It is Sue's birthday. She is twenty-two.

CHAPTER 26

I have been in a position to compare the traumatic results of adoption with the comparatively simple remedy of early safe abortion. In my view there is no contest.[1]

I awoke one morning to a golden world. Through every floor-to-ceiling window, the ethereal gold of the sky had melted into the liquid gold of the sea and the house seemed to hang in air, weightless and insubstantial. The saffron leaves of the liquidambar were all on fire. Autumn had arrived.

The past few months had been climactic. Through her best friend, I had come as close as I ever would to the enigmatic woman who was Charmian Clift. I had found Toni Burgess to be a loyal and loving friend to me. To my mother she had been a sympathetic, loving, non-judgmental refuge. Charmian had felt safe with her. In the early days of their friendship, the two young women had obviously been very similar in many ways. No flight of fancy was too wild, no exaggeration too great for them. Rather than bringing each other down to earth, they spurred each other on to greater heights. Their emotions soared and plunged, they laughed and wept together.

Despite their love, probably *because* of their love, Toni had seen Charmian with clear eyes, and never tried to hide any aspect of her from me. I was sometimes distressed by the things she had to tell me, but I wanted to know it all, the worst and the best. She had given me beads for the necklace of my mother's life by the handful: brightly sparkling, multicoloured beads—and black, black beads.

She had known Charmian Clift the private person, as distinct from Charmian Clift the writer and public figure.

The private person had once said to her friend about her marriage: 'We created a myth, George and I, and now I have to keep on living it.'

When I thought about it, it was true. So much of her life had a mythic quality.[2] The romance of her barefoot childhood beside a wild beach was encapsulated in her desire to lie star-baking under the night sky until she turned silver. Her marriage—beautiful young girl marries older, golden-boy war correspondent—was the stuff of Hollywood movies. Her instant success as a very young woman with their prize-winning collaborative novel *High Valley* catapulted her into the world of fame and glamour she had always wanted. She and George added myth to myth by turning their backs on that glamorous, sophisticated world, 'dropping out' a decade before such a thing became popularised. Their life with their children on a remote Greek island, in the days before the creative world began to dream of Greek islands, was the ultimate myth, romanticised and publicised, until Hydra became synonymous with her name. She created a final myth for herself, through her weekly columns. She became the warm, wise, witty Charmian Clift.

A guru figure. Tens of thousands of newspaper readers hung on her words. Her words gave hope, even changed lives.

She had confided in Toni about this too: 'There is this woman, Charmian Clift. And I have to dress up as her and go out and *be* her.'

Perhaps I now had more clues to the elegy Martin had written for his mother. It had haunted me from the day I first read it, and its dense imagery still defeated me. Part two begins: 'You're wearing yourself again'.[3]

In the programme Nadia Wheatley and Garry Kinnane had made for Radio Helicon, Martin had said about his mother:

> *But there was a side to her, or I should say, a core to her, which is so private that I don't think I ever really knew it—all the years I knew her, and I'm not entirely sure that my father did, although I'm sure that he came much closer to it than anyone else. She needed people too. She needed my father above all. But I think she needed them on her terms. In fact in a sense, she wanted... she wanted to cheat. She wanted to have it both ways. She wanted to be able at any instance to run into wherever that core was at the centre of herself and slam the door, pull up the drawbridge, bang down the portcullis and come out when she felt good and ready.*[4]

That solitary self forms the core of each of us. Some of us so cover and clothe and camouflage that core that we never know it. Some of us spend our lives in motley and bells distracting and diverting ourselves away from it. Some of us nourish it, cause it to grow and use it as a storehouse when the world temporarily fails us. Some of us plunge into it—fatally.

When was the first time I discovered the essential aloneness of my journey through life? Was it when I struggled under the hands of nurses, trying to see my baby who had been born dead? Afterwards I had written:

> *One thing has emerged clear and strong—whatever happens to you, good or bad, you are by yourself. The experience is yours and you can only convey it to others, even beloved others, through words. They can only accompany you to the entrance. Once through that threshold, you are on your own.*

Or was it when I sobbed the night away in the long wet grass, having failed to drown my fourteen-year-old self in six inches of fish-pond water? Or even earlier in Camperdown Children's Hospital, as a six year old who was refusing to eat, when huge looming shapes in white tried to push feeding tubes into the veins that crossed my ankle bones, and I screamed and screamed and screamed for a mother who did not come? Or was it immediately after the torsion and pressure, the relentless crushing of my expulsion from that original Eden, the womb of my mother?

'Toni, why did she have me at all? Why didn't she have an abortion?'

We were sitting together in a Mosman coffee shop. I had asked Toni to find for me the various places where Charmian had lived the latter part of her life. The Raglan Street house I knew well, but others I could not find. We had spent the morning driving and walking streets in Mosman and Neutral Bay.

'Why didn't she have an abortion?' I repeated my question.

There was a silence. 'There would have been no question

of an abortion. Let me tell you a story. You know, I nearly died having my first baby. We both nearly died. I had brummy kidneys and was Rh negative, so when I fell pregnant again straightaway, I just knew I couldn't risk it. So I had an illegal abortion.'

'But surely abortion would have been legal for a reason like that,' I said.

'No. Not in those days. You couldn't get a legal one, even as a married woman. I told Charm what I was going to do, and she was absolutely horrified. Horrified. She offered to come with me, but I refused and she watched me go with eyes like saucers.'

'Why?' I asked. 'On the grounds of morality? Or because it was dangerous?'

'No. Neither of those reasons. Because of *guilt*. She didn't understand how I could bear the guilt.'

★

It was March 1965—the tag-end of summer. The heat vibrated and shimmered above everything. The wide brown river was running sluggishly, meandering from muddy shoal to muddy shoal. Huge snagged tree stumps thrust their jagged roots up through the water's flow. Willows hung their long green hair dispiritedly over the river's margins. Not a breeze stirred the drooping leaves.

Sue and Doug were in love. They had become a couple. To be spoken of in a single word: Doug-and-Sue. Sue-and-Doug. They were living in a lovers' charmed circle of gazing eyes, touching hands, draped arms, entwined bodies, entwined lives. In the house she rented with two other girls, he frequently shared her lumpy double bed. Between them they owned a black-and-tan kelpie pup, a grey-and-white half-Persian kitten, a red mini-van (Doug's), a grey Honda 50 c.c. motor scooter (Sue's), a pair of yellow-checked double blankets and an electric frypan. They were going to be married at the end of the year.

The brazen bowl of the summer sky had sent them out to the river. Shaking back her wet shoulder-length hair, Sue climbed up on a fallen log on the river bank. Doug climbed up beside her, cigarette in hand, and pulled her towards him. His face relaxed into lines of contentment as he inhaled deeply and blew out a cloud of blue smoke, which made a halo around his head in the still air.

'What do you think? Will we apply for a coastal school? Even if it's inland a little bit, we'll be able to live *right* on the coast, and travel a few miles if we have to. You want to get married in your church in Mosman I suppose—St Clement's? We'll have all the long summer holidays for a honeymoon.'

'Doug . . .' she was trying to get the words out.

'Our mothers are going to love it . . . proper white wedding, bridesmaids, flowers, your church choir singing. You watch what will happen. Dad will have us organised into buying a house before we can blink. And with both of us working . . .' He shook his head. 'Sometimes I think we do these things more for other people than for ourselves.'

'Doug.' At last she blurted it out. 'Stop! Stop it! I'm pregnant.'

There was a shocked silence.

'How can you be? We've been careful. Are you *sure*?' He threw the cigarette into the river and put his arms around her. She buried her head in his shoulder, unwilling to look into his eyes.

'I'm pretty sure. I've just had brown stains instead of a period, and I'm feeling sick already. What are we going to do?'

'God. I don't know. See a doctor first. You might be wrong.'

But she was not wrong.

The shame of it. That was what was hard to bear. The tremendous disappointment of her parents. Their boasted-about daughter, the art teacher, so clever, so talented, earning a good salary for herself. They'd been so proud of her. She couldn't face them, especially her father and her godmother, Edna Shaw. They were so religious, so conservative and so moralistic. If she really was an illegitimate child herself, and Aunt Edna knew it, how would *she* feel? The bad blood coming through? Could she ever look any of them in the face again? Her mother? She would react badly at first, but probably end up supportive.

And what about their marriage, hers and Doug's? What chance would it have if they had to get married in a hurry and start their life together with a baby before they'd even really got to know each other? Before they had become adjusted to whatever married life was. Neither of them wanted children for a long time. She certainly didn't. She had never been particularly maternal—never picked up other people's babies and cooed over them.

She would have to stop teaching, become merely a housewife and a mother. Just when she was beginning to find some rewards for all those years of study. She would have to give up her most important possession—her independence! Her sense of self. She wasn't ready to do that yet. She had seen too many marriages where the husband and wife had nothing to bind them together but their children. She didn't want hers to be like that. She had been known to ride around the town on Doug's shoulders. Their friends laughed about their future, imagining the two of them as a tall old man carrying a white-haired old woman on his shoulders, whooping it up! She loved Doug, and she wanted it to be that way. She wanted to give them both every chance.

As the days went on, her morning sickness increased. She would frequently turn her back on her class, her face to the blackboard, and try to control the hot rising flood. Or tears would well up and have to be fought back. Often tiredness would engulf her like a wave. Food would not stay down, and she grew steadily thinner. It was harder and harder to go to school every day. There was only one thing in her life that was real to her. Her focus had narrowed down to the microscopic, parasitic being that was beginning to grow inside her. A parasitic being that was going to ruin the rest of her life.

Among well brought up girls, sex was not a topic for discussion, not even between best girlfriends. Some boys may have talked, but girls pretended that they were not doing it, even when they were sharing a man's bed. Sandy and her boyfriend had come to stay one weekend. Sue had discovered her in the morning washing their sheets. She had not made the obvious inference, but only assumed that her friend was being a considerate guest. (It was twenty years later that Sandy told her that that was the occasion she had lost her virginity.) If sex was a taboo topic, how impossible it was to talk about the ultimate sexual disaster—illicit pregnancy. When Sue vomited, as she did frequently now, her flatmates thought she had a particularly virulent gastric virus.

The only person she could talk to was Doug, but his focus was just as narrow as hers, and they could only try vainly to comfort each other. But there was no comfort to be had.

Finally she could bear it no longer. She and Doug were lying on the lumpy bed in the hot night, the only light the glowing tip of his cigarette.

'I can't think of this as a baby. It won't be a baby for a long time yet. I've seen pictures of embryos. At the moment, it's more like a little budding growth inside me. I'm not going to ruin my life, both our lives, for a thing no longer than my thumb. I'll have an abortion. But I don't want to have one here. Do you know of anyone in Sydney who does them?'

In his first year out Doug had taught at a very tough Sydney boys' school, where the street-wise pupils had taught him more than he had taught them. He knew of a chemist who had contact with a Macquarie Street specialist who made a separate fortune in his consulting rooms at the weekend.

They travelled down to Sydney late at night, after a Bachelors and Spinsters ball, over winding roads made dangerous by heavy fog. Doug drove, his eyes fixed on the only thing visible, a few feet of yellow centre line, while Sue tried hard not to be sick. They slept for a couple of cramped, miserable hours in the car in a suburban park, waiting for the sun to come up. The abortion was so expensive that they could only afford to stay at a motel for one night. They had decided to save it for afterwards, when they had been given back their lives.

Sue's appointment was for nine o'clock, and the nausea that rose scaldingly in her throat was not just morning sickness. It was the nausea of humiliation and fear. The nurse was crisp, condescending and rude. But this was nothing new. Sue had already been mentally and physically humiliated by a succession of doctors as well as the chemist who had arranged this. She accepted it all as her punishment for getting pregnant. Woman's lot.

Having counted out the money, Doug was motioned to a seat in the waiting room. Sue was ushered into the consulting room. Naked except for a hospital gown, her knees were bent and her feet strapped wide apart in stirrups. The nurse swabbed her and the doctor loomed over her with nameless instruments in his hand. She squeezed her eyes shut. *Just let it be over soon, and I'll never do it again*, she prayed to a God she no longer believed in.

The pain was sudden and violent. Metal on soft flesh. She screamed and threw her hands up above her head.

'No! No!' The nurse was holding her down. 'Be quiet and put your arms down, or we'll never be able to do this.'

Once again a violent, searing pain that went on and on, as if the entire contents of her uterus, indeed the uterine walls themselves, were being scalded and scraped and jerked out of her, scalded and scraped and jerked. She began to sob.

'Stop that noise. We've nearly finished now.'

She heard the doctor's voice but she couldn't see his face. Her eyes were shut tight. She bit her bottom lip to stop herself from crying out, and tried to move her consciousness up, up into the top part of her body, away from the pain. It was still there, the scalding scraping pain, again and again, but if she concentrated she could will herself above it. But she couldn't stop the tears that streamed down the sides of her face into her hair and onto the plastic-covered pillow.

At last it was over. She leant over and was sick into a kidney bowl that the nurse held up for her. She took a few sips from a glass of water. Bleeding profusely into a large sterile pad, she shakingly dressed herself again, listened to the nurse's instructions '... any sign of infection... raised temperature... to your local doctor...' She didn't mind the blood. It was good blood. The blood of life to her. Her life given back to her. Not without pain. But she could accept that now. That was part of her punishment. Her mind knew the good thing, but her body remembered the bad thing. She couldn't stop shaking and racking sobs convulsed her. The nurse held her arm to keep her from falling as she led her out to where Doug was waiting.

Doug put his arms around his wife-to-be while tears trickled down his cheeks. It was the first time Sue had ever seen him cry.

'I know exactly why she had to give me up,' I told Toni. 'If it was shameful in my day to have a baby before marriage, what must it have been like in *her* day? She wrote one of her pieces on abortion. Needless to say it was not published at the time, but she said, "Unmarried mothers are still, to our abiding shame, the subjects of lewd jokes and smoke-room sniggering."[5] And that was in the sixties, too. It's only very recently that I have been able to tell friends about my abortion. I still don't dwell on it. Actually I have no regrets. I think I did the most sensible thing. The argument that an embryo is in fact a baby leaves me cold. It's a potential life—that's all. If I had borne that baby, I wouldn't have had the three daughters I have now. Different people would have been in the world, and that's neither here nor there. I had the same dilemma as Charmian, but I made a different choice.

'As it was we got married in St Clement's, Mosman, in December 1965, with bundles of wheat painted gold tied amongst the flowers. The choir I had sung in for so many years sang for us and no-one except Doug and I knew that it all could have ended so differently.'

'Shane got married in that church, you know.'

'Yes, I did know that. I looked up the church records. Married by the same minister as I was, as it happened. I had these romantic thoughts of my voice imprinted into the molecules of the brick arch over the chancel during all the years I had sung there. I imagined it being breathed out for my mother to absorb when she sat in the front pew at my sister's wedding. But it didn't happen that way, did it? Charmian was already dead when Shane married.'

'Yes, she was. The reception was going to be in the Raglan Street house. Charmian had great plans for doing up the house. But it ended up being held at the Crookes'. Poor little Shane. She wanted her mother to help her choose her wedding dress, but Charm was not at all interested. The whole thing, a conventional white wedding, was just too suburban for her. Shane asked me to help her, and Charm was very relieved.'

The thought flicked through my mind that Charmian Clift would have been equally unimpressed with her elder daughter's suburban white wedding: homemade Thai silk wedding dress (hours of painstaking sewing), matching homemade pillbox hat and veil, gold spray-painted wheat, full choir and all. My adoptive parents, however, particularly Dad, had almost burst with pride.

It was the second-last day of December, 1965, when

Suzanne Shaw took Douglas Arthur Chick for better for worse, for richer for poorer, in sickness and in health.

In December 1965 the worst was confirmed. George needed to have major thoracic surgery. His TB had recurred, and he had been in hospital since August. Charmian had to hold the family together. She was inordinately proud of the fact that it was *her* writing that was bringing in the daily bread. She had moved herself and the children from the large house near Balmoral to a small shiny new flat in a block of units near Neutral Bay Junction. The flat had a view up Middle Harbour and was easier to look after, cheaper to rent and closer to a shopping centre. Jason had been sent away to stay with relations in Victoria until the crisis passed. Shane was now a working girl and Martin was waiting for the results of his Leaving Certificate.

Charmian was drinking heavily just to cope. Toni would sometimes arrive at 7.30 a.m. to keep her from starting on whisky for breakfast, and would drink with her later in the day at The Oaks. Taxis or friends' cars were her usual method of getting about and Toni would often accompany her to Royal North Shore Hospital to visit George. It was a time of extreme stress and great anxiety.

CHAPTER 27

... birthparents care deeply for the life they create. The decision to relinquish that life for someone else to parent is an unforgettable decision. This decision can result in a lifetime of grief and despair, the trauma of which some birthparents have described as 'a psychological amputation'.[1]

We were walking along Balmoral Beach, Toni and I, in a sharp autumn wind. A party of old ladies from a rest home were settling themselves on a bench, adjusting rugs over their knees, opening packets of sandwiches, unscrewing thermos lids, while others of the group, too frail to brave the bitter wind, stayed in the hospital bus, eating their lunch in the warm behind the glass. As we hurried past them, Toni drew in her breath with a hiss and sketched a cross, and I burst out: 'Oh God, don't let that happen to me. I want to be an extremely eccentric old woman. I hope I go nova. I'm never going to be herded into a bus with a lot of other grey and docile old women. Dylan Thomas had it right. You know,

Do not go gentle into that good night
Old age should burn and rave at close of day;
Rage, rage against the dying of the light.'[2]

Toni joined in the last line, shuddered and said, 'How Charm would have hated being old. She *loathed* the idea of getting old. She hated being middle-aged. She couldn't stand losing her beauty.'

I had read her words on the subject:

> *One goes around for so long believing that every little physical set-back or deterioration is temporary, can be retrieved—the torn nail, the grey hair, the loose tooth, the muscle that sags on the bone, the broken vein, the laughter lines and the worry lines. 'When I get time,' one says. Or: 'I must do something about that.' 'Later,' one says.*
>
> *. . . I swear that inside every forty year old and fifty year old there is still a twenty year old, and this double identity makes for all sorts of confusions.*[3]
>
> *Who really wants to relinquish beauty, which is a joy and a delight and should not be so fragile and perishable?*[4]

'Toni, wouldn't she have been content to be thoroughly eccentric and interesting?'

'No. No. Not Charm. Her youth and beauty were part of her. She had been very beautiful, and had known she was very beautiful. She had been at home in her own skin.'

Martin had expressed similar thoughts:

> *Her worries about ageing did become more and more apparent. I think it wasn't so much a matter of looking at the young and envying them for being young, as just looking at the young and looking at the mirror and drawing conclusions which were, I think, considerably exaggerated by her, but which were unavoidable. Certainly her own physical beauty had always been very much part of her personal myth, as it were.*[5]

'What about the men, Toni—the affairs?' I asked the question diffidently. Even with regard to a mother one has never known, sex is one of the most difficult topics. 'Has the whole thing been exaggerated? What motivated her? Was it merely physical? George's impotence? Or was it a total disregard for conventional morality? Or was it part of a power-gambit? *See, I still have what it takes!*'

'Well, I can only really speak about her when she was back here in Sydney. And no, it hasn't been exaggerated. She never had brief casual affairs when she was sober, but at the end she was seldom sober. So booze played a part. No, I don't think it was physical. I think her confidence was at a very low ebb. George had nearly destroyed it. She needed constant reassurance—that she was beautiful, that she was lovable. She would sometimes tell me, after a fleeting affair with someone who didn't matter at all, "But he said he *loved* me, Antonia. He loved me," as though that was enough.'

'Oh God, how sad.'

We sat on a bench as clouds raced across the face of the sun, brushing indigo shadows across the ultramarine of the water. I gave her the print I had made of a still young and beautiful Charm standing in her kitchen on Hydra. Charm standing looking at the camera but not seeing it. Charm in a reverie.

'I've seen her look like that so often. It's so typical. So sad. I'll have to frame this. It *is* her.' Toni stared at the photograph then shook the memory free with a sudden sigh.

'Toni,' I said, 'it seems strange to me that she is often thought of as a tragic figure, when the blazing, talented, ambitious, beautiful, triumphant girl that she was would seem to have suggested another future entirely.'

'Oh, darling, it's the long-running Greek tragedy.'

'Hubris and retribution? The revenge of the gods?' I asked.

'Exactly.'

'It's strange, Toni, but Mum had a favourite quotation. I don't know where she got it, but in her old age it could bring tears to her eyes when very little else could. She used to say: "Why didst thou promise such a beauteous day, and let me travel forth without my cloak?" My adoptive mother meant it as a metaphor for her own life, but it expresses equally well the life of my natural mother. I feel that she must have been born with a skin too few, without a protective covering.'

I shivered. I asked yet another question that turned into two questions, three questions.

'Do you think Charmian was ever happy? When did it all go wrong? Was it when she had me? Her childhood seemed very happy if we go by her writing.'

'Perhaps it was.'

'Apparently George thought that those staring silences, when she just went away inside herself, and her inexplicable tears, were because of giving up a child. At least that's what the Kinnane book says. It certainly fits in with everything I've read about women who have to give away their babies.'

'So it seems.'

'But surely you were happy as young girls falling about laughing in the Bondi flat?'

'Oh, yes, particularly when George wasn't there. When we were making clothes or Christmas decorations, or something like that, or wheeling our babies out in the sun. But George didn't want a suburban wife. He'd already had one of those and left her. He wanted this beautiful, sophisticated young girl on his arm.'

'A trophy?'

'Exactly. If ever Charm did anything he considered suburban, he came right down on her. They had a family saying: *No more antirrhinums*.'

'What on earth is an antirrhinum?'

'A snapdragon.'

'Oh, I see.' And as I thought of my autumn garden, I did see.

'So do you think that George shaped her in a sense?'

'In a sense, yes. Not that she wasn't a very definite person in her own right. But he was concerned with his status and image, and he wanted her to fit it.'

'But in *Clean Straw For Nothing* he—or his character, David Meredith—comes across as a deeply thoughtful, self-analytical man, who knows himself for a failure.'

'He was dishonest in that book. In reality George liked to associate with success, big name artists and so on. That humble self-abasement wasn't George Johnston. Look, I was in the house once when Charm was speaking to a friend on the telephone. George called out to her, "Don't ask them around! Don't encourage them! We didn't come back to Australia to clutter up our lives with nobodies!" And there was I in the same room, a nobody if ever there was one.'

'But she loved the somebody side of her life too, didn't she?'

'She *always* loved life—all of it—the glamour, the clouds, the smell of the sea, the swoop of the gull.'

We both turned to look out at the sea. A swooping seabird's flight would always suggest my mother to me.

Toni continued, 'She loved the excitement and prestige of her life. Of course, she loved it—who wouldn't love it? Winning the literary prize, being an overnight success, the open house parties on Saturday nights. George was well-known, had his own column. He invited anyone who was anyone in the creative world. He was well into status, even in those early days. They were mostly older than Charm and adored her. She was like a flower—a lovely, beautiful fresh flower, open to the sunshine. And they were the sunshine! Of course she loved it. The painters and poets and musicians and writers who came. People like William Dobell, fresh from New Guinea with a roll of sketches under his arm; people like Peter Finch. Now *he* was yummy.' The corners of her small, full mouth quirked up. 'But I think the gilt had worn off the gingerbread with George even before they went to London.' She gave a half smile. 'Of course, as I've told you, I'm biased. I was *her* friend, not his.'

'I don't know about London,' I said, 'but I'm certain she was happy on Kalymnos. The photos and her letters to Cedric and *Mermaid Singing* all show it. To me, her happiness sings out. I'm sure that's why I love that book so much.'

'Well, after all, Charm was the one who wanted them to go to Greece.'

'Then perhaps for a little while she did find what she was looking for. I hope she did. I wonder how long that something went on? Hydra sounds a different story altogether.'

'She wrote to me sporadically from Hydra, you know. In one letter she told me that she had lain out at night on the cliffs under the stars, looking up at the sky and raging, "What about *me*? Who am I?"'

'And by the time she came back to Sydney it was too late? The damage had been done?'

Toni just nodded. The smoke from her cigarette blew away from us on the sharp edge of the wind. When she spoke it was with deep emotion.

'People just don't realise. George had done his job on her too well—*no more antirrhinums!* In hindsight I see that she was frightened. George was a trained journalist. He would be all right. But what would happen to her? And when he got ill she was frightened. It all fell on her. She just wasn't equipped to cope with the mundane things of life—the children and their problems, George's illness.'

'Yet in Greece in the early years she coped splendidly with terrible physical conditions, lack of sanitation, bedbugs, small children with jaundice and no doctor—that sort of thing. And it seems that on Hydra she coped with constant visitors and often with peasant-like poverty.'

'Yes, but that was all romantic. Greece was an exotic place. The Greek people were exotic, strange beings. It was all part of her romantic vision. By the time she got back here, she was still off in her imagination with the unicorns, but the fight had gone out of her. The minutiae of daily life left her quite bewildered. Like Shane's wedding. It was too much for her to cope with. Much of the time she looked bewildered—totally bewildered.

'She had been talking about killing herself long before she actually did it. Once when George had been taunting her, along the lines of, *Look, I'm a sick man, see what you're doing to me*, she said to me, "I'll die before he does."'

We both stared out to sea, Toni with her memories, me with the gathering weight of my mother's bewilderment and sadness.

I broke the silence. 'I'm sorry, Toni. I'm always forcing you to remember things you've probably worked hard to

forget. But she is just so complicated and contradictory and difficult to understand. After the last time I saw you, when you gave me a fair idea of how bad things really were for her towards the end, I went home absolutely wrung out. Exhausted. And I was only listening. But you—you were reliving your life in telling me. You must have been drained dry!'

'It's extraordinary, my darling,' Toni said. 'When I talk about it, it's as though I were young again. I feel that she's never grown older and neither have I. Here, you know,' she pointed to the blue ruffled water with its racing cloud shadows, the encircling rocks, the scrubby bush and slab-like blocks of flats built almost down to the edge of the rock, 'This is exactly the same as it was, and I feel about forty years old.'

'I know just what you mean. It's the same for me. When I am here, I feel twenty—and my boyfriend is lying down there on the sand waiting for me to come back from the kiosk with two ice-creams. This dipping in and out of time is very strange. When I went home after I saw you last time, I re-read some of her essays which, thanks to Nadia, are dated. I read them knowing just what was going on in her life at the time, knowing what despair she was experiencing. And I felt again exactly what I had felt at the beginning when I hardly knew anything. I still had the one big question: how could she have written what she did? The essays were just as full of warmth and sparkle and joy and generosity as they had been the first time I read them. Toni, tell me—how did she do it?'

'My darling, I don't know myself how she did it. I only know that she did. She still had it, that magic core that she could draw on. And despite the fact of her saying that *that* Charmian Clift was a fraud, it wasn't. It was real and it was true.

'She decided to write a piece on Paddy's market,[6] and she wanted me to come to the market with her. She rang me and said, "Antonia, I shall ring you very early in the morning to be sure that you wake up. I know what you're like in the mornings. Then I'll collect you in a cab."

'So she did, and it was one of the most extraordinary mornings of my life. We wandered around, knocked out by the sights and the colours, and the sounds and the scents. The markets were so piled with produce, such a wealth, all fresh and dewy and heaped up. Vegetables and fruit and flowers. And people. Swarthy Greeks and Italians in leather aprons, nuns in black and white. We were carried away. We couldn't help ourselves. There was a wall of cauliflowers, crisp and curled and beautifully heaped and she said, "Let's buy half a dozen cauliflowers each," and we looked at each other and burst out laughing. "Whatever will we do with a dozen cauliflowers?" We had breakfast in a truckies' pub. "You and I, we enjoy the low life," Charm put it. Then we walked up George Street, our arms full of roses, behind a Greek woman. "Now there's a woman, Antonia," Charm said. "There's a real woman! She doesn't shave and deodorise. She just lets everything grow."

'So we started to fantasise about letting everything grow—our head hair, our underarm hair, our pubic hair. You can imagine! We kept topping each other's fantastic images until, in our imaginations, we were lying in the sea and letting our long, long hair float around us like seaweed. And of course we were still falling about with laughter.

'The point is that it was just the way it had been when we were girls. *That* Charm was still there, but in increasingly fewer and fewer patches. When we had that marvellous, marvellous morning that was such fun I'll never forget it, when she wrote that piece, she was at a very low ebb.' She paused. 'George was in hospital. Charm was raddled, she was addled, she was misbehaving.' Her right eyebrow soared. 'But she could still do it.'

'So how did she write, Toni?'

'She got up very early in the morning. About five o'clock. That market piece was exactly as it had happened. She didn't exaggerate at all. In fact she toned it down if anything.

'You know that quote in Kinnane's book on George, where he says that I stayed with her all night while she talked out her fear of writing the piece? Well it's quite wrong. We might have sat up *one* night, when she was in the Neutral Bay flat. She said, "What am I going to write about?" Her head in her hands. George in the hospital, while she tried to cope with everything. Out of that night came the essay on drinking tea, I think.[7] But you mustn't get the idea that she needed me, or anyone, to help her. She didn't rely or lean on anybody. She was fanatical about getting it right. She was inordinately proud of her professionalism, proud as a kid with a lollipop of the fact that she had never missed a deadline. She used that fact as the final word in arguments with George. She would look him straight in the eye and say very slowly and deliberately, "In any case, I have *never* missed a deadline!"

'Sure she might sometimes say to me, "What shall I write about this week?", but only in the way that anyone might. My answer often used to be, "I don't care what you write about, but don't write about me!" '

An awful thought surfaced. 'Toni, how do you feel about *me* writing about you then?'

'I'm appalled, to be honest. To me, my life has been an ordinary life, and I wouldn't let anyone else do it, but I can see that you have to. You *need* to. This book is going to be about your life. You're your mother's daughter! And not just in your broad cheekbones and green eyes and wide mouth. She would have done exactly what you're doing. Without a qualm. In fact, she's probably sitting up there on a cloud right now and cheering you on!'

Martin had said that his mother drafted and redrafted and that the Charmian Clift who appeared each week in the *Sydney Morning Herald* revealing details of her life and sharing her thoughts with her readers was a clever literary persona.[8] Toni knew that some of her pieces were written straight off, pieces that expressed a Charmian Clift who was real to her. Rodney Hall in his introduction to *The World of Charmian Clift* writes:

> *And, by the way, if anyone asks—the answer is yes, she was exactly the way these essays suggest. She created herself on paper much better than anyone else could.*[9]

Once again she had affected different people in her life very differently. To a much greater extent than anyone I have ever known, she was different things to different people. In fact she *was* different people. It was one of the first things to strike me about my mother. My journal was full of my confusion.

George understood this about Charmian. There is a

moving scene in *A Cartload of Clay* where, after the suicide of his wife, Cressida (who is, of course, Charmian), George's alter ego David Meredith says:

> *Nothing now could be subtracted from his experienced history with Cressida, nor from his knowledge of these many women who were one woman . . .*[10]

The next time I saw Toni we sat over lunchtime sandwiches and cappuccinos in a coffee shop in Balmain. It was a lunchtime that was to continue for the rest of the afternoon. A sliding glass door was open to a narrow balcony where red geraniums blazed away in the foreground. A row of restored terraces in greys and ochres slashed a strong diagonal across the background.

'You know, my darling,' she was saying, 'in this book you just *must* let people know what it was like to have an illegitimate child in the forties. Nowadays there is no social stigma to having a child when you are unmarried, and there are benefits to allow girls to keep their babies. People just won't understand how terrible it was then.'

'Well actually, Toni, I've been spending a lot of time trying to discover just what it was like. And it isn't easy to find out. I've spent days in libraries to no avail, and yesterday I visited the Post Adoption Resource Centre in Paddington.'

I passed across the table a photocopy of two pages from a little booklet published two years ago. It was the recollections of a nurse who had worked at Crown Street in 1946–47.

'There,' I pointed.

> *Adoption Babies.*
> *Matron Shaw maintained that 'all babies are*

> *entitled to be cuddled by their mothers and to be breastfed for at least their first couple of weeks. Every mother is entitled to cuddle her own baby before giving it up for adoption and she owed the baby that bit of "mothering".'*[11]

'Oh my God,' said Toni, her eyes widening and filling with tears. 'Oh, poor Charm.'

We both wiped our tears. But our eyes kept filling up.

'I can see Charmian's face in front of me now, her big green eyes with the tears welling out of them and rolling down her cheeks. She cried and cried, and I just held her. She said she'd walked the streets looking into the faces of little girls, wondering, always wondering if... But to have held and fed her baby for two weeks, and then to have had to give her up. How could she have borne the pain?'

'How could any woman? But of course, from my point of view it's wonderful to know that she held me—that's if this policy was in force three to four years earlier. Certainly Matron Shaw was there then, and I can't imagine her ideas would have been more rigid earlier. Things changed later, in the fifties, when the mothers were packed off straight after the birth to convalesce at Wakehurst, and the babies were sent to the adoption nursery. But a mother was allowed to see the baby behind the nursery glass before she went. I think it was after my Aunt Edna had retired that the horrible business of the pillow on the mother's chest came in, so that she could *never* see her baby.'

'How terribly, terribly sad.' Toni's eyes filled yet again. 'I can see why you're excited—because it means your mother knew you, and you knew her, if only for two weeks. But for Charmian... giving you up must have been unbearable pain.'

'So you have no recollection of her ever saying anything about it?'

'No. You have to understand that this was the only time we talked about it. I never felt I could bring it up, and the only time she did, after that sad scene in the late forties in the Bondi flat, was the time in the sixties that I've told you about.'

Yes, I did understand. It was certainly not something you could talk about, even with your best friend. Girls were told they had committed their sin, made their tragic mistake. Now they had to forget it, put it out of their minds, go off and start life anew.

I gave Toni some of the photocopies to read that dealt with illegitimacy and adoption while I settled back in my chair and thought about what I had discovered.

The Post Adoption Resource Centre was set up to coincide with the advent of the new *Adoption Information Act* to provide a service for people affected by the Act—adopted people, birthparents and adoptive parents. It is attached to The Royal Hospital for Women, and when Crown Street Women's closed, its records dealing with adoption went there. Unfortunately there are no casework records earlier than the sixties.

I made an appointment with the manager of the Centre, social worker Margaret McDonald. She and Petrina Slaytor, also a social worker with expertise in this field, listened to my story with the attention and interest that it always elicits. But not with tears. They must have heard hundreds of adoption stories by now. At the point in the story where my parents told me the lie about a mother who died in childbirth and a father who was killed in the war, they looked at each other knowingly.

'That was a very common story at that time,' they said.

They did not have answers to my questions about what policies and practices were in force at Crown Street when I was born, but they set me loose on a vast collection of books, newspaper articles, clippings from the *Women's Weekly* and *Woman*, articles about my adoptive aunt and godmother, Matron Shaw, from 1947 on, booklets prepared for annual dinners, annual reports and so on.

What these showed very clearly was the social climate surrounding illegitimacy and unmarried motherhood.

One article from 1947, titled 'How We Treat Unmarried Mothers', reported an interview with Matron Shaw and quoted her as saying, 'Only good girls have babies. The bad ones know how to get rid of them.'

The same article informed the reader that at Crown Street the girls all wore wedding rings, and were called Mrs Jones or Mrs Smith or some such alias. There was some pride expressed in the fact that the girls were not called by their Christian names as in some institutions. The unmarried girls worked as domestics in the hospital and lived in a pre-maternity section which had recently been built to accommodate thirty women, and it was proudly pointed out that the unmarried mothers had the same food as hospital patients.

Toni had remembered Charm telling her about living at the hospital and washing hospital floors, so I now knew where she had hidden herself, at least in the last months of her pregnancy.

The last two paragraphs were revealing:

> *The girls who create this tragic problem for themselves are from no one social group. Some are stupid, some intelligent. Some come from wealthy homes, others from slum terraces. But women who*

> *deal with these girls say most come from unhappy homes where the parents are divorced or have remarried. Most of the girls, feeling unwanted in their homes, are longing for affection.*
>
> *Unfortunately the general public treats the problem of the unmarried mother as most do venereal disease—as something not to be spoken of aloud. Few of the hundreds of charitable goodwill organisations in Australia cater for the unmarried mother, who gets very little assistance unless she is able to work for it.*[12]

Despite being a progressive and compassionate view for that time, to modern ears the whole article has a patronising ring.

Another extract from *Woman*, dated 1948, told of the financial assistance the unmarried mother could expect. A Commonwealth Maternity Bonus of fifteen pounds (thirty dollars) as a one-off payment, and a child welfare allowance of ten shillings (one dollar) per week, not granted unless the mother was prepared to name and summons the father. The woman would receive food relief of up to seventeen shillings (one dollar seventy-five) per week during pregnancy. This was given in the form of cash orders, which some shops refused to redeem.[13]

There were only three options for a girl who wanted to keep her baby. Firstly her family could support her. Apparently this was not uncommon at Crown Street, which was based on a poor, inner-city area where extended families were the rule, and the grandmother looked after the baby while the mother went out to work. Secondly she could find accommodation and some kind of work which would let her bring the child with her. Domestic work was really the only option here. Thirdly she could find accommodation and work while boarding the child out in a foster home until such time as she could make a home for her baby. This option was to all intents and purposes giving up the child, at least temporarily, without an actual adoption taking place.

I was told that there were between five and six hundred illegitimate births per year at Crown Street—an average of over ten every week. Middle-class girls and girls from country towns faced extreme social stigma. In fact I was told of one woman who had been kept by her mother in a small country town. She had experienced a horrendous childhood, and had been known to all as the town bastard.

Private adoptions, like mine and my adoptive brother's, seem to have been common. In another article, from 1953, Matron Shaw says:

> *I can remember many cases when a married mother had lost several babies through difficult childbirth and wanted to adopt one while still in hospital. In very worthy cases like these we could come to an agreement with the Child Welfare Department that these mothers could immediately adopt illegitimate children still in the hospital and start feeding them themselves.*
>
> *Within a matter of two weeks these mothers could take the baby home as if it were their own. All adoption papers were completed before they left the hospital. I cannot remember a single case of unhappiness on either side afterwards.*[14]

I had been told of obstetricians who chose the pick of the babies for their infertile patients. And nursing sisters who creamed off the babies with the 'best points' (whatever these were) for the private adoption list, leaving the rest for couples who applied through Child Welfare. Paediatricians could also stop a child being adopted because of something in its social background—if its mother had suffered a mental breakdown or was an alcoholic, for example. There was a strong belief in bad blood. Authority figures had tremendous and largely unquestioned power.

In 1947 the *Women's Weekly*'s 'Medico' column had this advice for the adoptive parent on the subject of whether to tell the child about the adoption:

> *You certainly should... When old enough to understand the child should be told of how the choice was made, and then never mentioned again.*[15]

When I first found the recollections from Crown Street from 1946–47, describing how the unmarried girls were required to breastfeed their babies before giving them up, I showed it to Petrina Slaytor.

'I wondered if she'd even seen me. Just to know that she had seen me means so much to me. Now, if this is true! I feel this enormous joy. Isn't it ridiculous that a woman of nearly fifty, with grown children of her own, should find it so incredibly moving to know that her mother had held her and fed her for two whole weeks all those years ago?'

'No, not ridiculous at all,' she said. 'We have an intense need to know where we belong, where we come from. We have quite elderly people in here, knowing it is too late to find their mothers—but they're looking for possible brothers and sisters. The urge to know is very, very strong.'

'You know,' I said to her, 'I would be crying buckets of tears right now, except that I'm all cried out. I've cried buckets so many times over the last year.'

'Many's the time I've cried with the girl as she signed the papers to adopt out her baby when I knew she didn't really want to,' Petrina said. 'Now, some of the younger women direct their anger at us, the social workers, but we have to operate within the framework of the times.'

'We can't do anything but operate within the framework of the times,' I said. 'And now the times have changed. For a start, premarital sex isn't thought of as something sinful, like it was when I was young. In fact these days a girl who doesn't experiment is regarded as an oddity, at least by her peers. Now there aren't too many girls who give up their babies I should imagine.'

'Oh, adoption as we knew it is a thing of the past.'

'And these days it is financially possible for a single girl to keep a child. Barely possible, but it can be done. I'm a high school teacher and we see a bit of it. Far from being stigmatised, single mothers are glamorised by other girls. Some pregnant girls stay at school as long as possible, a focus of interest for their friends, and when the baby is born they bravely come back to do their Higher School Certificate or whatever. Often it is the girl's mother who is the brave one. She ends up bringing up the baby.'

'Yes, it's all changing. We're a part of history, you and I. Everything has become so much more open.'

'Oh, absolutely. When I was a child, secrecy and concealment were the order of the day. There was so much that was never talked about, that wasn't quite *nice*. People in authority, usually men, thought they knew what was best for others. And the others, often women, didn't know how to question it. Now, more and more, people know their rights and make their own decisions.'

'Yes,' said Petrina. 'Women today have a great deal more control over what happens to their bodies.'

I thought again of my nineteen-year-old mother leaving the hospital empty-handed, while her baby went to the adoption nursery. I thought of her going back home to Kiama, 'for a number of reasons'. This impetuous girl who had tried to fly, her wings now clipped. I wondered if her mother had comforted her—or had she refused to discuss the matter, and told her to put it behind her and start again? Was that why she joined the army? To put it all behind her? Could any girl put such a thing behind her, let alone one with the passion and fire and imagination of Charmian Clift?

Toni looked up from her reading, took off her glasses and looked me in the eye.

'Tell me, Sue, how do you think of her? As your mother?'

'Oh, definitely as my mother.'

'Even though you were brought up by another woman?'

'I have *two* mothers. One who gave me life and the genetic things I share with her, and one who loved me and brought me up. It's not because she's a well-known person. It wouldn't matter if she was Mary Smith, I would feel the same. Everything I've found out proves that. What I feel is the same thing all searching adopted people feel. The person who gave birth to you *is* your mother. She is part of you, in a way the mother who brought you up can never be. If it was only that one thing I share with Charmian—that way of looking at every beautiful thing in the world as if it was totally fresh and new—if it was only that—that would be enough to make me certain she was my mother.'

CHAPTER 28

There will always be wives who prefer complete domesticity to the risks and hazards of competing in a world that is tough, fast and demanding. And why not, if that is satisfying to them? But for the rest of us, let's get on with the busy bustle of bazaar and town gate if we choose, and the satisfaction of earning our fine linens and purples ourselves.[1]

Tomorrow is Mother's Day. Danni and Kristy are both home for the weekend. Gina's phonecall has already come through. It is, as the girls wish it to be, the most homey and nostalgic of evenings. The weather is cold and the copper fire-hood over the hearth contains within its proscenium arch a hypnotic world of flaming leap and swirl. With a sense of high theatre, rain is drumming and hammering at the iron roof and cascading from the eaves just beyond the reflecting rectangle of the easterly window. We all know that, still further out there in the blackness, the surf will be running a high white wall from the island to the headland, but we can't hear its fury. We are eating home-made pumpkin soup around the fire. From the CD player, Haydn's Trumpet Concerto in E Flat is brassily resonating around the room. It is my daughters' Mother's Day gift to me. The cat is curled up in the crook of Danni's knees, and the dog, who is terrified of thunder, is taking refuge under the dining room table, hemmed in by a forest of protective highly polished chair legs.

This is a time I will remember. A time I am glad that I am a mother.

It was not always so.

It was January 1971. Charmian had been dead for eighteen months. Doug had been promoted, and we were sent to a new country town on the Northern Tablelands. Our first daughter was fifteen months, our second three months old, and I thought I was pregnant again. I should have felt fulfilment in being a mother, especially after losing an earlier child, but instead I felt rather like a female animal—a milk-sodden, breeding animal curled around her litter in a dark, hidden den.

My friends and family were far away. It was a very small country town, where no-one seemed to share my interests. I felt an outsider looking in. Teaching would have given me some intellectual stimulation and companionship, but that was an impossibility. After all, I had two babies to look after.

I could never be one of the Rotary wives, or the Country Women's Association and church-on-Sunday set, which was the way to acceptance for a young woman in a small town. There was no chance to paint or express myself at all. There was no time. Doug was at work all day, and at night he was studying for a post-graduate degree. The strength of my feeling of being trapped with young children frightened me. Most of all I hated the sense of losing myself, of becoming *only* the wife of Doug Chick, the mother of Gina and Danni Chick. I began to insist that people address letters to me as *S. Chick.* Mrs D. Chick? That way lay annihilation.

Fortunately I was wrong about being pregnant again. But having been one of two siblings I had long decided that at least three, preferably four, would give each child some kind of choice of companion. To reinforce this decision the shock of Doug's brother's death had made a mere two seem like a fragile hold on posterity. So we decided we might as well have the third soon in any case, on the principle of getting it all over at once.

My youngest daughter was born in the base hospital of the nearest large town. This town was over one hundred miles away down a precipitous mountain road. Kristin was born with severe talipes of the right foot: in other words, a club foot. Her pathetic little leg looked more like a hockey stick with toes than a human limb. I left hospital after three days, but she stayed for the first month of her life, having physiotherapy daily with a specialist in preparation for the operation she was to undergo when she was three months old. She finally came home to her parents and her excited expectant sisters, now aged almost-two and almost-three, on condition that she be taken back to the large town once a week for further physiotherapy and plaster changes.

So every Friday for three months I would pack my three

babies into the car (two of them in nappies, the oldest not securely toilet-trained yet) for a nightmare two-hundred-mile five-and-a-half-hour round trip. Five-and-a-half hours of driving that is. We drove in miles in those days. As well as three babies, I packed Bluey, a dirty ragged piece of cotton jersey from a pair of blue pyjamas that the eldest could not live without. I also packed Pee-oh, a soiled blue-and-white gingham-covered baby pillow that the middle one could not live without; and Bibby-Bear, a disgracefully mauled teddy that they both loved and fought over. I packed food in an esky for the two bigger babies and me, bottles of formula for the youngest (at a pinch the eldest could hold the bottle for her baby sister), a thermos of hot milky tea for me, bibs for all the children, nappies for two babies, spare pants for the eldest, spare clothes for all of them, plastic bags for food scraps, other plastic bags for dirty nappies. I loaded in toys and books and crayons in a forlorn hope that the bigger ones might amuse themselves on the journey. Into the station wagon went towels, soap and wet washers in plastic bags, pillows and bedding for naps; a folded down pram, with carrying seat above for the almost-two-year-old—the almost three-year-old would have to walk, or sit in the pram on top of the baby. Two Safe-and-Sound baby seats, thank heavens, were already fixtures in the back seat of the station wagon, so I only had to put in the baby basket for accommodation. Oh and a potty for the eldest, with my fingers crossed for good luck. Sam, the black and tan kelpie, was paranoid about being left behind, so she packed herself as soon as I opened the tailgate, and only needed a water bowl from me. To get all of that little tribe stowed away in the car without one of them playing in the mud, or poking her sister in the eye, or wetting her pants, or being sick down the front of her dress—or worse still my dress—took a miracle of luck and life-form engineering. But that was only the start.

It took two and three-quarter hours to drive down those mountain bends and through one coastal town to the regional centre. The baby had been fed, so, with luck, she slept, if fitfully because of her uncomfortable plaster. The other two were another matter. They were raring to go. Both very early talkers, they were at the stage of asking questions, over and over and over again. Even when answered logically and with calmness and patience, they could ask the same question twenty-seven times. Twenty-seven times *each*. I counted once.

'Why is that windmill broken, Mummy?' (Stationary windmills were *broken*, rotating ones were *fixed*. Crescent and full moons were similarly categorised.)

'Why windmill bwoke, Mummy?'

'Waa . . . a-waaa . . . a-waaa,' from the newly woken baby.

'The windmill isn't broken, love. The vanes aren't rotating because the wind isn't blowing.'

'But why is the windmill broken, Mummy?'

'Yes, why it bwoke?'

'Waaa . . . a-waaa . . . a-waaa . . .'

'It only goes around when the wind is blowing, love. It isn't broken. There just isn't any wind today. See, the trees aren't blowing. Could you gently pat the baby?'

'WAAA . . . a-WAAA . . . a—.'

'No, *gently*.'

'But *why* is the windmill broken? I want a *fixed* windmill.'

'Bibby-Bear wants fixed one too. Why it bwoke, Mummy?'

The rest of the day can be inferred, as long as you include three stops before the bottom of the mountain, a temperature in the high thirties with humidity of ninety per cent on the coastal plain, lunch and a drink of water for the dog in a park (a park with a river for the dog to get wet in and two toddlers to fall into if not watched), mother, pram, babies and dog-on-a-lead trailing through the streets of the regional centre, looking by this time not unlike the local hippies who stared at them. Add the delights of finding public toilets, only to discover that the eldest didn't want to go just then, trying to find somewhere to change a baby, a doctor's waiting room, a baby screaming with pain, demonstrations on how to torture the baby's foot outwards, more screaming, then the whole trip in reverse. *Now* the eldest wanted to go.

We often arrived home after dark. The three babies would have just gone to sleep as I drove into the town limits. They woke up crying the minute the engine stopped. After I had handed them over to an anxiously waiting husband, I would start. Crying.

There was no room for Sue, the individual, in all of this. She just had to wait her turn. The trapped feeling would not go on for ever. Reason told me this, but I could still feel her wings fluttering and battering themselves against the bars of this cage of love.

That Charmian had felt similar feelings, I was certain. She had said as much herself, firstly about her time in Sydney in the late 1940s when she and George were living in the ugly brick block of flats at Bondi:

> *At this point I should have taken wings and started to fly but at this point also, of course, I was involved in having children, and for many, many years I had this dual thing, the frustrations that are inevitable with any creative person being tied and bound and at the same time struggling, beating one's head against a wall to do what one wants to do. I*

> *think those are terribly difficult years for any young woman and for a young woman who wants to write or paint or do something else, even more so.*[2]

And in the early 1950s, after the family had moved to England:

> *I liked England, I was very happy in London, excepting that again there was the feeling of being bound and constrained, held by little children in an apartment or taking them to school or bringing them home or walking them in parks, and I felt that I was an outsider looking in, never part of it, never part of the London I wanted to be part of, because I wasn't free . . . I did very little work of my own because I didn't have time, also in a sort of sense, in some peculiar sense, I felt at that time I was losing my identity completely. I wasn't quite sure who I was . . .'*[3]

And then yet again about the early years in Greece in 1955 and 1956:

> *I wanted to do my own work in my own way. This was probably very egotistical but most writers have this. In any case I didn't have time because I was the one who had to learn the Greek and I was our interpreter and I was our cook, and I had this awful problem on my hands of two small children who were lost and bewildered and lonely in a foreign country, and it took about a year to adjust all that. Then I found out that I was going to have another baby, and this plunged me back into a long, long tunnel that I thought I'd just got clear of.*[4]

These feelings, which would have been unacceptable in a mother of her generation, could only have deepened her resentment with her lot. Her resentment towards George and the children, and therefore her guilt.

Marjorie, on the other hand, of a generation even earlier than Charmian's, and childless as well, had fashioned her whole life around her adopted son and daughter. On the surface she had found her fulfilment through them. Society approved.

As for me, the daughter of the two of them, the seasons passed and things began to look better. Magically, the best possible medicine for my ailment materialised: a three-day-a-week teaching job. The high school music teacher was leaving and, in this small town, there was no-one who could replace her. Well, music was within my ken.

I bought an acoustic guitar, taught myself to play it, found a grandmotherly woman to look after my babies and went back to work. Until I developed calluses on my fingertips, they regularly opened up on the keys of the school piano, making a shiny bright red mess, to the great excitement of the roomful of children of farmers, railway fettlers and meat workers and rabbiters.

I thought I might need to grow calluses on my heart, also. But my grandmotherly woman loved my children, and they loved her, and I came home to a tidy house and the vegetables peeled for dinner and the baby bathed and pinkly asleep and the other two delighted to see me. And most important of all I was Sue Chick, the music teacher, with a life of the mind again. I was myself. The pulse of life came surging back.

In my desperate need for social contact, I had made brief forays on the outskirts of women's life in this town, which consisted in the main of coffee mornings and tennis afternoons with a rush home in the middle of the day to cook husbands' hot lunches when they walked home from work or came in from the paddocks. None of this could I share. However, by moving in inexorable circles around the heavenly bodies of my small children, I had managed to connect with some fellow satellites and together we existed in that special firmament expressly created for isolated young mothers in isolated small places. Now, with my new sense of identity in finding a work niche for myself, I also carved out a social niche.

One of the town's chief organisations was a charitable money-raising one which specialised in big production-line public dinners. Never a cook, though a willing enough washer-upper, there was little scope here for me. But when the dinners expanded to dinners with concerts, I found my salvation: producer, director, singer, actress and set painter. We put on an Old Time Music Hall. There were enough frustrated Thespians in the town and on the staffs of the primary and high schools to gather together a cast, but sheet music was more difficult, and there was a small matter of top hats. Brisbane was the closest city, but it could have been Betelgeuse for all the chance I had of getting there.

In my weekly letter to my mother, I mentioned my problems. The reply came back promptly.

> *Dearest Daughter!*
>
> *I can see your grimace at this title, sounds like 'lolly' and various other terms that you do not care for.*
>
> *Anyway I procured the music you asked for but bought two of them at Palings and they did not have the Henery the Eight one, so had to buy it in the big book to get it and it had one in the other books, so sorry to spread your money so, but there may be some other tunes you can use. Unfortunately one cannot change music or patterns.*

I had a good laugh at your letter. I know what you mean about not having anyone to laugh with. Aunt Edna went home again a few days ago and at last we have the house free. The conversation for the last few weeks. Talk about trivia. 'Has the Archbishop cut his toenails yet?' 'Are the bowels of the Canon working properly after his fright?' It nearly drives me up the wall. I really think there should be a firm like Rentokil for old people. 'Stop Age', 'End It' or 'Blast 'em Out!' for people over a certain age. Voluntary, of course.

We'll bring the hats up ourselves. If you'll have us. Don't forget to let us know. About the hats. See you soon, I hope. Dad sends his love.

Lots of love to you all, darling,

Ma.

Mum was now seventy, still trying to give up smoking, and Dad seventy-five, still trying to understand Mum. Until the year before he had been working part-time with the same firm where he had started as an office boy of fifteen. He was lost without his job and welcomed any opportunity for a little jaunt.

At my end of New South Wales, rehearsals were going well and the kitchens of the good country cooks bubbled and steamed with the delicious scents of new recipes. They had not quite decided on the menu for the big night.

Mum and Dad were due to arrive the next day with the top hats in time for dress rehearsal. The two elder children were excited to the point of dementia. *How many more sleeps until Nan and Grandpa come? Only ONE?*

When the day dawned, I had to persuade three-year-old Gina to go to preschool as usual. I walked her around the corner, with Kristin in the pram and two-year-old Danni holding onto the handles, to the little fenced-in enclosure with its white-painted child-heaven. And mother-heaven, I have to admit. Gina ran off happily enough when she saw her friends. The baby, the two-year-old and I walked back home, past the prunus in pale pink spring blossom, down the hill and under our own archway of ancient, interlacing pin oaks, budding now with tiny shoots of intense green. As I was putting the kettle on the stove, the phone rang.

'Hello... Mum! Where are you?... At *what* railway station? What on earth's happened?... Dad had an accident on the outskirts of Sydney? You left the car at a garage and came on in the train? But you'll have been up all night. It's a terrible journey... What? You got a sleeper... Oh, the train's about to leave again. OK. I'll meet you at the station at eleven-thirty. See you then, you poor things.'

The four of us were there to meet the train. The girls let out a shriek of delight when they saw their grandparents. Two grey-haired figures climbed down from the carriage wearing top hats and broke into a soft-shoe shuffle along the platform.

During the week after Mother's Day, Doug and I were in Sydney to celebrate Vanda's fiftieth birthday and to see the Henry Moore exhibition at the Art Gallery of New South Wales. We had also arranged to have dinner with Roseanne at a little Italian place just round the corner from her house. We were sitting upstairs, outside on the terrace despite the autumnal wind. The never-quite-dark of the city sky loomed behind the block-like apartments opposite with a mushroom-coloured broodiness. Just visible above the terrace wall, a tattered palm leaf whipped backwards and forwards like a searching triffid.

But Roseanne had brought a bottle of good wine and the food was authentic. I loved sitting outside in the elements. And I loved talking to my sister-in-law again. We asked about her daughter, who was pregnant.

'What if she has a girl? How strange it must feel, Roseanne, to be the mother of a mother of a daughter.' I tried to imagine how it would feel. Womb to womb to womb again.

'I don't know yet how it's going to feel,' she said. 'Ask me again when she's had the baby. If it's a girl. But I'm convinced it's going to be a boy.'

As it usually did, the conversation got around to Martin. I never tired of hearing about this fascinating brother I had never known. Roseanne talked again about how as a child he had hated to hear his parents fight, hiding his head under his pillow.

'He wrote about them in one of his poems. You know the one? Where he likens them to barracudas?'

'No,' I answered. 'Tell us.'

'It's called 'Biography', and begins:

> *About love and hate and boredom they were equally barracudas, took an arm or leg quick as winking.*'[5]

There were tears in her eyes as she said to me: 'You missed out on all that fun. Weren't you lucky?'

The next day Doug and I were eating out again. This time at Doyles at the Fishmarkets with Toni Burgess. Gulls wheeled and dipped and quarrelled noisily over scraps under the white iron tables. Their masts oscillating like demented metronomes, small boats jinked and skittered at their moorings and overhead the grey clouds raced diagonally in shredded streams across the torn blue sky. But we all wanted to sit outside and be part of the wild day.

'Darling,' Toni said, 'thank you for my beautiful red roses. I was feeling so depressed and there was a banging at the door and the dogs went crazy, you know how they do, and there they were. *Exquisite* red roses.'

'Seeing both my mothers are dead and it was Mother's Day, I hoped you wouldn't mind,' I said.

'Mind? It was lovely. You know, you look *so* like your mother sitting there. It's unnerving. You're more like her than any of her other children. Isn't that strange?'

'And me the illegitimate one she gave away. It's ironic, isn't it?'

'She would have loved to see you. Loved to have had a daughter like you. She was disappointed in Shane. She'd always expected to produce a raving beauty of a daughter, and she considered Shane plain.'

'But Shane was most attractive,' protested Doug, memories of many photographs in his mind.

'Charm didn't think so. She said to me once, when we

were talking about Shane: "But I have another daughter, you know."'

'Oh, poor Shane,' I said. 'What a difficult mother to live up to. She wouldn't have thought me beautiful either, I can assure you.'

'Well there certainly could have been a lot of conflict about it. She put Shane down, you know. She was jealous of her youth. I said to her, "Darling, we all have our turn. Now it's hers."'

Toni looked at me closely. 'You're very lucky, darling,' she said, her raised eyebrows tracing dramatic triangles into her hairline. 'Very lucky. I loved your mother dearly, but I didn't see her through rose-coloured glasses. She made her choices and you were very very lucky that she didn't choose to keep you.'

CHAPTER 29

. . . it is the interplay between hereditary and environmental factors that is significant.[1]

One of the greatest tasks that life offers is the riddle of identity. 'Who am I?' is the question we hope to have answered before our journey is completed.

> *My face is cold turned up to the stars. Inexorable and orderly they move across heaven, star beyond star, nebula beyond nebula, universe beyond universe, wheeling through a loneliness that is inconceivable. Almost I can feel this planet wheeling too, spinning through its own sphere of loneliness with the deliberation of a process endlessly repeated, a tiny speck of astral dust whirling on into the incomprehensibility of eternity. How queer to cling to the speck of dust, whirling on and on, perhaps at this moment even upside down. There's no comfort in the stars. Only darkness beyond darkness, mystery beyond mystery, loneliness beyond loneliness.*

> *Wrapped in its own darkness and mystery and loneliness the child in my body turns, as though to remind me of mysteries closer to hand. And I go spinning on through space, enveloped by mystery, enveloping mystery, ignorant as a sheep as to why I am being used in this way. On the dark little terrace under the dark mountains I have a childish desire to shake my fists and shout into the impossible emptiness between those wheeling stars, 'This is all very well, but who am* I?[2]

This lovely evocation of the questioning being was written by my mother on Hydra, when pregnant with her fourth child, Jason. She was thirty-two years old.

For me, the first child of her body, the question is complicated by the fact that she gave me away. In finding her and trying to understand her, I am, of course, trying to find and understand the missing parts of myself.

All adopted people have questions that must be answered before they can hope to meet the challenge of 'Who am I?' They must come to terms with their heredity and re-evaluate it against their upbringing, their environment.

I have read my mother's words many times over, listened to her voice on tape, seen a brief, blurred image of her on videotape and many, many sharp images of her in still photographs, some of which I have printed from negatives myself. On my shelves are books she has owned, inscribed with her name. I have looked at her manuscripts and her notes, even some shopping lists, in the National Library. I have talked to some of her friends and acquaintances. Her best friend and I have talked and laughed and wept together. I know a lot about Charmian Clift. In fact I know far more *about* her than I do about Marjorie Shaw, my adoptive mother, whom I was close to for forty-two years. Yet knowing is not knowing.

My adoptive mother is a series of living memories, translucent layer after translucent layer of them, from the time her arms gingerly cradled me as she took me from Matron Shaw at the entrance to Crown Street Hospital. My senses have all been engaged by her. I can still see the old-woman web of soft, dry, wrinkled skin on her blotchily rouged cheeks, feel it against my cheek. I can feel her horny hands rubbing camphorated oil into my bony chest in the middle of the night when I was ill. I can smell her cigarette smoke, all the sweeter because she thought Dad didn't know she was smoking. I can hear her bitter tongue, raised in anger at some injustice to the Irish or to women. I can taste the mess of mashed potato, carrot and spinach flavoured with Marmite that she called 'tasty' in an effort to get her food-faddist daughter to eat vegetables. I may not know too much about her history but I *know* her.

Nevertheless I want everything. I want the impossible. I want to know my natural mother with my senses, as well as with my intellect. I still find it painful to read about, or watch a documentary on, reunion. I still have to fight back the tears. I still yearn for what I can never have—the living woman. The mother who gave me birth.

The nature and nurture question affects all adoptive people. I am struggling to understand the aspects of myself that come from my heredity, and those that come from my upbringing. How one has reacted with the other. Of course it is nearly impossible to use the analytical knife cleanly, especially on oneself. For me the issue is: where do I fit between my two mothers?

How does an organism born with its own genetic imperatives react to an opposing environment?

There is a well-known experiment where a fowl's egg is put under a broody duck with her own eggs. When the eggs hatch, the chicken does not know it is not a duckling.

Instinctively the chicken follows the mother duck to the water with the ducklings. But no further. While the duck family dabbles and up-tails happily, the chicken stands cheeping hysterically at the water's edge. If it were human we would say it was having an identity crisis. How then does an adopted child, given one set of genes from two natural parents, fit into a home where the environment has been both consciously and subconsciously arranged by surrogate parents with totally different genetic imperatives?

In an ideal home where the child carries the genes of the parents who love and rear her, environment should reinforce heredity—the two things working together in harmony. The way the child is, the way she acts, the things she wants out of life, are likely to appear all of a piece, right, inevitable and unremarkable. (Of course, it is not always the case, but it is at least probable.)

In a home with adoptive parents, even with all the love in the world, the heredity of the child could well be at odds with her environment. It would not be surprising if the child is out of kilter. To belong to the family environment, that child might have to subdue her sensed, but unacknowledged, core. On the other hand, she might reject the environment at great peril and become an outcast, a rebel. Into her identity structure, at a very deep level, below consciousness, she must integrate two sets of parents, one genetic, one environmental. With her head she knows a great deal about one set and nothing at all about the other. But every cell of her body is imbued with another knowledge.

It would indeed be remarkable if an adopted child did not have specific problems to do with her identity.

I tried to explain this idea to a friend who is a courageous idealist, not afraid to stand alone for a principle. From when she was a girl, her father encouraged her to do whatever she thought was right, and supported her through the ensuing consequences. Because of the stands she takes, she has often been lonely, but she knows where that loneliness comes from and is willing to pay that price. She is a perfect example of nature and nurture working towards the same ends.

She listened on the other end of the phone as I fumbled around with words, trying to get my thoughts straight.

'Look, Sue,' she finally burst out impatiently, 'you could have been brought up in a grey house by grey people and you still would have blasted out of there!'

Would I?

The best birthday present I ever gave Mum was a big fertiliser bag full of cow pats and an industrial hard hat. The cow pats were soaked in a forty-four gallon drum of water and the resultant soup ladled onto the roots of the roses at precisely the right moment. The hard hat, dinged and scored, was donned whenever Mum had to go under the house. Bent right over she would hang out the washing on a wet day, or look for a couple of lengths of two-by-four and a roll of chicken wire to knock together into a frame for the sweet peas. If she forgot where she was (which she frequently did) and straightened up suddenly, the resulting bang could be heard all through the house above.

When I am standing at the back of the shed in what used to be the chook yard, happily shovelling horse manure, kitchen scraps, sawdust and grass clippings into my compost tumbler, my face grubby with smears of rich, pungent dung, her image comes immediately to mind.

When I stop motionless in my composted and flourishing garden, trowel hanging limp from my dangling arm, overwhelmed by the plump swelling beauty of buds, softly

furred like a summer peach, or the dancing dazzle of reflected light from the water in the birdbath or the dappled leopard pattern on the tall straight trunk of the native frangipani, wet and polished after rain, I feel like Charmian's daughter.

There is no conflict here. Nature and nurture complement each other.

But when I was appointed the delegate from my district to a Teachers' Federation Annual Conference, and was talking to Mum about the right of workers to withdraw their labour, she said, 'Never let Dad hear you talking like that. He still thinks you vote Liberal.'

And when my eldest daughter was born and I still believed enough to want her christened, I chose a very dear friend of mine to be her godmother. She happened to be a Methodist. My church, the Church of England, would not permit her to have any function within it. I was furious at the sectarianism and petty hypocrisy that caused one Protestant sect to consider another one unworthy, and I severed all ties with my church. I refused to have my daughter or any subsequent children christened at all.

I can still hear Mum's exasperated voice: 'Stop dramatising yourself! Of course she must be christened. What does it *matter* who is godmother? Let David's wife be godmother. What will the relations think? I've already told the neighbours. Do it for the social reasons. Do it to make your father happy.'

But unlike Mum, I have never been any good at pretending. I can't do or not do things to keep other people happy if I am convinced of my beliefs. Once convinced, I am almost naive in my honesty. Here I can find echoes of the mother I never knew.

There is much controversy over this issue of heredity and environment, and one of the ways it had been researched is by studying pairs of identical twins (with, of course, identical genetic material) who have been separated when very young and reared in different environments.

Presumably characteristics that are identical, or at least very similar, will be hereditary, while differences will have been caused by their upbringing in different environments.

Physical characteristics are the most striking in their similarity: it is self-evident that identical twins look identical. But some areas of similarity are quite surprising.

All people have a characteristic mood, basically happy, melancholy, optimistic or whatever. Twins reared apart share that same basic mood. Most separated twins laugh alike, describe symptoms in the same way, smoke similar numbers of cigarettes, choose similar creative pursuits and sometimes even marry the same number of times. They frequently have the same mannerisms and nervous habits such as nail biting, grimacing, snickering, tapping their fingers.[3]

This finding about mannerisms goes a long way to explain a fascinating detail described in *Looking For Lisa.* A relinquished son met his birthmother, who had subsequently married his father. The young man had a nervous habit of twisting holes 'in the bottom of his pockets, the corners on the bottom of the shirts and the corners of his sheets and pillowcases'.[4] His father had exactly the same habit.

When first I looked at photographs of Charmian and saw myself so distinctly, I was amazed at how the signs of ageing were so similar. The way the muscles of the face had let the flesh loosen on the same place along the bone, the criss-crossing of lines on the neck, the frown line between the brows, the vertical cracks in the lips, these things were amazingly similar. Her bottom teeth, which, like mine, were straight in younger days, had moved closer together by median migration, and overlapped slightly. My heredity was obviously determining the physical characteristics of my ageing pattern.

When I saw the little envelope with its quote from Yeats in my mother's hand on Toni's noticeboard, I saw my own handwriting. And my eldest daughter's handwriting. That was eerie. Totally unexpected.

In the studies on twins, environment also had its own strong part to play. Personality, more than any other area, is affected by environment: 'Family influences show clearly in attitudes, values, and choice of mate.'[5]

Of course it is a very complex issue. We aren't lifeless puppets, dancing to the strings of heredity and environment with no will of our own. Choice comes into it.

'The true cost of anything is what we have to give up in order to have it. It is the path not taken,'[6] or, in the bolder language of a Spanish proverb: 'Take what you want,' says God, 'and pay for it.'

For all our similarities my mother and I are very different. We have made opposing life-choices. With very different outcomes. Her nature and the call of her talent led her to live close to the creative edge, to turn her back on security and safety. To live the big life with all its dangers. She reaped its rewards for a time, using her abilities to their fullest and being loved and feted for so doing. The price she paid for it was her own life when it became intolerable to her.

My nature, which could have been similar, with its extremes of highs and lows, has been modified by family influences. Like a majority of women, I have chosen the little life. The safe life. The life of paid mainstream work. The life of concentration on hearth and husband and loved children. The rewards I have reaped are very different to those of my mother. The coin I have paid for this is my talent and my ambition, and the biggest question of my life has always been whether the price has been too high.

Both genetic and environmental forces are extremely powerful agencies in the formation of a human being. There is an ongoing controversy as to which has more importance.

Conservative opinion at its most polarised has, at times, made out that heredity is all. It is all a matter of breeding. Blood will out. From this extreme view come philosophies of elitism: racial superiority, rigid class systems, private schools, IQ tests, even many fairytales. For a society that believed this, it would be an act of great charity or foolhardiness to adopt an illegitimate child. No matter who adopted her, the baby daughter of a wild, passionate, pagan girl would in her turn fling her hat over the windmill.

Progressive opinion at its extreme has, at times, believed that environment is all. A newborn baby is a blank slate waiting to be written upon. Equality can be achieved by social change. Take away from the privileged and give to the underprivileged and a just and equal society will be the result. Equality of opportunity will mean equality of outcome. Adoption in a society that believed this would be an excellent option because the adopting parents could impress their attitudes and beliefs on the child. When adopted by middle-aged, conservative, church-going parents, the baby daughter of a wild, passionate, pagan girl would be a model of rectitude and conformity.

Both views are extreme. It is in the wide space between them, with its inevitable conflicts, that adopted children have to find their way.

This is the key to my dilemma.

For the first time in my life and with a certain resigned acceptance, I understand why I have never belonged. Not to my upbringing. Not to my genetic inheritance. It is one of the difficulties of being adopted.

At last I can explain the dichotomies of my life. I know I can fly, should fly, must fly, but doubt that my wings will get me off the ground. The Charmian in me says *Do it, and to hell with the consequences*, the Harold-and-Marjorie says *Do it if you must but be careful, don't fly high, and make sure the beds are made first*.

As a young girl, bursting to express myself, I felt repelled by the 'arty' world that I brushed up against. It seemed to me then to be pretentious, immoral, foul-mouthed, smelling of garlic and just plain unwashed-dirty. My straight-laced, conventional, religious upbringing saw to that.

As a young woman full of ideals of equality in marriage, I felt equally repelled by the suburban, conventional world to which marriage and motherhood seemed to relegate me. I was desperate to be myself. My genes saw to that.

I realise now that I have spent my life charting a course in the gap between two different modes of existence—occasionally, especially in my youth, braving the border guards to sightsee for a while in one country or the other. Was it really me, mother-of-three, who dived naked from the high board into the street-lamp-lit swimming pool of my small, ultra-conservative country town? The pool manager was a friend (an out-of-towner like us) and we were all smoking pot and skinny-dipping inside the cage of cyclone wire. Was it really me, mother-of-three and run off my feet, who cooked elaborate four-course dinners that took me all day to prepare (and I *hate* cooking) for people I didn't particularly like, and have never seen since? In comparison with either of these opposites, the sea of not-belonging has seemed like a good place to sail. It is my great good fortune that I have not had to sail alone.

In navigating these straits, this passage, over the years, there are certain qualities, possessions, beliefs that I have let slip overboard. They have drifted easily away. I mislaid God long ago, left behind when I finally understood what Charmian had experienced on Hydra under her universe of stars—the total aloneness of each human being. Any desire to take a mind-altering substance slid painlessly over the side the night when, high on cannabis sativa, I tried to pin a nappy on my baby, only to find she was melting under my hands. I am in the process of shoving out by brute force my concerns with other people's opinions. Once I cared desperately to be liked by everyone. Next, I only cared that the people who mattered to me thought well of me. Now I would be well content if my own good opinion were enough.

Today, yes, I look like Charmian Clift, but even more I look like (oh horrible words) a middle-aged suburban matron. One among thousands. No-one would give me a second glance as I wheel my trolley full of groceries to the checkout.

But in my visits to the houses where many of Charmian's

friends have made their homes, I have found... myself. Original paintings and prints and photographs on walls of whitewashed mudbrick or white painted shiplap timber or white painted plaster. Books in their dozens, in their hundreds, stacked along shelves. A pleasant clutter of precious objects scattered on window ledges and tabletops. Rooms with a sense of space and ease. Busy workrooms or studios.

Our sprawling house, painted the same green as the gum trees that surround it, contains the world I have made for myself. Not quite true. Doug is a little bit responsible, but on the whole it is mine. Open plan rooms on different levels, paintings and my photographs on the walls, thousands of books read and re-read, spilling off the shelves, pots and precious objects on every surface. Objects that are precious to me: a set of delicate Shelley bone china coffee cups that were a wedding present to Marjorie and Harold; a large, rough, free-form terracotta bowl made for me by a past student; shells and bones and feathers and water-rounded stones. If I had a Rembrandt in my kitchen I don't think it would feel too out of place.

The windows make picture frames containing a sparkling blue and green day, a dramatic lightning-filled sky reflected in sullen water, or a dark and moonless night with the light of one little fishing boat moving slowly across the space. My studio has a half-finished painting sitting on the easel gathering dust, my darkroom can be assembled at a moment's notice and in Doug's study the computer is set up with this manuscript in its incomprehensible memory, ready to leap onto the screen.

I don't clatter away at a little typewriter like Charmian Clift, but perhaps, in writing this book, I have discovered something else about her.

When I am writing, present time and place cease to exist.

I am totally alone, inside the skins of the people I am writing about, or moving and breathing in a time far removed from the present, or re-experiencing and reshaping overwhelming emotion. When I am not writing, more often than not I am thinking about writing. The garden is full of weeds and spiders have woven webs over the broom closet, and I am shamefacedly glad that any problems my children are experiencing are being solved, or not solved, hundreds of miles away from me.

But when, after weeks of struggle, a difficult chunk of the book has finally come out right, I feel like Moses coming down from the mountain with The Word. If I found a tribe of Israelites passing around a jug of fermented grape juice, dancing and laughing and singing and making love around a Golden Calf in my living room, I would be very much inclined to join them.

CHAPTER 30

The name is the symbol of her lost identity.[1]

Today is my first birthday. My first birthday as the daughter of Charmian Clift. A year ago today I opened a brown manila envelope that had been carelessly lying on the dining room table.

I was in the mood for symbolism. I drove the half-hour trip to my nearest town and stopped the car outside the old courthouse, its mellow red and ochre brick glowing warm in the thin winter sunshine. A scattering of people leaned against walls or car bonnets, or sat dejectedly on Indian-red iron seats. Two young women, faces hopeless, shoulders hunched, rocked a squalling baby in a hand-me-down pram. A middle-aged woman with a grim set face sat beside a boy of fifteen or so, both staring straight ahead. A group of familiar youths in checked flannelette shirts, tracksuit pants and ugh boots raised embarrassed faces in greeting as I passed.

'G'day, Miss. You gotta go to court too, have ya? What've youse been up to, eh?' Their voices were loud, harsh and uncertain, the breaking voices of adolescent boys not yet in control of pitch or volume. Their brave laughter held a note of strain.

The plane trees I walked under were bare and cast irregular, spiky shadows on the curved geometry of brick paving. The dark-suited magistrate and a pretty, well-dressed court secretary were walking towards me under the vine-clad archway that led to the Registrar's Office. In that office, over a year ago, I had paid my one hundred and seventeen dollars and filled out an application for my original birth certificate.

I pushed at the shining brass crescents that form the handles for the glass doors.

'Are you being attended to?' A young blonde girl in an embroidered jumper came up to the counter.

'No, not yet. I want to make a change to my name by deed poll. I presume I do it here?'

'Just one moment and I'll find out for you.'

By the filling-in of a form and the payment this time of seventy-five dollars, I added to the name my adoptive parents had given me, *Suzanne*, and the name my husband had given me, *Chick*, the name my natural mother had given me, *Jennifer*. I was now legally *Suzanne Jennifer Chick*, and had to practise my new signature accordingly at the foot of the form.

When I walked back to the car the group of boys was disappearing into the courthouse. The windscreen-filtered sun warmed my hands on the steering wheel as I made a U-turn in the wide street, negotiated the roundabout and turned right at the lights into the highway that led home. The winter paddocks rolled past. My thoughts rolled with them.

In the last couple of days the media had been full of the news of the tragic death of the *enfant terrible* of Australian painting, artist Brett Whiteley. He was only fifty-three, and had lived his life with fierce, obsessive intensity. He was addicted to heroin, and had tried many times to pull himself free. He had said of himself that people with great gifts often derail because of their need to ride close to the edge.

Great gifts. Ride close to the edge. How much it reminded me of Charmian Clift. Her life and her death.

So much that I see and hear these days makes me think of her.

What an incredible year it has been for me. So much emotion. So much to analyse and synthesise. So much to assimilate.

David, my brother, had recently rung from Melbourne to tell me that he had changed his mind and applied for his birth certificate, only to find it had a veto on it. His birthmother had left a message. The text of this message was like a slap in the face. It was brutally short: *There are no medical problems in the families, and I want no further contact*. He had the information on his birth certificate: her name, her age at his birth, and where she had lived and the name she had given him—*David*. That was the full extent of his knowledge. His problem is the exact opposite of mine. I had to struggle through an avalanche. He has to build on next to nothing. Of course, he is going to try to find out what he can, short of contacting her. But he was hurt, I could tell, by this second rejection. Empathy brought a prickle to my eyes. I winged to him all my support for the difficult journey he was just beginning.

Who are we, anyway? Where do we fit on a scale from who we think we are, inside our own skins, to who other people think we are? My natural mother was at once an exceedingly private individual and an exceedingly public one. Aspects of this individual are revealed in her writing—hints of the private one, vistas of the public one. Everyone who has ever read her work has opinions about who she was. But who can ever know how she saw herself?

As I read articles and books and talked to people over the past year, it became ever clearer to me that most people saw her in ways that reflected themselves. I have seen this phenomenon often in art students attempting their first portrait. It is inevitably more like the student than it is like the model. Feminists saw Charmian as a feminist. Marxists saw her as a Marxist. Political activists claimed her. Jewish people revelled in her part-Jewishness. Those with strong working-class connections thought she would have done better in a working-class suburb, away from the snobbery of Mosman. Mosman people loved the woman who opened art exhibitions, wrote beautifully and spoke with an English-accented voice. Many men saw her as a desirable woman. Some women saw her as a threat. Those who liked to see only the bright and beautiful in life concentrated on the early happy years. Others saw only the desolation and tragedy of the late years. Women who had stayed in their own kitchens, bringing up their families, saw the Charmian Clift of the Thursday columns, the one who spoke directly to them and gave them hope, as the real one. The sophisticated saw her stylishness, the down-to-earth her peasant qualities. Me, I was no different. Unless I monitored myself very closely, I saw what I wanted to see.

I was with Toni Burgess not long ago, looking through a box of photographs that I had copied or printed from Johnston negatives. There was one, a family shot taken with a cheap camera, of an obviously middle-aged Charmian in her Raglan Street kitchen, in a dressing-gown, hair tied back, eyes slitted against the steam rising from whatever she was stirring in the saucepan for breakfast. She was totally unglamorous. I instantly loved that photo. She looked just like a mother.

How hard, how hard the lot of a highly talented woman who tries to fly out of the magic circle. How the hands reach out to pull her back down to earth. Here were mine, more than twenty years after her death, wanting to clutch at her. Can such a woman's freedom come only at the cost of those who need her?

I thought sadly about the increasing part that alcohol had played in the last years of her life. And about the part it had played in her death. One eerily self-prophetic line she had written about seventeen months before her death I will never forget. The first time I read it, the page was wet with my tears:

> *A whole human life of struggle, bravery, defeat, triumph, hope, despair, might be remembered, finally, for one drunken escapade.*[2]

Who was this woman who gave me life? How did she come to deal death to herself? She was a writer of great talent, compassion and warmth. A romantic girl who grew into a woman of ambition, mind and spirit. A woman whose physical beauty proved as ephemeral as physical beauty has always been, but whose soul was large and generous and made to last. A woman who earned the love her public gave her. A 'Yea Sayer'[3] to life who ended her life with the ultimate 'Nay.'

Was she then truly an Icarus, her blazing wings lighting and warming the space around her until, consumed, she fell? Was she a woman trapped in a myth of her own making, unable to break free except by suicide? Was her death an accident, a *cri de coeur*? Was she simply, at heart, a desperately sad woman, broken at last by the cumulative guilts and griefs of her woman's life? A woman, who, woman-like, finally tidied up her life before the mess could become too great, in the only way she could? Can we ever know? Suicide is the supreme mystery.

Were her light and darkness the two sides of the one coin,

each one an inseparable part of the other? How can I presume to understand her?

What is certain is that, for me, the story, the necklace of her life, is not finished yet. I will continue to add to it. I may even discard some of its links, change its pattern slightly. There are tales I have not yet heard, papers I have not yet read, photographs I have not yet seen, people I have not yet met. One more viewpoint, one more anecdote, one more bead.

What I do understand is her effect on me. My life has been changed. Completed. This is the best way to describe it. In finding my natural mother, I have set free a self that had always been there, but has never been certain of its provenances. Charmian Clift has given this part of me permission to exist. To come out. What I do with this self will occupy me for the rest of my life. Curiously and quite unexpectedly, I have also found again the mother who adopted me, loved me and brought me up. I can love her with new understanding. I have found a kind of peace in unravelling the threads of my being and tracking them back to their several sources: my genes, my upbringing, and my own life-choices.

The salt smell, the rhythmic beat and the turquoise and white beauty of the bay rushed towards me to welcome me home. The resident sea-eagle soared alone on effortless wings, high above the distant cliffs, impervious to the cloud of harrying small birds. Oh, it was a day for symbolism.

My garden reached out towards me too. The liquidambar tree spread its bare tracery to the clear blue of the sky. As I opened the car door, the strong sweet scent of daphne and jonquil arose in waves and bore me with it—up the side path, brushing past the hakea, around their roots little violet heads peeking up from a green mat, through the gate and into the back garden. Christmas the dog raced ahead of me, banner waving, and Mrs Cat, pennant high, rubbed her old head around my ankles as I walked. She and I sat side by side on the green garden-seat in the winter sun and surveyed our realm. *Zit-zit, zit-zit*, the little pairs of finches in the aviary called anxiously to each other. *Where are you? Where are you? I'm here. I'm here.* Two crimson rosellas, male and female, landed with bell-calls on the birdbath, taking no notice of us. The old cat, memories of her days as a fearless hunter stirring, twitched her tail and laid back her ears. But my stroking hand cut memory short.

The sweet pea seedlings caught my eye. It was time to tie them up. They had reached the trellis and were ready to be on their way. I had just finished untangling the twining green tendrils, and tying them one by one, when a deep voice called from the back door.

'I'm home, Suzie. Ready for a cup of tea?'

'I'll just wash my earthy hands and I'll be in.'

On the oval pine table, amongst our steaming mugs and crumb-scattered plates, were a couple of bills and a handful of travel brochures.

'I stopped in at the travel agent on my way home. If we're going to meet Roseanne in Greece, we'd better start doing some thinking about it.'

For some time we had been planning to spend a year in Europe, after our youngest daughter finished university and we were free. All our children had been overseas, on school trips or exchange plans, but neither Doug nor I had ever been out of the country. Now we had even stronger reasons for going: to follow whatever trail my mother had left in Greece. Now it was our turn.

Even through the garishness, the over-intensified blue of

the sky and sea in the brochures, the song of the sirens could be faintly heard.

I'm coming, I whispered to them in my head. *I'm coming. Soon.*

It was indeed a day for symbolism.

'By the way, Doug,' I said, pushing back my chair as I stood up. 'Could you please find me your electric drill and the buffer attachment? I'm going to polish this chair.'

POSTSCRIPT
TO THE SECOND EDITION

A sharp autumn wind was at work cleaning the streets in Sydney's Kings Cross. The car looked incongruously dirty as it drew up outside a plush hotel: awning, braided commissionaire, liveried parking attendant. Four doors flung open simultaneously and out scrambled a middle-aged man, very tall, with a grey-flecked dark beard and hazel eyes enmeshed in smile lines; a middle-aged woman of average height with dark hair tied back in a black band; three long-legged young women, two dark, the third blonde, dressed and made-up in opposing styles; one young man in T-shirt, stubbies and thongs with his hand in a cast (the result of surgery); and lastly a black and white spaniel-cross with her head in a pink plastic bucket (also the aftermath of surgery). A shower of used tissues swept out with the dog and blew up the gutter too fast to retrieve. Before the door could be slammed a handful of hay followed the tissues.

The parking attendant tried unsuccessfully to control his grin as he held open the driver's door to allow the dog to jump back in, then got in himself and kicked aside the shoes and defunct biros from under the accelerator and swung the car towards the nether regions of the hotel's parking lot.

Inside the hotel in a room off the lobby, a TV crew was fiddling with lights and sound levels. The journalist stood and held out her hand as the group walked in.

'Hi. You must be Gina, Danni and Kristin. Which is which? Pleased to meet you, Doug, I feel I know you. Hello Suzanne, I'm very glad to meet you. I loved your book. No Kristin, I don't mind at all if your boyfriend watches the interview. It's all going to be pretty informal. He can sit over here with Doug. Now, Suzanne, what do you like to be called?'

'Sue will be fine.'

'OK, Sue it is. Now, the way I'd like to do this is . . .'

The phone rang. It was the fifteenth time that afternoon. A woman's voice.

'I have something that I think you might be interested in. When I was younger I did a business course. I lost my Pitman shorthand book and picked up a second-hand one. I've had it for donkey's years. It's old and battered. Inside the front cover is the date nineteen thirty-something and the name Charmian Clift. Underneath the name is handwritten:

is nuts
and as ugly as sin.

'It's got drawings—cartoon sort of drawings. I expect she did them too. It obviously belonged to your mother. Would you like to have it?'

The line of people waiting to have their books signed was a long one. The literary lunch had been packed, and I thought everything had gone well. I had brought my mother's old shorthand book that, as promised, had arrived in the post. People had been fascinated by the way it had come to me and by the drawings inside. One was a caricature: small slanty eyes, jutting cheekbones and enormous mouth—Charmian's face expressed with a teenager's hypercritical vision. I had burst our laughing when I first saw it. Many years ago I too had made a drawing of myself very like this, and only recently I had seen a similar self-portrait pinned to my eldest daughter's noticeboard.

The woman standing in front of my author's table was taking a couple of photographs, sepia-toned with age, out of an envelope.

'I wondered if you'd like to see these,' she said.

'These' were images of a room in a business college—long wooden tables, one behind the other, at right angles to the wall. At the first desk, looking up with a rebellious expression on her face from under a tangle of hair, was my teenage mother. This was the desk where she had doodled the savage drawings and written the bitter lines in the book I had beside me right now.

The phone was ringing again. This time it was a man's voice. What he had to say riveted my attention.

'I definitely know who your father was and I can tell you his name. And he wasn't a stage designer.'

I was working my way through the pile of mail on the dining room table. A letter from a fellow adoptee, two from women who had been forced to give up babies. From the correspondence that filled my letterbox, it was obvious that adoption was not a minor issue. There was one envelope containing photographs of my mother in the army, photographs I hadn't seen before. And another fat envelope packed with pages from a lecture pad. This was a letter from a woman who thought that we might be sisters—that her father (long dead) might be my father also. His name was the same one I had been given by my caller. The letter mentioned someone who could confirm the story, someone who had known Charmian Clift well in the sixties and, under extraordinary circumstances, had heard about my conception and birth from her. The name was familiar. It was the name of the caller from a few days before.

Was the impossible about to become possible? Was I going to find my father also?

The lady was in her nineties but her voice on the other end of the line was firm and clear. She had a story to tell me. In the early 1940s she had been the secretary at Crown Street Women's Hospital and a close friend of Matron Shaw. She had known about Charmian Clift, her Christmas Day baby and the adoption.

'But what you don't know, my dear, is that Christmas after Christmas Charmian used to come back to the hospital with a parcel, baby clothes she'd made herself and so on, for Matron Shaw to hand on to her baby.'

Exhausted. Down. Empty. All I wanted was to flop on the bed and sleep. There were still piles of letters I hadn't answered and phone numbers jotted on the backs of envelopes that I had yet to ring. In a few weeks we were flying overseas. I hadn't even begun to organise myself for a whole year on the other side of the world. I had given nearly forty interviews in four and a half days—my first experience of the other side of the looking-glass world of print, radio and television media. Today every interview had run over time and now there was only time for a quick shower and an even quicker flinging on of clothes and make-up. I still hadn't written my speech. I would have to do that in the car.

I really couldn't be bothered—I didn't want to drag myself to this book launch. But Doug and the girls and their men were ready. And, after all, it was *my* book launch. We would have to go.

The pub had a string of lights outside. Music, laughter and the smell of cigarette smoke wafted out to the street. Inside at a downstairs table were two familiar faces—Toni Burgess talking to her daughter through the customary blue haze. A meeting of daughters took place. I downed a quick drink. Friends from my country town made their way over to give me a quick hug before moving upstairs. My publishers came across and were introduced to Toni and my family. Pat Lovell, the celebrated film producer who was launching the book, gave a friendly wiggle of her fingers as she crossed the room with her daughter. Cedric and Wendy smiled and waved as they climbed the stairs.

It was time to begin. Like well-trained sheep dogs, a couple of sound engineers cut me out of the upwardly moving crowd and proceeded to thread a bodymike under my shirt, through my bra and out at my collar.

'Now don't forget you're live, love. Come and see us if you want to go to the loo and we'll switch it off. This thing picks up every sound!'

They too went upstairs.

My tiredness began to lift. I walked alone upwards, around the bend in the staircase. Only a few steps to go. I felt the bubbling beginning of a fountain of energy—adrenalin pumping through my veins.

A hubbub of voices. A scent of fresh flowers and after-shave and perfume. The sudden blinding of TV lights. The popping of flashes as my head emerged over the railing. The room full of delighted smiles. A glass of champagne thrust into my hand. An open copy of my book and a pen. The fountain soared upwards and upwards . . .

I was flying.

NOTES

Chapter 1

1 Linda Burgess, *The Art of Adoption*, Acropolis Books, Washington D.C., 1976, p. 81.

Chapter 2

1 Arthur D. Sorosky, Annette Baran, Reuben Pannor, *The Adoption Triangle: The Effects of the Sealed Record on Adoptees, Birth Parents, and Adoptive Parents*, Anchor Press/Doubleday, Garden City, New York, 1978, p. 87.

Chapter 3

1 Kate Inglis, *Living Mistakes: Mothers who consented to adoption*, George Allen & Unwin Australia Pty Ltd, North Sydney, 1984, p. 18.

Chapter 4

1 New South Wales Department of Community Services, *Adoptees and Birthparents Guide to Searching, Adoption*, 1990, p. 17.
2 P. D. Eastman, *Are You My Mother?*, Random House, 1960.
3 Charmian Clift, 'Taking the Wrong Road', *The World of Charmian Clift*, William Collins Pty Ltd, Sydney, 1989, p. 20.
4 New South Wales Department of Community Services, op. cit., p. 12.
5 ibid., p. 22.
6 ibid., p 17.

Chapter 5

1 Sorosky, Baran and Pannor, op. cit., p. 96.

Chapter 6

1 Kathleen Silber and Phylis Speedlin, *Dear Birthmother, Thank You For Our Baby*, Corona Publishing Co., Texas, 1982, p. 62.

2 Charmian recounts these family details in 'A Portrait of My Mother', *The World of Charmian Clift*, op. cit., p. 80ff.

Chapter 7

1 New South Wales Department of Community Services, op. cit., p. 21.

2 Diana Bradshaw, Barré and Bobbie Clift's daughter, remembers hearing her parents discussing this. In 1947 her mother's sister, Marie, with her little daughter, Gaye, visited Barré and Bobbie at Kiama when George and a pregnant Charm were staying there in the family home with Amy (Charmian's mother). Amy was uncharacteristically horrid to the child and told her son to get rid of their visitors at once. Bobbie was very upset on behalf of her sister and her niece but Barré had an explanation for his mother's strange behaviour: George also had a daughter called Gae, living with her mother in Melbourne and she was much the same age as this little girl. Amy was terrified that George would become nostalgic for his daughter and decide to go back to his wife, leaving Charm to bear another illegitimate child.

Chapter 8

1 New South Wales Department of Community Services, op. cit., p. 22.

2 Garry Kinnane, *George Johnston: A Biography*, Thomas Nelson Australia, Melbourne, 1986, pp. 73-4.

3 In fact statistics from the Post Adoption Research Centre's newsletter, *Branching Out*, confirm this. Eighty-one per cent of telephone enquiries the Centre receives are from women; in the UK in the first seven years after adopted adults became entitled to their original birth certificates, 66% of certificates were issued to women. *Branching Out*, vol. 1, no. 4, May 1993, p. 3.

4 Charmian Clift, *Mermaid Singing*, William Collins Pty Ltd, Sydney, 1988, p. 190.

5 ibid., p. 11.
6 George Johnston, *Clean Straw for Nothing, A Cartload of Clay* (one-volume edition), William Collins Pty Ltd, Sydney, 1989, p. 54.

Chapter 9

1 Charmian Clift, 'A Rembrandt in the Kitchen', *The World of Charmian Clift*, op. cit., p. 45.

Chapter 10

1 Charmian Clift, *Mermaid Singing*, op. cit., p. 13.
2 These letters are mis-dated January 1954 and March 1954 by C. C. At this time the Johnstons were still in London. It is my belief that the first mistake was one many of us make on starting a new year. The second may have occurred when she consulted her letter-file and automatically copied the date of the last letter.

Chapter 11

1 Charmian Clift, *Peel Me a Lotus*, William Collins Pty Ltd, Sydney, 1988, p. 49.
2 Charmian Clift, *Mermaid Singing*, op. cit., p. 31.
3 Charmian Clift, letter to Cedric and Pat Flower.
4 Charmian Clift, 'Christmas', *The World of Charmian Clift*, op. cit., p 62.
5 ibid., p. 63.
6 ibid., p. 63.
7 Charmian Clift, *Mermaid Singing*, op. cit., p. 72.
8 Charmian Clift, letter to Cedric and Pat Flower, 5 January 1954.
9 Hazel de Berg, interview with Charmian Clift, 8 June 1965, tape no. deB 105, Oral History Collection, National Library of Australia.
10 Charmian Clift, letter to Cedric and Pat Flower, 5 January 1954.
11 5 January 1954.
12 1 March 1954.
13 Charmian Clift, *Peel Me a Lotus*, op. cit., p. 32.
14 ibid., pp. 45–6.

Chapter 12

1 Kate Inglis, op. cit., p. 188.
2 Charmian Clift, 'Long Live Democracy', *Being Alone With Oneself*, Collins Angus & Robertson Publishers Pty Ltd, North Ryde, 1991, p. 66.

Chapter 13

1 Sorosky, Baran and Pannor, op. cit., p. 25. Many ancient cultures practised adoption, including the Mesopotamian one referred to here.
2 The *Sydney Morning Herald*, 12 July 1969.
3 Nadia Wheatley and Garry Kinnane 'George Johnston and Charmian Clift', broadcast on ABC Radio National's *Radio Helicon* programme, 14 July 1986.
4 Garry Kinnane, op. cit., p. 278.
5 quoted in Garry Kinnane, op. cit., p. 266.

Chapter 14

1 Charmian Clift, 'Getting Away From it All', *The World of Charmian Clift*, op. cit., p. 168.
2 Charmian's ashes were lost. There is no memorial to her at all except for her writing.

Chapter 15

1 New South Wales Department of Community Services, op. cit., p. 9.
2 Elizabeth Jane Howard, *The Sea Change*, World Books, Britain, 1961.
3 George Johnston, *Clean Straw for Nothing, A Cartload of Clay*, op. cit., p. 387.

Chapter 16

1 Charmian Clift, *Peel Me a Lotus*, op. cit., p. 64.
2 George Johnston, *Clean Straw for Nothing, A Cartload of Clay*, op. cit., p. 176.
3 Charmian Clift, *Peel Me a Lotus*, op. cit., p. 64.
4 ibid., p. 42.
5 Charmian Clift, 'My Husband George', *Pol* magazine, August 1969.
6 Garry Kinnane, op. cit., p. 281.

Chapter 17

1 New South Wales Department of Community Services, op. cit., p. 18.
2 Charmian Clift, 'Where My Caravan Has Rested', *The World of Charmian Clift*, op. cit., p. 36.

Chapter 18

1 Charmian Clift, 'On Coming to a Bad End', *The World of Charmian Clift*, op. cit., p. 242.

Chapter 19

1 Charmian Clift, 'On Coming to a Bad End', *The World of Charmian Clift*, op. cit., p. 242.
2 Charmian Clift, *Peel Me a Lotus*, op. cit., pp. 68–9.
3 Garry Kinnane, op. cit., p. 188.
4 Hazel de Berg, op. cit.
5 Charmian Clift, 'Old Acquaintance Be Forgot', *The World of Charmian Clift*, op. cit., p. 192.
6 Charmian Clift, 'An Old Address Book', *The World of Charmian Clift*, op. cit., p. 53.
7 ibid.
8 Charmian Clift, *Peel Me a Lotus*, op. cit., p. 150.
9 ibid., p. 127.
10 Garry Kinnane, op. cit., p. 183.
11 Charmian Clift to David Higham, May 1959 and 23 July 1959, quoted in Garry Kinnane, op. cit., p. 183.
12 George Johnston to David Higham, 23 July 1959, quoted in Garry Kinnane, op. cit., p. 183.
13 Interview with Charmian Clift rebroadcast by Nadia Wheatley and Garry Kinnane in 'George Johnston and Charmian Clift', op. cit.
14 Garry Kinnane, op. cit., p. 189.
15 George Johnston, *Clean Straw for Nothing, A Cartload of Clay*, op. cit., p. 202.
16 Charmian Clift, 'My Husband George', op. cit.
17 ibid.

Chapter 20

1 Charmian Clift, 'Men', *Trouble in Lotus Land*, Collins/Angus & Robertson Publishers Australia, North Ryde, 1990, p. 25.

Chapter 21

1 Charmian Clift, 'What'll the Boys in the Back Room Have?', *Trouble in Lotus Land*, op. cit., p. 295.
2 Silber and Speedlin, op. cit., pp. 8–9.

Chapter 22

1 Charmian Clift, 'An Old Address Book', *The World of Charmian Clift*, op. cit., p. 52.

Chapter 23

1 Charmian Clift, 'A Sense of Ease', *Being Alone With Oneself*, op. cit., p. 196.

Chapter 24

1 Charmian Clift, 'On Tick and Tock', *Being Alone With Oneself*, op. cit., p. 265.
2 ibid., p. 267.
3 Hazel de Berg, op. cit.
4 Charmian Clift, *Mermaid Singing*, op. cit., p. 90.
5 ibid., p. 93.
6 ibid., p. 95.
7 Nadia Wheatley and Garry Kinnane, 'George Johnston and Charmian Clift', op. cit.

Chapter 25

1 Charmian Clift, 'Coming Home', *Images in Aspic*, William Collins Pty Ltd, Sydney, 1989, p. 3.
2 Garry Kinnane, op. cit., p. 228.
3 ibid., p. 211.
4 Charmian Clift, 'My Husband George', op. cit.
5 Rodney and Bet Hall, July 1993.
6 Rodney Hall, introduction to *The World of Charmian Clift*, op. cit., p. 11.
7 Charmian Clift, 'On Being A Home-Grown Migrant', *Trouble in Lotus Land*, op. cit., p. 100.
8 ibid., p. 100.
9 Charmian Clift, 'Coming Home', *Images in Aspic*, op. cit., p. 2.
10 ibid., p. 1.
11 ibid., p. 5.
12 ibid., p. 6.
13 Charmian Clift, 'On Debits and Credits', *Trouble in Lotus Land*, op. cit., p. 17.
14 Charmian Clift, 'On Lucky Dips', *Trouble in Lotus Land*, op. cit., pp. 22–3.

15 Charmian Clift, 'Christmas', *The World of Charmian Clift*, op. cit., p. 61.

Chapter 26

1 Joss Shawyer, *Death by Adoption*, Cicada, Auckland, 1979, p. xii.

2 George and Charmian's writing as well as their lives (and the media attention given to them) all combined to create the myth. To a greater or lesser extent they used each other's stories and images in their writing. Thus the story (which his family denied) that George had been regularly beaten as a child; the childhood stories about Charmian marching barefoot across the cunjevoi, water jets squirting up around her; Charmian lying star-baking on the night beach, hoping to turn silver (see 'Feeling Slightly Tilted?', *The World of Charmian Clift*, op. cit., p. 200); Charmian not wearing shoes—'until she was thirteen,' he said—'not quite true,' she said (see 'Saturnalias, Resolutions and Other Christmas Wishes', *Trouble in Lotus Land*, op. cit., p. 93).

We might think that these latter images are mainly George's view of Charmian, because he drew on them heavily to create Cressida Morley (the character who represents Charmian in George's trilogy). And Cressida Morley is known to the reading public. So how did Charmian Clift see herself? In her essays and novels she gives us the occasional glimpse of a romantic, wild and pagan girl. But in the remaining drafts of her unfinished novel, *The End of the Morning*, she was developing the stories about this remembered self to create an autobiographical character, a stormy petrel, Miranda (who she sometimes refers to also as Christine) Morley. Unfortunately *this* romantic, wild and pagan girl has never seen the light of public day.

3 Martin Johnston, 'Letter to Sylvia Plath: *i.m. c.c.*', in *The Sea-Cucumber*, University of Queensland Press, 1978.

4 Nadia Wheatley and Garry Kinnane, 'George Johnston and Charmian Clift', op. cit.

5 Charmian Clift, 'Death by Misadventure', *Being Alone with Oneself*, op. cit., p. 192.

Chapter 27

1 Silber and Speedlin, op. cit., p. 112.

2 Dylan Thomas 'Do Not Go Gentle into That Good Night' in Daniel Thomas (ed.) *Dylan Thomas: The Poems*, J. M. Dent & Sons, London, 1971, p. 207.

3 Charmian Clift, 'On Being Middle-Aged', *Trouble in Lotus Land*, op. cit., p. 119.
4 ibid., p. 121.
5 Nadia Wheatley and Garry Kinnane, 'George Johnston and Charmian Clift', op. cit.
6 Charmian Clift, 'The Private Pleasures of a Public Market', *The World of Charmian Clift*, op. cit., p. 104.
7 Charmian Clift, 'The Joy of a Good Old Cuppa', *Trouble in Lotus Land*, op. cit., p. 127.
8 Nadia Wheatley and Garry Kinnane, 'George Johnston and Charmian Clift', op. cit.
9 Rodney Hall, introduction to *The World of Charmian Clift*, op. cit., p. 12.
10 George Johnston, *Clean Straw for Nothing, A Cartload of Clay*, op. cit., p. 392.
11 Archina Thornton in Pamela Hayes (ed.) *Some Recollections of Working at Crown Street, The Women's Hospital*, March 1990.
12 *A.M.*, April 1949, p. 12.
13 *Woman*, 12 January 1948, p. 21.
14 'Women's Move on Adoption Laws', *Women's Weekly*, 7 October 1953, p. 18.
15 'Medico: Adopting A Baby', *Women's Weekly*, 10 May 1947, p. 40.

Chapter 28
1 Charmian Clift, 'What Price Rubies?', *Trouble in Lotus Land*, op. cit., p. 43.
2 Hazel de Berg, op. cit.
3 ibid.
4 ibid.
5 Martin Johnston, 'Biography', in *The Typewriter Considered as a Bee-Trap*, Hale & Iremonger, Sydney, 1984, p. 26.

Chapter 29
1 Sorosky, Baran and Pannor, op. cit., p. 97.
2 Charmian Clift, *Peel Me a Lotus*, op. cit., p. 52.
3 Susan L. Farber, *Identical Twins Reared Apart: A Re-analysis*, Basic Books, Inc., New York, 1981, p. 269.

4 Libby Harkness, *Looking for Lisa*, Random House Australia, Milsons Point, 1991, p. 192.
5 Susan L. Farber, op. cit., p. 270.
6 Jean Shinoda Bolen, *Goddesses in Everywoman*, Harper Colophon, New York, 1985, p. 281.

Chapter 30

1 Linda Burgess, op. cit., p. 81.
2 Charmian Clift, 'What Are You Doing It For?', *Being Alone With Oneself*, p. 40.
3 Charmian Clift, 'My Husband George', op. cit.